SEEKING
ALIVENESS

*Daily Reflections on a New Way
to Experience and Practice
the Christian Faith*

Brian D. McLaren

Faith
Words

NEW YORK   NASHVILLE

FaithWords
Hachette Book Group
1290 Avenue of the Americas, New York, NY 10104
faithwords.com
twitter.com/faithwords

First Edition: November 2017

FaithWords is a division of Hachette Book Group, Inc. The FaithWords name and logo are trademarks of Hachette Book Group, Inc.

The publisher is not responsible for websites (or their content) that are not owned by the publisher.

The Hachette Speakers Bureau provides a wide range of authors for speaking events. To find out more, go to www.hachettespeakersbureau.com or call (866) 376-6591.

This author is represented by Creative Trust, Inc.

Library of Congress Cataloging-in-Publication Data has been applied for.

ISBNs: 978-1-4789-4747-9 (trade paperback), 978-1-4789-4746-2 (ebook)

Printed in the United States of America

LSC-C

10 9 8 7 6 5 4 3 2 1

CONTENTS

Part III: Alive in a Global Uprising

Part IV: Alive in the Spirit of God

INTRODUCTION

What we all want is pretty simple, really. We want to be alive. To feel alive. Not just to exist but to thrive, to live out loud, walk tall, breathe free. We want to be less lonely, less exhausted, less conflicted or afraid...more awake, more grateful, more energized and purposeful. We capture this kind of mindful, overbrimming life in terms like *well-being*, shalom, *blessedness, wholeness, harmony*, life to the full, and *aliveness*.

The quest for aliveness explains so much of what we do. It's why readers read and travelers travel. It's why lovers love and thinkers think, why dancers dance and moviegoers watch. In the quest for aliveness, chefs cook, foodies eat, farmers till, drummers riff, fly fishers cast, runners run, and photographers shoot.

The quest for aliveness is the heartbeat that pulses through the Bible—and the best thing about religion, I think. It's what we're hoping for when we pray. It's why we gather, celebrate, eat, abstain, attend, practice, sing, and contemplate. When people say, "I'm spiritual," what they mean, I think, is simple: "I'm seeking inner aliveness."

Many older religious people—Christians, Muslims, Jews, and others—are paralyzed by sadness that their children and grandchildren are far from faith, religion, and God as they understand them. But on some level, they realize that religion too often shrinks, starves, cages, and freezes aliveness rather than fostering it. They are beginning to see that the only viable future for religion is to become a friend of aliveness again.

Meanwhile, aliveness itself is under threat at every turn. We have created an economic system that is not only too big to fail, it is too big to control—and perhaps too big to understand as well. This system disproportionately benefits the most powerful and privileged 1 percent of the human species, bestowing upon them unprecedented comfort, security, and luxury. To do so, it destabilizes the climate, plunders the planet, and kills off other forms of life at unprecedented rates.

The rest, especially the poorest third at the bottom, gain little and lose much as this economic pyramid grows taller and taller. One of their greatest losses is democracy, as those at the top find clever ways to buy votes, turning elected governments into their puppets. Under these circumstances, you would think that at least those at the top would experience aliveness. But they don't. They bend under constant anxiety and pressure to produce, earn, compete, maintain, protect, hoard, and consume more and more, faster and faster. They lose the connection and well-being that come from seeking the common good. This is not an economy of aliveness for anyone.

As these tensions mount, we wake up every morning wondering what fool or fiend will be the next to throw a lit match—or assault, nuclear, chemical, or biological weapon—onto the dry tinder of resentment and fear. Again, this is a formula for death, not a recipe for life.

So our world truly needs a global spiritual movement dedicated to aliveness. This movement must be *global*, because the threats we face cannot be contained by national borders. It must be *spiritual*, because the threats we face go deeper than brain-level politics and economics to the heart level of value and meaning. It must be *social*, because it can't be imposed from above; it can only spread from person to person, friend to friend, family to family, network to network. And it must be a *movement*, because by definition, movements stir and focus grassroots human desire to bring change to institutions and the societies those institutions are intended to serve. Such a movement can even begin with one person: you.

I believe that the story of the Bible is largely the narrative of God working to bring and restore aliveness—through individuals, communities, institutions, and movements, especially movements started by individuals. In the biblical story, for example, Moses led a movement of liberation among oppressed slaves. They left an oppressive economy, journeyed through the wilderness, and entered a promised land where they hoped to pursue aliveness in freedom and peace. Centuries after that, the Hebrew prophets launched a series of movements based on a dream of a promised time…a time of justice when swords and spears, instruments of death, would be turned into plowshares and pruning hooks, instruments of aliveness. Then came John the Baptist, a bold and nonviolent movement leader who dared to challenge the establishment of his day and call people to a movement of radical social and spiritual rethinking.

John told people he was not the leader they had been waiting for; he was simply preparing the way for someone greater than himself. When a young man named Jesus came to affiliate with John's movement through baptism, John said, "There he is! He is the one!" Under Jesus's leadership, the movement grew and expanded in unprecedented ways. When Jesus was murdered by the powers that profited from the status quo, the movement didn't die. It rose again through a new generation of leaders like James, Peter, John, and Paul, who were full of the Spirit of Jesus. They created learning circles in which activists were trained to extend the movement locally, regionally, and globally. Wherever individual activists in this movement went, the Spirit of Jesus was alive in them, fomenting change and inspiring true aliveness.

This fifty-two-week compilation of daily reflections is adapted from my book, *We Make the Road by Walking*. My prayer is that it will be a resource for this emerging spiritual movement in service of aliveness. It is essentially a retelling of the biblical story and a reintroduction to Christian faith. It is organized around four major themes chronicled in Scripture whose common thread is the "quest for aliveness." It begins with the book of Genesis and finishes in the book of Revelation.

At the beginning of each week you'll find a few Bible passages listed that you can read in any responsible translation, such as the New Revised Standard Version. Then you'll see some key verses (or a single verse) from these Bible passages printed out in their entirety on which you can sharpen your focus, and possibly commit to memory. Your enjoyment of that week's daily reflections will be enriched if you take the time to read the passages and verses upon which they are based. Of course, the line of interpretation and application I have chosen is one of many possible responses to each text. At times, it may differ from the interpretation you have heard in the past; you are asked only to give it an honest and open hearing, and you should feel free to prefer another interpretation.

There are five to seven reflections per week to be read over fifty-two weeks—a personal resource for your own thinking and rethinking. Then there is a thought or practice for the day. You can use this "Today" section to set the tone for your inner conversation throughout the day, to guide you in what to notice, and to keep you alert for opportunities to do good. One of my mentors likes to say that "Learning is not the consequence of teaching; it is the consequence of thinking and doing." The "Today" section invites you to think and do in response to what you feel God is saying to you through the daily reflection.

If you're a seeker exploring Christian faith, or if you're new to the faith and seeking a good orientation, here you'll find the introduction to the central theme of the Bible I wish I had been given. If you're a long-term Christian whose current form of Christianity has stopped working and may even be causing you and others harm, here you'll find a reorientation from a fresh and healthy perspective. If your faith seems to be a lot of talk without much practice, I hope this book of reflections will help you translate your faith into meaningful, creative action.

I

ALIVE IN THE STORY
OF CREATION

You are entering a story already in process. All around you, things are happening, unfolding, ending, beginning, dying, being born. Our ancient ancestors tried to discern what was going on. They conveyed their best wisdom to future generations through stories that answered certain key questions:

Why are we here?

What's wrong with the world?

What's our role, our task, our purpose?

What is a good life?

Is there meaning and hope?

What dangers should we guard against?

What treasures should we seek?

From the Hopi to the Babylonians, from Aztecs to Australian Aboriginals, from the Vikings in Europe to the Han in China to the Yoruba in Africa to the ancient Hebrews of the Middle East—human tribes have developed, adapted, and told powerful creation narratives to convey their best answers to key questions like these. Of course, their language often sounds strange to us, their assumptions foreign, the details of their culture odd or alien. But if we listen carefully, mixing their ancient wisdom with our own, we can let their stories live on in us. We can learn to be more fully alive in our time, just as they learned in theirs. In that spirit, we turn to the creation narratives of the ancient Hebrews.

WEEK ONE

AWE AND WONDER

Scripture Readings

> Genesis 1:1–2:3
> Psalm 19:1–14
> Matthew 6:25–34

Key Verses—Psalm 19:1-4

> *The heavens are telling the glory of God; and the firmament proclaims*
> *God's handiwork.*
> *Day to day pours forth speech, and night to night declares knowledge.*
> *There is no speech, nor are there words; their voice is not heard;*
> *yet their voice goes out through all the earth, and their words to the end*
> *of the world.*

DAY ONE: *The Great Surprise*

Big bangs aren't boring. Dinosaurs aren't boring. Coral reefs aren't boring. Elephants aren't boring. Hummingbirds aren't boring. And neither are little kids. Evolution isn't boring. Magnetism and electricity aren't boring. $E = MC^2$ might be hard to understand, but it certainly isn't boring. And even glaciers aren't boring, although their dramatic pace is at first quite hard for us to perceive. And God, whatever God is, must not be boring, either, because God's creation is so amazingly, wonderfully, surprisingly fascinating.

The first and greatest surprise—a miracle, really—is this: that anything exists at all, and that we get to be part of it. Ripe peach, crisp apple, tall mountain, bright leaves, sparkling water, flying flock, flickering flame, and you and me...here, now!

On this, the first pages of the Bible and the best thinking of today's scientists are in full agreement: It all began in the beginning, when space and time, energy and matter, gravity and light, burst or bloomed or banged into being. In light of the Genesis story, we would say that the possibility of this universe overflowed into actuality as God, the Creative Spirit, uttered the original joyful invitation: *Let it be!* And in response, what happened? Light. Time. Space. Matter. Motion. Sea. Stone. Fish. Sparrow. You. Me. Enjoying the unspeakable gift and privilege of being here, being alive.

Today: Pray, "God, help me be awake to beauty, wonder, and delight wherever they appear."

DAY TWO: *Here We Are*

Picture the unfolding of creation. Imagine how uncountable nuclei and electrons and sister particles danced and whirled. Imagine how space dust coalesced into clouds, and how clouds coalesced into galaxies, and how galaxies began to spin, sail, and dance through space. Imagine how in galaxy after galaxy, suns blazed, solar systems twirled, and worlds formed. Around some of those worlds, moons spun, and upon some of those worlds, storms swirled, seas formed, and waves rolled. And somewhere in between the smallest particles and the largest cosmic structures, here we are, in this galaxy, in this solar system, on this planet, in this story, around this table, at this moment—with this chance for us to breathe, think, dream, speak, and be alive together.

Today: Think of yourself as surfing on the leading edge of a magnificent creation that has been unfolding for billions of years.

DAY THREE: *A Common Amazement*

The Creator brought it all into being, and now some fourteen billion years later, here we find ourselves: dancers in this beautiful, mysterious choreography that expands and evolves and includes us all. We're farmers and engineers, parents and students, theologians and scientists, teachers and shopkeepers, builders and fixers, drivers and doctors, dads and moms, wise grandparents and wide-eyed infants.

Don't we all feel like poets when we try to speak of the beauty and wonder of this creation? Don't we share a common amazement about our cosmic neighborhood when we wake up to the fact that we're actually here, actually alive, right now?

Today: When you slip out of aliveness and into autopilot, remind yourself that you're "actually here, actually alive, right now!"

DAY FOUR: *God's Representatives*

Some theologians and mystics speak of the Creator withdrawing or contracting to make space for the universe to be...on its own, so to speak, so that it has its own life, its own being and history. Others imagine God creating the universe within God's self, so the universe in some way is contained "in" God, within God's presence, part of God's own life and story. Still others imagine God creating an "out there" of space and time, and then filling it with galaxies, and then inhabiting it like a song fills a forest or light fills a room or love fills a heart. Interestingly, some scholars believe the Genesis story echoes ancient Middle Eastern temple dedication texts. But in this story, the whole universe is the temple, and the Creator chooses to be represented by human beings, not a stone idol.

Today: Think of the universe being in God. And then think of God filling the universe like a song. And then ponder the wonder of God being with you, in you, right now!

DAY FIVE: *All Matter Matters*

The romance of Creator and creation is far more wonderful and profound than anyone can ever capture in words. And yet we try, for how could we be silent in the presence of such beauty, glory, wonder, and mystery? How can we not celebrate this great gift—to be alive?

To be alive is to look up at the stars on a dark night and to feel the beyond-words awe of space in its vastness. To be alive is to look down from a mountaintop on a bright, clear day and to feel the wonder that can only be expressed in "oh" or "wow" or maybe "hallelujah." To be alive is to look out from the beach toward the horizon at sunrise or sunset and to savor the joy of it all in pregnant, saturated silence. To be alive is to gaze in delight at a single bird, tree, leaf, or friend, and to feel that they whisper of a creator or source we all share.

Genesis means "beginnings." It speaks through deep, multilayered poetry and wild, ancient stories. The poetry and stories of Genesis reveal deep truths that can help us be more fully alive today. They dare to proclaim that the universe is God's self-expression, God's speech act. That means that everything everywhere is always essentially holy, spiritual, valuable, meaningful. All matter matters.

Today: Pick one thing—a bird, a sunset, stars, a leaf, a loved one, your own reflection in a mirror—and listen for the whisper of God in it.

DAY SIX: *The Creator's Language*

If you ask what language the Creator speaks, the best answer is this: God's first language is full-spectrum light, clear water, deep sky, red squirrel, blue whale, gray parrot, green lizard, golden aspen, orange mango, yellow warbler, laughing child, rolling river, serene forest, churning storm, spinning planet.

A psalmist said the same thing in another way: The universe is God's work of art, God's handiwork. All created things speak or sing of the God who made them. If you want to know what the Original Artist is like, a smart place to start would be to enjoy the art of creation.

Today: Practice looking at creation as God's art gallery.

DAY SEVEN: *Participants in Creation*

Genesis tells us that the universe is good—a truth so important it gets repeated like the theme of a song. Rocks are good. Clouds are good. Sweet corn is good. Every river or hill or valley or forest is good. Skin? Good. Bone? Good. Mating and eating and breathing and giving birth and growing old? Good, good, good. All are good. Life is good.

The best thing in Genesis is not simply human beings, but the whole creation considered and enjoyed together, as a beautiful, integrated whole, and us a part. The poetry of Genesis describes the "very goodness" that comes at the end of a long process of creation...when all the parts, including us, are working together as one whole. That harmonious whole is so good that the Creator takes a day off, as it were, just to enjoy it. That day of restful enjoyment tells us that the purpose of existence isn't money or power or fame or security or anything less than this: to participate in the goodness and beauty and aliveness of creation. And so we join the Creator in good and fruitful work...and in delightful enjoyment, play, and rest as well.

So here we are, friends. Here we are. Alive!

And this is why we walk this road: to behold the wonder and savor this aliveness. To remind ourselves who we are, where we are, what's going on here, and how beautiful, precious, holy, and meaningful it all is. It's why we pause along the journey for a simple meal, with hearts full of thankfulness, rejoicing to be part of this beautiful and good creation. This is what it means to be alive. Amen.

Today: Whenever you can, pause to consider "the beautiful, integrated whole" of Creator and creation, together.

WEEK TWO

BEING HUMAN

Scripture Readings

Genesis 2:4–25
Psalm 8
Mark 3:1–6

Key Verses—Psalm 8:3–6

> *When I look at your heavens, the work of your fingers, the moon and the
>   stars that you have established;*
> *what are human beings that you are mindful of them, mortals that you
>   care for them?*
> *Yet you have made them a little lower than God, and crowned them with
>   glory and honor.*
> *You have given them dominion over the works of your hands; you have
>   put all things under their feet...*

DAY ONE: *Wild and Fascinating Stories*

Two eyes are better than one, because they make depth perception possible. The same goes with ears. Two ears make it possible to locate the direction of a sound. And we often say that two heads are better than one, because we know that insight from multiple perspectives adds wisdom.

The same is true with stories. We can best think of the Bible not as one tidy story with many chapters but as a wild and fascinating library with many stories told from many perspectives. On any given subject, these multiple stories challenge us to see life from a variety of angles—adding depth, a sense of direction, and wisdom. So we're given four gospels to introduce us to Jesus. We're given dozens of parables to illustrate Jesus's message. We're given two sections or testaments in which the story of God unfolds. And right at the beginning, we're given two different creation stories to help us know who we are, where we came from, and why we're here.

Today: Reflect on why multiple stories are better than one.

DAY TWO: *The First Creation Story*

According to the first creation story, you are part of creation. You are made from common soil… *dust,* Genesis says; *stardust,* astronomers tell us… soil that becomes watermelons and grain and apples and peanuts, and then they become food, and then that food becomes you. As highly organized dust, you are closely related to frogs and tortoises, lions and field mice, bison and elephants and gorillas. Together with all living things, you share the breath of life, participating in the same cycles of birth and death, reproduction and recycling and renewal. You, with them, are part of the story of creation—different branches on the tree of life. In that story, you are connected and related to everything everywhere. In fact, that is a good partial definition of God: *God is the one through whom we are related and connected to everything.*

In the first creation story, we learn two essential truths about ourselves as human beings. First, *we are good.* Along with all our fellow creatures, we were created with a primal, essential goodness that our Creator appreciates and celebrates. And second, *we all bear God's image.* Women and men, girls and boys, toddlers and seniors and teenagers, rich or poor, popular or misunderstood, powerful or vulnerable, whatever our religion or race, whatever our gender identity or marital status, whatever our nationality or culture… we *all* bear God's image, no exceptions.

Today: Pray, "God, help me see you as the one through whom I am related and connected to everyone and everything."

DAY THREE: *Image Bearers*

What is the image of God? An image is a small imitation or echo, like a reflection in a mirror. So if we bear the image of God, then, like God, we experience life through relationships. Like God, we experience love through our complementary differences. Like God, we notice and enjoy and name things—starting with the animals, our companions on the Earth. Like God, we are caretakers of the garden of the Earth. And like God, we are "naked and not ashamed," meaning we can be who we are without fear.

Back in ancient times, this was a surprising message. Yes, kings and other powerful men were seen as image bearers of God. After all, since they were powerful, rich, sophisticated, and "civilized," they could reflect God's power and glory. But in Genesis, the term is applied to a couple of naked and "uncivilized" hunter-gatherers, a simple woman and man living in a garden with no pyramids or skyscrapers or economies or religions or technological inventions or even clothing to their credit! Centuries later, Jesus said something similar: The Creator loves every sparrow and every wildflower, and so how much more precious is every person—no matter how small, frail, or seemingly insignificant? Every woman, man, and child is good! Every person in every culture has value! Every person bears the image of God!

Today: Keep your eyes open for people who may be considered (or consider themselves) insignificant. See them with dignity, bearers of the image of God.

DAY FOUR: *A Second Creation Account*

The second creation account, which many scholars think is a much older one, describes another dimension to our identity. In this second account, the possibility of "not-good" also exists. God puts the first couple in a garden that contains two special trees. The Tree of Life is theirs to enjoy, but not the Tree of the Knowledge of Good and Evil. The Tree of Life is a beautiful image—suggesting health, strength, thriving, fruitfulness, growth, vigor, and all we mean by *aliveness*. What might that second tree signify?

There are many answers, no doubt. But consider this possibility: The second tree could represent the desire to play God and judge parts of God's creation—all of which God considers good—as evil. Do you see the danger? God's judging is always wise, fair, true, merciful, and restorative. But our judging is frequently ignorant, biased, retaliatory, and devaluing. So when we judge, we inevitably *mis*judge.

Today: Look for times today that you judge this or that as good or evil, beautiful or ugly, annoying or okay, normal or weird. And consider how your judgment could be *mis*judgment.

DAY FIVE: *The Danger of Judging*

If we humans start playing God and judging good and evil, how long will it take before we say this person or tribe is good and deserves to live, but that person or tribe is evil and deserves to die, or become our slaves? How long will it take before we judge this species of animal is good and deserves to survive, but that one is worthless and can be driven to extinction? How long until we judge this land is good and deserves to be preserved, but that river is without value and can be plundered, polluted, or poisoned?

If we eat from the second tree, we will soon become violent, hateful, and destructive. We will turn our blessing to name and know into a license to kill, to exploit, and to destroy both the Earth and other people. God sees everything as good, but we will accuse more and more things of being evil. In so doing, we will create in ourselves the very evil we claim to detect in others. In other words, the more we judge and accuse, the less we will reflect God…and the less we will fulfill our potential as image bearers of God.

Today: Notice people in your life who don't judge or accuse and reflect on how you feel in their presence.

DAY SIX: *Join In*

The second creation story presents us with our challenge as human beings. We constantly make a crucial choice: Do we eat from the Tree of Aliveness—so that we continue to see and value the goodness of creation and so reflect the image of the living God? Or do we eat from the Tree of the Knowledge of Good and Evil—constantly misjudging and playing God and as a result mistreating our fellow creatures?

It's a good and beautiful thing to be an image bearer of God. *But it's also a big responsibility.*

We can use our intelligence to be creative and generous, or to be selfish and destructive.

We can use our physical strength to be creative and generous, or to be selfish and destructive.

We can use our sexuality to be creative and generous, or to be selfish and destructive.

We can use our work, our money, our time, and our other assets to be creative and generous, or to be selfish and destructive.

Think of your hand. It can make a fist or it can extend in peace. It can wield a weapon or it can play a violin. It can point in derision or it can reach out in compassion. It can steal or it can serve. If the first creation story is about the gift of being human, the second story is about the choice all humans live with, day after day. To be alive means to bear responsibly the image of God. It means to stretch out your hand to take from the Tree of Aliveness—and to join in God's creative, healing work.

Today: Ponder the immense responsibility and opportunity of being human, of being alive, of being you.

WEEK THREE

A WORLD OF MEANING

Scripture Readings

> Psalm 145:1–16
> Proverbs 8:1–36
> John 1:1–17

Key Verses—John 1:1–5

> *In the beginning was the Word, and the Word was with God, and the Word was God. He was in the beginning with God. All things came into being through him, and without him not one thing came into being. What has come into being in him was life, and the life was the light of all people. The light shines in the darkness, and the darkness did not overcome it.*

DAY ONE: *An Unfolding Pattern*

Okay. Pay attention.

> 1, 6, 11, 16, 21, 26, 31 … What comes next?
> 1, 4, 2, 5, 3, 6, 4, 7 … What comes next?
> 1, 2, 3, 5, 8, 13, 21, 34 … What comes next?
> I, space, L, O, V, E, space, Y, O … What comes next?

You know the answers because you are paying attention to the pattern.

It becomes more obvious the longer you live that all life is full of patterns. Reality is trying to tell us something. Life is speaking to us. There's lots of mystery out there, to be sure, and no shortage of chaos and unpredictability. But there's also lots of meaning … messages trying to find expression, music inviting us to listen and sing, patterns attracting our attention and interpretation. The chaos becomes a backdrop for the patterns, and the mysteries seem to beckon us to try to understand.

Sometimes the universe feels like this:

> 71, 6, 2, -48, -213, 9 … random numbers with no pattern.
> Or…
> G, M, B, O, I, space, Q, H, Z, space, P … random letters with
> no meaning. Or…
> 1, 1, 1, 1, 1, 1, 1, 1, 1 … sameness or repetition going nowhere.

But above and behind and beyond the sometimes confusing randomness of life, something is going on here. From a single molecule to a strand of DNA, from a bird in flight to an ocean current to a dancing galaxy, there's a logic, a meaning, an unfolding pattern to it all.

Today: Notice when patterns—musical patterns, architectural patterns, visual patterns, etc.—seize your attention, and think of those patterns as an artist's signature on his or her works of art.

DAY TWO: *Pay Attention*

Like wood, reality has a grain. Like a river, it has a current. Like a story, it has characters and setting and conflict and resolution. Like poetry, it has syntax and structure, so letters are taken up in words, and words are taken up in phrases and sentences, and they're all taken up in a magnificent pattern of beauty and meaning that we can glimpse and savor, even if it's too big and deep to fully comprehend. Creation reveals wisdom through its patterns. It reveals wisdom about its source and purpose, and about our quest to be alive…if we are paying attention.

Of course, we often struggle to know how to interpret those patterns. For example, if a tornado destroys our house, an enemy army drops bombs on our village, a disease takes away someone we love, we lose our job, someone we love breaks our heart, or our best friends betray us, what does that mean? Is the logic of the universe chaos or cruelty? Does might make right? Do violence and chaos rule? Is the Creator capricious, heartless, and evil? If we had only our worst experiences in life to guide us, that might be our conclusion.

Today: Recall times in your life when you were tempted to interpret your life only in terms of painful experiences.

DAY THREE: *What Jesus Shows Us*

The Gospel of John adds a profound insight to the creation stories we find in the Book of Genesis. John had a special term for the pattern of meaning God has spoken or written into the universe. He called it *Logos,* which is often translated in English as "Word." We find *logos* in words like biology, anthropology, and psychology—the logic of life, human development, or the human personality.

This Word or *Logos,* he said, was "made flesh" in a man named Jesus. In other words, if we want to know what God is like and what the universe is about, we should pay special attention to the logic, meaning, wisdom, and patterns found in the life of Jesus. He communicated the *logos,* or logic, of God in his teachings. He lived the *logos,* or pattern, of God in his life. He showed the *logos,* or essence, of God in the way he treated others. From his birth to his death and beyond, John believes, Jesus translates the logic or meaning or pattern or heart of God into terms we humans can understand: skin and bone, muscle and breath, nerve and action.

Today: Ponder Jesus as revealing the pattern or logic or *logos* of God.

DAY FOUR: *A New Way to Live*

So, inspired by Genesis, we are guided to look for the pattern, meaning, wisdom, and logic of God woven into galaxies, planets, forests, fields, plants, animals, you, and me. In John's gospel, we are inspired to look for the pattern in a poor man traveling across the land with a band of students and friends, telling stories, confronting injustice, helping people in need. If we learn and trust the wisdom that comes in creation and in Jesus, we will live our lives in a new way, John says. We will discover God as our loving parent, and we will encounter all other creatures as our relations, our relatives, in one family of creation.

Of course, we have other options. For example, many of us live by the logic of rivalry. Under this logic, the cosmos is a huge battlefield or coliseum in which participants can survive only by competing, defeating, deceiving, displacing, or killing their rivals. In this universe, the strongest survive, the ruthless are rewarded, the kind are killed, and the meek are crushed. You'd better fight, or you'll be trampled.

Others of us live by the logic of compliance. Under this logic, the cosmos is a big organization ruled by powerful bosses, and your job is to learn the rules and comply. Stay in your allotted place, do what you're told, curry favor in the "inner circle" of power, and the logic of compliance will work in your favor. You'd better play it safe, or you'll get in a lot of trouble.

Today: Look for evidence of people living by the logic of rivalry and compliance.

DAY FIVE: *Creation Possibilities*

While some think of the universe as a battleground full of violent rivalry or as an organization demanding fearful compliance, others think of it as a giant machine demanding that they live by the logic of mechanism—action, reaction; cause, effect; stimulus, response. You can use the mechanisms of the universe to seek whatever pleasure, power, and security you can during your short life. But in the end, there is no meaning to the machine, so you'd better grab whatever moments of fleeting pleasure you can. That's all there is or ever will be.

Clearly, the creation stories of Genesis and John offer us a powerful alternative to the logic of rivalry, the logic of compliance, and the logic of meaningless mechanism.

They dare us to believe that the universe runs by the logic of creativity, goodness, and love. The universe is God's creative project, filled with beauty, opportunity, challenge, and meaning. It runs on the meaning or pattern we see embodied in the life of Jesus. In this story, pregnancy abounds. Newness multiplies. Freedom grows. Meaning expands. Wisdom flows. Healing happens. Goodness runs wild.

So here we are, alive and paying attention. We discern patterns in life. We interpret those patterns and we open ourselves to the possibility of a creative *logos* of love and wisdom that runs through the universe like a current and can play in our lives like a song.

Today: Pray, "God, help me live by the logic of 'creativity, goodness, and love.'"

WEEK FOUR

THE DRAMA OF DESIRE

Scripture Readings

> Genesis 3:1–13
> Psalm 32
> Philippians 2:3–11

Key Verses—Psalm 32:1–5

> *Happy are those whose transgression is forgiven,*
> > *whose sin is covered.*
> *Happy are those to whom the Lord imputes no iniquity,*
> > *and in whose spirit there is no deceit.*
> *While I kept silence, my body wasted away*
> > *through my groaning all day long.*
> *For day and night your hand was heavy upon me;*
> > *my strength was dried up as by the heat of summer.* Selah.
> *Then I acknowledged my sin to you,*
> > *and I did not hide my iniquity;*
> *I said, "I will confess my transgressions to the Lord,"*
> > *and you forgave the guilt of my sin.* Selah.

DAY ONE: *Wrong Choices*

In the ancient wisdom of storytelling, Genesis tells us that we are part of God's good creation. It then tells us we have a special responsibility as God's reflections or image bearers. It tells us that in order to reflect God's image, we have to desire the Tree of Life, not the tree that feeds our pride so that we think we can play god and judge between good and evil.

Of course, we know what happened. The story of Adam and Eve doesn't have to be about literal historical figures in the past to tell us something very true about us, our history, and our world today. We humans have consistently chosen the wrong tree. Instead of imitating and reflecting God as good image bearers should do, we start competing with God, edging God out, playing god ourselves. We reject the Creator and choose another model instead: a snake (the story says), who seems to represent a subtle and dangerous desire to choose rivalry and violence over harmony and well-being.

In Genesis, after feeding on the Tree of Knowledge of Good and Evil, Adam and Eve suddenly feel a change come over them. Perhaps they each fear that the other will judge them for being different, so they fashion crude clothing to hide their sexual differences. When God approaches, they no longer see God as a friend but as a rival and threat. So they hide from God in fear. When God asks what has happened, they blame each other and refuse to admit their mistake. Soon they face a harder life of pain, competition, sweat, labor, frustration, and death— East of Eden, outside the beautiful garden that was their home.

Today: Look for signs of people fearing judgment and hiding from one another or God. Don't judge them but instead feel compassion for them.

DAY TWO: *Losing Our Divine Perfection*

Adam and Eve's two sons repeat the mistakes of their parents. The older brother—we might say he is "more advanced"—becomes an agriculturalist. His life is wrapped up in fields, fences, ownership, barns, and accumulated wealth, with all the moral complexity they bring. The younger brother—we might say he is "more vulnerable" or "less developed"—is a nomadic herdsman. He can't own land or accumulate wealth, because he moves constantly with his herds to wherever the fresh grass is growing. Their different ways of life are expressed in different forms of religious sacrifice. They soon become religious rivals, competing for a higher degree of God's favor. The perceived loser in the competition, Cain, envies and resents his brother.

Sometime later, we can imagine Abel leading his flocks into his brother's field. At that moment Cain, his resentment simmering, no longer sees a brother: He sees a trespasser, an enemy. He plays god and judges his brother as evil and therefore worthy of death. Abel soon becomes the first victim of violence, and Cain the first murderer. So we humans quickly turn from reflecting the image of a creative, generous, life-giving God. With Adam and Eve we become graspers, hiders, blamers, and shamers. With Cain and Abel we become rivals, resenters, murderers, and destroyers—the very opposite of God's image.

Today: Grasper, hider, blamer, or shamer...rival, resenter, murderer, or destroyer—monitor whether you feel a pull toward any of these primal human behaviors seen in the Adam/Eve and Cain/Abel stories.

DAY THREE: *Know What's Broken*

What do these ancient stories of Adam and Eve and Cain and Abel mean for us today?

They help us know what's broken with our world: something in us human beings.

And they help us know what's broken in human beings: something in our desires.

And they help us know what's broken with our desires: We have stopped imitating God's good desires to create and bless and give life. Instead we've started imitating the prideful, competitive, fearful, and harmful desires we see in one another...the desire to acquire what someone else has, the desire to compete and consume, the desire to judge as evil those who get in our way, even the desire to harm or kill those who are obstacles to our desires.

Today: Be sensitive to the pull of imitating the desires of others.

DAY FOUR: *The Path of Death*

Think about how much imitation runs our lives.

Somebody hits or criticizes you and what do you want to do? Hit them back! Criticize them back!

Somebody buys a new shirt or a new TV and what do you want to do? Buy an even better shirt or bigger TV!

Somebody moves to a bigger house in a different neighborhood and what do you desire? To get an even bigger house in an even better neighborhood!

And what happens if you can't get what you desire? You'll be tempted to cheat, steal, lie, harm, or maybe even kill to get what you desire.

Now, there's nothing wrong with desire. The question is, whose desires are you imitating? To be alive is to imitate God's generous desires...to create, to bless, to help, to serve, to care for, to save, to enjoy. To make the opposite choice—to imitate one another's desires and become one another's rivals—is to choose a path of death.

If we imitate our way into that rat race, we will compete rather than create, impress rather than bless, defeat rather than protect, dominate rather than serve, and exploit rather than respect. As a result, we will turn our neighbor first into a rival, then an enemy, and then a victim.

Today: Pray, "God, help me to imitate your desires to create, to bless, to help, to serve, to care for, to save, to enjoy."

DAY FIVE: *The Drama of Desire*

We all live in this drama: the drama of desire. We have the opportunity to imitate God's generous and good desires on the one hand—and we have the temptation to imitate selfish, fearful, envious human desires on the other hand.

Think of all the advertisers who are trying to influence our desires. Think of all the politicians who are eager to mold our desires so they can manipulate us for their advantage. Think of all the potential rivals who are glad to engage us in competition—their desires against ours. What's true of us as individuals can also be true of us as groups; both personally and socially, we are caught in the drama of desire.

Today: Notice how advertisers and politicians try to mold your desires.

DAY SIX: *A Different Way of Life*

That's another reason Jesus is so important to us: because he modeled a different way of life. He gave us a down-to-earth example of God's creative self-giving. True, Adam and Eve grabbed for the chance to be like gods—judging others as good or evil, exploiting rather than preserving the Earth, competing with each other rather than loving and serving each other. But Jesus didn't grasp at godlike status. He humbly poured himself out for others—in service, in suffering, even to the point of death. He even gave us a way of remembering his attitude of self-giving: He said that his life was like food, like bread and wine, and he freely gave himself for us. His constant invitation—"Follow me"—could also be expressed as "Imitate me."

To be alive is to be mindful that we live in the drama of desire. We can imitate one another's competitive desires, and so be driven to fear, rivalry, judging, conflict, and killing. Or we can imitate God's generous desires…to create, bless, help, serve, care for, save, and enjoy. At this moment, let us turn toward God, not as rivals who want to play God, but as image bearers who want to imitate and reflect God. Let us humbly and fervently desire the right kind of desire.

Today: Pray, "God, help me desire what you desire!"

WEEK FIVE

IN OVER OUR HEADS

Scripture Readings

> Genesis 4:1–17; 6:5–8;
> 7:1–5; 8:1; 9:7–17
> Psalm 51
> James 4:1–8

Key Verses—Psalm 51:1–5

> *Have mercy on me, O God,*
> *according to your steadfast love;*
> *according to your abundant mercy*
> *blot out my transgressions.*
> *Wash me thoroughly from my iniquity,*
> *and cleanse me from my sin.*
> *For I know my transgressions,*
> *and my sin is ever before me.*
> *Against you, you alone, have I sinned,*

and done what is evil in your sight,
so that you are justified in your sentence
and blameless when you pass judgment.
Indeed, I was born guilty,
a sinner when my mother conceived me.

DAY ONE: *The Crisis of Desire*

In the ancient Genesis stories, our species was created in the image of God—to reflect God's character faithfully in the world, both to our fellow creatures and to one another. Soon, though, we wanted to be little gods ourselves. We wanted to judge good and evil for ourselves, to decide who would live and who would die, who would rule and who would be enslaved. Consumed by the desire to grasp what others had, we became rivals of God and our neighbors. That crisis of desire has led to great shame, pain, suffering, violence, counterviolence, and fear...in our lives, our communities, and our world. Today's headlines tell the same story in a hundred different ways.

In the Genesis story, the descendants of Cain, the first murderer, started building cities, and those cities reflected the violence of Cain. As city-states competed with one another and defeated one another, the winners created growing empires that elevated a few to godlike status and reduced most to oppression and slavery. The situation became so unbearable that in the story of Noah and the flood, God felt sorry for making the world in the first place. Eventually God decided to wipe the whole slate clean and start again. Maybe Noah's descendants would do better than Adam's had.

Today: Notice when you or others feel like giving up and starting over.

DAY TWO: *Storytelling Seeks Truth*

Although many people think of the Noah story as a cute tale of animals and a boat ride, those who think more deeply find it deeply disturbing. The image of violent oppressors and innocent victims drowning together seems only to make a bad situation worse. At the very least, one would think God would have more creativity, moral finesse, and foresight than to create a good world only to destroy it because it went so bad so (relatively) quickly. Shouldn't God be better than this?

To properly understand this story—and others like it—we need to remember that ancient cultures were oral cultures. Few people were literate, and oral storytelling was to them what reading books, using the Internet, going to concerts, and watching movies and TV shows are to us today. Ancient stories had a long life as oral compositions before they were ever written down. As oral compositions, stories could evolve over time. In a sense, writing them down ended their evolution.

For ancient people in oral cultures, a story was like a hypothesis. A good and helpful story, like a tested hypothesis, would be repeated and improved and enhanced from place to place and generation to generation. Less helpful stories would be forgotten like a failed theory, or adjusted and revised until they became more helpful. Sometimes, competing stories would stand side by side like competing theories, awaiting a time when one would prevail—or both would fail, and a new story would arise with more explanatory power. In all these ways, storytelling was, like the scientific method, a way of seeking the truth, a way of grappling with profound questions, a way of passing on hard-won insights. As our ancestors deepened their understanding, their stories changed—just as our theories change.

Today: Ponder the idea of a story as a theory that can be tested and improved over time.

DAY THREE: *God's Character Revealed Further*

In light of the ways stories engage with other stories and evolve over time, we can reconsider the story of Noah as an adaptation of even older stories from the Middle East. In one of those earlier versions, a gang of gods unleashed a catastrophic flood as a personal vendetta against some noisy people who kept the gods awake at night. Ancient Jewish storytellers would have found that story repulsive. So they adapted it to reveal more of God's true character, replacing many vindictive gods who were irritable from lack of sleep with one Creator who unleashes a flood to flush out human violence.

That's certainly a step in the right direction, but the process doesn't have to end with the Noah story. After all, God's violence doesn't really solve anything in the Noah story, since Noah's family quickly starts cooking up more trouble so that soon things are just as bad as they were before the flood. We can't help but wonder: Shouldn't God be better than that? To answer that question, we need to bring in another story. Later in Genesis, in the story of Joseph, God responds to violence in a very different way—not with more violence, but with kindness. Another big step in the right direction!

Today: Instead of seeing something as simply wrong, try to see it as a step up from something even worse, and imagine what the next step forward might be.

DAY FOUR: *A Giant Step Forward*

The ancient world was filled with huge structures—towers and pyramids and temples and the like—that were built with slave labor. Just about everyone in those days assumed that the gods chose a few high-echelon people to sit pretty at the top of the pyramid. The masses were destined to be slaves at the bottom, sweating to make bricks or haul stones or irrigate fields so that the elite could have a nice day. Everyone assumed that the gods supported these slave-based economies of empire, and everyone understood that the towers, pyramids, and temples both pleased and honored the gods of the status quo.

But in the Tower of Babel story, the storytellers realize that the living God must be better than that. So in their story, tower building is exposed as another form of rivalry with God. God opposes their soaring ambition of assimilation and domination. God diversifies the languages of the Babylonian empire so that its ambition of global empire fails, memorialized forever in an unfinished tower. This new version of an old story is a big step in the right direction. Later, when we come to the story of Pentecost in the Acts of the Apostles, we'll see another giant step forward, revealing God even more beautifully and fully.

Today: Pray, "God, help me always be open to the possibility—no, the certainty—that you are better than I currently understand you to be."

DAY FIVE: *A Deeper Vision*

As we progress through the biblical library, stories interact with one another again and again. Together they reveal an ever fuller and deeper vision of God. We come to know a God who consistently refuses to support a pyramid economy with a few at the top and the masses at the bottom. We come to trust a God who consistently opposes the oppressors and consistently takes the side of the humble, the vulnerable, and the poor. We eventually come to understand God as one who consistently prefers nonviolence over violence, equality over dominance, and justice over injustice. Taken together, these stories make one of the most audacious claims in all of history: The living God doesn't uphold the status quo...but repeatedly disrupts it and breaks it open so that something better can emerge and evolve.

Today: Whenever you see injustice in the status quo, remind yourself that God wants to disrupt it "so that something better can emerge and evolve."

DAY SIX: *An Even Better Story*

Do you see what's happening? Generation after generation, people are telling stories that improve upon previous stories and prepare the way for even better stories to emerge. The process leaps forward in the story of Jesus. He comes proclaiming the message of the commonwealth—or kingdom, or alternative economy—of God. He shows how in God's way of arranging things, the last are first and the first are last. Leaders serve, and the humble—not the arrogant—inherit the Earth. In word and deed, in parable and miracle, Jesus shows that God is at work in history to heal what is broken—on the personal level of individual lives, and on the societal level of economics and government, too. And he proclaims God not as a reactive avenger who sweeps away the innocent with the guilty but as a forgiving, merciful, gracious parent who loves all creation with a perfect, holy, faithful, compassionate love.

No wonder he told people to "repent"—which means to "rethink everything." No wonder Jesus was known as a brilliantly creative and original storyteller.

Today: Look for ways to rethink everything and tell better stories.

DAY SEVEN: *Retell the Ancient Stories*

Like the parables of Jesus, the Adam and Eve, Cain and Abel, flood, and tower stories in Genesis don't have to be *factually* true to tell an *actual* truth about us and our civilization. Those ancient stories courageously expose how all civilizations were founded on violence and oppression, producing luxury and ease for a few but exhaustion and degradation for the many. They warn us that unjust structures are unsustainable. They advise that floods of change will sweep injustice away and internal conflicts will thwart arrogant ambitions. They promise that in the long run, justice and reconciliation will prevail over injustice and rivalry.

If we aren't careful, we can grow comfortable and complacent with a status quo of injustice, oppression, and violence. That's why we are wise to gather often and retell these ancient stories. Rather than being conformed to this world and its mixed-up priorities, we can seek together to be transformed by a different and better story so we can join with God in the healing of our world.

To be alive is to join God in caring about the oppressed, the needy, the powerless, the victims, and the vulnerable. To be alive is to believe that injustice is not sustainable and to share God's desire for a better world. To be alive is to look at our world and say, "God is better than that!"—and know that our world can be better, too. *And so can we.*

Today: Pray, "God, help me join you in the good and beautiful things you are doing to write a better story."

WEEK SIX

PLOTTING GOODNESS

Scripture Readings

Genesis 12:1–9
Galatians 3:6–9
Mark 11:15–19

Key Verses—Galatians 3:6–9

The Scriptures say that God accepted Abraham because Abraham had faith. And so, you should understand that everyone who has faith is a child of Abraham. Long ago the Scriptures said that God would accept the Gentiles because of their faith. That's why God told Abraham the good news that all nations would be blessed because of him. This means that everyone who has faith will share in the blessings that were given to Abraham because of his faith.

DAY ONE: *God Is Blessing the World*

According to the ancient stories of Genesis, God is up to something surprising and amazing in our world. While we're busy plotting evil, God is plotting goodness.

Yes, sometimes we humans try to rope God into our dark plots and use God to help us scramble to the top of the pyramid, where we can dominate over others. Yes, we sometimes try to enlist God to condemn those we want to condemn, deprive those we want to deprive, even kill those we want to kill. But God isn't willing to be domesticated into our little nationalistic deity on a leash who will "sic 'em" on our command. While we plot ways to use God to get blessings for ourselves, God stays focused on the big picture of blessing the world—which includes blessing us in the process.

Today: Bring this thought to mind throughout the day, that God is not a little nationalistic deity, but rather the Creator of all who loves all people everywhere, no exceptions.

DAY TWO: *Abram and Sara*

Consider the story of God choosing a man named Abram and a woman named Sara. They are from a prominent family in a great ancient city-state known as Ur, one of the first ancient Middle Eastern civilizations. Like all civilizations, Ur has a dirty little secret: its affluence is built on violence, oppression, and exploitation. Behind its beautiful facade, its upper classes live each day in luxury, while its masses slave away in squalor.

God tells this couple to leave their life of privilege in this rich and powerful civilization. He sends them out into the unknown as wanderers and adventurers. No longer will Abram and Sara have the armies and wealth and comforts of Ur at their disposal. All they will have is a promise—that God will be with them and show them a better way. From now on, they will make a new road by walking.

God's promise comes in two parts. In the first part, Abram and Sara will be blessed. They will become a great nation, and God will bless those who bless them and curse those who curse them. That's the kind of promise we might expect. It's the second part that's surprising.

Not only will they be blessed, but they will be a blessing. Not only will their family become a great nation, but all the families on Earth will be blessed through them.

Today: Notice the different ethnicities of people you meet today, and remind yourself that each is included in God's promise to bless all the families of the earth.

DAY THREE: *A Unique Identity*

Abram and Sara and their descendants are given a unique identity indeed. They will be a unique *us* in relation to all the other *thems* of the world. No, their identity will not be *us at the top* of the pyramid and *them at the bottom*, or vice versa. Nor will their identity be *us assimilated into them*, or *us assimilating them into us*. Nor will it be *us against them, us apart from them*, or *us in spite of them*. No, Abram and Sara's unique identity will be *us for them, us with them, us for the benefit and blessing of all*.

That "otherly" identity—*us for the common good*—wasn't intended only for Abram and Sara's clan. It is the kind of identity that is best for every individual, every culture, every nation, every religion. It says, "We're special!" But it also says, "They're special, too." It says, "God has a place for us and a purpose for our lives." But it also says, "God has a place and purpose for others, too." When we drift from that high calling and start thinking only of *me*, only of *our* clan or *our* nation or *our* religion, our sense of identity begins to go stale and sour, even toxic.

So the story of Abram and Sara's unique identity tells us something powerful about God's identity, too: God is not the nationalist deity of one group of "chosen" people. God is not for us and against all others. God is for *us* and for *them*, too. God loves everyone everywhere, no exceptions.

Today: Each time you look in the mirror today, tell yourself, "I have been blessed not to the exclusion of others but for the benefit of others."

DAY FOUR: *True Faith*

The story of Abram and Sara gives us a window into true faith. Faith is stepping off the map of what's known and making a new road by walking into the unknown. It's responding to God's call to adventure, stepping out on a quest for goodness, trusting that the status quo isn't as good as it gets, believing a promise that a better life is possible.

True faith isn't a deal where we use God to get the inside track or a special advantage or a secret magic formula for success. It isn't a mark of superiority or exclusion. True faith is about joining God in God's love for everyone. It's about seeking goodness with others, not at the expense of others. True faith is seeing a bigger circle in which we are all connected, all included, all loved, all blessed. True faith reverses the choice that is pictured in the story of Adam and Eve. In that story, Adam and Eve want to set themselves above everyone and everything else. True faith brings us back down to earth, into solidarity with others and with all creation.

Sadly, for many people, faith has been reduced to a list. For some, it's a list of beliefs: ideas or statements that we have to memorize and assent to if we want to be blessed. For others, it's a list of dos and don'ts: rituals or rules that we have to perform to earn the status of being blessed. But Abram didn't have much in the way of beliefs, rules, or rituals. He had no bibles, doctrines, temples, commandments, or ceremonies. For him, true faith was simply trusting a promise of being blessed to be a blessing. It wasn't a way of being religious: it was a way of being alive.

Today: Pray, "God, help me to be more fully alive."

DAY FIVE: *True Aliveness*

The Abram and Sara story not only tells us something about God's true identity and about the true nature of faith, it also tells us about true aliveness. If you scramble over others to achieve your goal, that's not true aliveness. If you harm others to acquire your desire, that's not true aliveness. If you hoard your blessings while others suffer in need, that's not true aliveness. True aliveness comes when we receive blessings and become a blessing to others. It's not a blessing racket—figuring out how to plot prosperity for me and my tribe. It's a blessing economy where God plots goodness for all.

Like all of us, Abram and Sara lose sight of this vision of aliveness sometimes. But even when they lose faith, God remains faithful. Through their mistakes and failures, they keep learning and growing, discovering more and more of God's desire to overflow with abundant blessing for all.

Are you ready to step out on the same journey of faith with Sara and Abram? Will you join them in the adventure of being blessed to be a blessing? Are you ready to make the road by walking?

Today: Say, "I am on a lifelong adventure of faith, being blessed to be a blessing."

IT'S NOT TOO LATE

Scripture Readings

Genesis 18:9–33; 22:1–14
Micah 6:6–8
Acts 17:19–34

Key Verses—Micah 6:7–8

Will the Lord be pleased with thousands of rams,
with ten thousands of rivers of oil?
Shall I give my firstborn for my transgression,
the fruit of my body for the sin of my soul?"
He has told you, O mortal, what is good
and what does the Lord require of you
but to do justice, and to love kindness,
and to walk humbly with your God?

DAY ONE: *The Impossible Is Possible*

Have you ever felt that it was too late? That things were so awful they could never get better, that you had failed so horribly and so often you could never, ever recover, that the situation was too far gone ever to be salvageable?

That was how Abram and Sara felt at one point in their lives. Like many couples, they had dreamed all of their lives of having children. But the years passed and no children came. They had received a promise from God that they would become a great family and that all people everywhere would be blessed through their descendants. But there was one problem: They had no descendants. When they were far too old to have children, you can imagine how they felt: It was just too late.

Then they received reassurance from God that they would have a child. No wonder, according to the Book of Genesis, Sara laughed when she first heard the promise!

However they felt at first, over time Abram and Sara came to believe that what seemed impossible was possible after all. When that impossible baby was born, guess what they named him? They named him Isaac, which means "laughter." And their names were changed, too, reflecting their new status as parents—from Abram and Sara to Abraham and Sarah.

Today: When you think something is impossible or "It's too late," imagine the sound of Sarah laughing.

DAY TWO: *Questioning Your Belief*

When Sarah finally has a baby after so many years of disappointment, you might expect a happy ending. But even after becoming parents when it seemed too late, Abraham and Sarah faced another huge challenge. They were about to overturn one of the most established assumptions about God.

Put yourself in their sandals. Imagine that you and everyone you know believes that God is a severe and demanding deity who can bestow forgiveness and other blessings only after human blood has been shed. Imagine how that belief in human sacrifice would affect the way people live, the way they worship, and the way they treat others. Now imagine how hard it would be to be the first person in your society to question such a belief. Imagine how much courage it would take, especially because if people think you're a heretic, you might be their next victim!

Today: Think about the courage it takes to question a misguided belief that everyone around you holds as sacred.

DAY THREE: *Acknowledge We Don't Know*

Questioning widely held assumptions about God can be a dangerous venture indeed. But if our assumptions aren't sometimes questioned, belief in God becomes less and less plausible. For example, biblical writers used the imagery of God sitting on a throne to express their belief that God was powerful and glorious, like an ancient king. Even though we may agree that God is powerful and glorious, does that mean we must believe that God's power and glory are exactly like those of ancient kings—who could often be insecure, capricious, vain, or vicious? Does it mean we must conclude that God has a literal gluteus maximus that rests on a really big chair floating up in the sky somewhere? Are we allowed to question or point out problems with these images and understandings that are widely held and emotionally comforting for many?

Perhaps we can agree that whoever and whatever God is, our best imagery can only point toward God like a finger. We can never capture God in our concepts like a fist. In fact, the more we know about God, the more we have to acknowledge we don't know. The bigger our understanding about God, the bigger the mystery that we must acknowledge. Our faith must always be open to correction, enhancement, and new insight. That's why humility is so essential for all who speak of God.

Today: Pray, "God, help me to remember that you are bigger and better than my best concepts of you, and help me always be open to expanding my understanding of you."

DAY FOUR: *Changing Your Theory*

The dominant theory of God in Abraham and Sarah's day taught that the gracious God who gives human life would also demand human life as a sacrifice. So when Abraham believed God was commanding him to kill Isaac, he was being faithful to a traditional model of how God and life worked. We might wish that Abraham had argued over this theory, just as he did when he believed God was about to destroy the cities of Sodom and Gomorrah. But strangely, what Abraham did for two cities he refrained from doing for his own son.

So one day Abraham led Isaac up a mountain. He piled stones into an altar, tied up his son, and placed him on the stones. He raised the knife and, once again, it seemed too late. But at that last possible instant, Abraham saw a ram nearby, its horns stuck in a thicket. Suddenly he realized that God had provided a ram to sacrifice in place of Isaac, his son. What a powerful new insight! Animal blood could please or appease their God as a substitute for human blood!

It was commonplace in the ancient world for a man to lead his son up a mountain to be sacrificed to his deity. It was extraordinary for a man to come down the mountain with his son still alive. Through that ancient story, Abraham's descendants explained why they had changed their theory or model of God, and why they dared to be different from their neighbors who still practiced human sacrifice. It wasn't too late to challenge widely held assumptions and change their theory of God!

Today: Think about old ideas of God that you have left behind for better ones.

DAY FIVE: *God Wants One Thing*

Many generations after ritualized human sacrifice was left behind forever and replaced by animal sacrifice, prophets and poets arose among Abraham's descendants who made a new shocking claim: God doesn't need animal sacrifices, either. They understood that God could never need anything *from* us, since God provides everything *for* us. Not only that, but they realized God isn't the one who is angry and hostile and needs appeasement. We humans are the angry ones! Our hostile, bloodthirsty hearts are the ones that need to be changed!

So over many centuries, led along by many teachers and prophets, Abraham's descendants came to believe that God wanted one thing from humanity...not sacrifice, whether human or animal, but this: to do justice, to love kindness, and to walk humbly with God. The only sacrifice that mattered to God was the holy gift of humble hearts and lives dedicated to his way of love.

Today: Repeat these words from the prophet Micah until you know them by heart: "Do justice, love kindness, and walk humbly with your God."

DAY SIX: *It's Not Too Late*

Remember: With faith, it's not too late. It's not too late for a dream to come true, and it's not too late to learn something new.

That's true for us today as we follow in the footsteps of Abraham and Sara, walking this road of faith together. We're still learning, rethinking, growing, discovering. In spite of long delays and many disappointments, will we dare to keep dreaming impossible dreams? In spite of the assumptions that everyone around us holds to be true, will we dare to ask new questions and make new discoveries—including lessons about God and what God really desires? It may seem as if it's too late to keep hoping, to keep trying, to keep learning, to keep growing. But to be alive in the story of creation means daring to believe it's not too late.

Today: Dare to keep dreaming impossible dreams. Dare to keep hoping, learning, and growing. Dare to believe.

WEEK EIGHT

RIVALRY OR RECONCILIATION?

Scripture Readings

> Genesis 32:22–33:11; 50:15–21
> Matthew 25:31–40
> Luke 10:25–37

Key Verses—Matthew 25:34–36

"Then the king will say to those at his right hand, 'Come, you that are blessed by my Father, inherit the kingdom prepared for you from the foundation of the world; for I was hungry and you gave me food, I was thirsty and you gave me something to drink, I was a stranger and you welcomed me, I was naked and you gave me clothing, I was sick and you took care of me, I was in prison and you visited me.'"

DAY ONE: *Competition and Conflict*

If you had siblings, how did you get along? The Book of Genesis is full of stories of brothers and sisters in competition and conflict. After the tragic story of Cain and Abel, we come to the story of Ishmael and Isaac. Ishmael was Abraham's first son, born not to his wife, Sarah, but to her Egyptian slave, Hagar. According to Genesis, there was a bitter rivalry between the two mothers and their two sons. Hagar and Ishmael were treated terribly, while Sarah and Isaac were given every advantage. God intervened and made it clear that even if Abraham and Sarah failed to love Hagar and Ishmael, God cared for them deeply.

Years later, Abraham's grandson Jacob was caught up in bitter sibling rivalry with his older twin brother, Esau. At the heart of their conflict was the belief that God loved Jacob and hated Esau. Based on this belief that he was uniquely favored, Jacob felt entitled to take advantage of everyone around him, especially his disfavored brother, Esau. He seemed to get away with his trickery again and again until, eventually, Esau grew so angry at Jacob that Jacob had to flee for his life. For many years, the two brothers lived far apart, maturing, but still alienated from each other. During this time, Jacob married two sisters—a favored one named Rachel and a disfavored one named Leah. Leah became the mother of six of Jacob's twelve sons, so her story had a happier ending than anyone expected.

After he became a rich and successful man, Jacob began a homeward journey. He learned that the next day he would be forced to encounter the brother he had wronged in so many ways so many years before. You can imagine how afraid he was. He had lived his whole life by trickery. Now his old tricks weren't working anymore. So all that night, he felt like he was in a wrestling match with God.

His sleepless night of inner wrestling seems like an image for the human struggle common to us all. Like Jacob, we wrestle to get our own way by trying to cheat or defeat anyone who has something we desire— including God. Like Jacob, we grapple with changing old habits, even when those habits aren't working for us anymore. Like Jacob, we agonize through the long night, held in a headlock of despair, fearing that it's too late for us to hope for a new beginning.

Today: Where in your life are you wrestling, struggling, agonizing, trying to break out of a "headlock of despair"?

Hour after hour through a long, dark night, Jacob wrestled. When the new day dawned, he rose from the struggle with two signs of his emergence into maturity as a human being. First, he received the blessing of a new name, Israel, which means "God-wrestler." And he received a hip injury that required him to walk with a limp, a lifelong memento of his long night of struggle.

Jacob was now ready—limping—to face his brother. Instead of trying to trick Esau as the old Jacob would have done, he sent Esau a huge array of gifts to honor him. When Jacob finally met Esau face-to-face, Esau had his chance. Now the older twin could finally get revenge on his upstart younger twin for all Jacob's dirty tricks in the past. Esau could treat Jacob to a taste of the disdain and contempt Jacob had repeatedly poured upon him.

But Esau surprised everyone. He made it clear that he wasn't holding a grudge. He desired no revenge, nor did he require any gifts or appeasement. He simply wanted to be reconciled.

Jacob was so touched that he said these beautiful words: "Truly, to see your face is like seeing the face of God, since you have received me with such grace." The upstart trickster had finally learned to see the face of God in the face of the one he formerly tricked and despised. He discovered God's grace in the one he had always considered disgraced. In the face of the other, he rediscovered a brother. In the face of the one everyone assumed God hated...God had been revealed. What a story!

Today: Think of a group of people who, like Esau, are considered disgraced, disguised, or inferior. Now imagine those people being the ones through whom God's face is revealed.

DAY THREE: *God's Good Intent*

Even though Jacob learned an important lesson in his encounter with Esau, sibling rivalry had a resurgence in the next generation. Jacob had twelve sons. One son, Joseph, was resented by his eleven brothers, because—as with Abel over Cain, Sarah over Hagar, Isaac over Ishmael, Jacob over Esau, and Rachel over Leah before him—Joseph was favored over them. In fact, Joseph dreamed that one day his brothers would grovel before him. Eventually, driven by the resentment of the disfavored, they plotted to kill him. At the last minute, however, they decided to sell him as a slave to some Egyptian traders instead. Through a dramatic series of temptations, delays, setbacks, and recoveries, Joseph rose from slavery to a place of honor in the court of the Egyptian Pharaoh.

Many years later, when a famine sent the brothers to Egypt as refugees, Joseph had his chance, just as Esau did: He could get revenge on those miserable brothers who treated him so badly. He could do to them what they had done to him. But Joseph, like Esau, made a different choice—not for revenge but for forgiveness. When his brothers groveled before him, as Joseph had dreamed they would when he was a boy, and when they offered to be treated as slaves rather than brothers, Joseph didn't gloat. He refused to play god, judge them evil, and sentence them to death or enslavement. Instead, he reinterpreted the whole story of their relationship. Their evil intent had been overshadowed by God's good intent, so that Joseph could save their lives. He had suffered and he had been blessed, he realized, for their benefit. So instead of imitating their resentful and violent example, he imitated the gracious heart of God. By refusing to play god in judging them, he imaged God in showing kindness to them.

In this way, Joseph—the victim of mistreatment by his brothers—became the hero. The one everyone cruelly rejected was the one whose kindness everyone needed. The one who was considered favored wasn't made superior so others could grovel before him; he was made strong so he could protect them, provide for them, and serve them.

In both the story of Jacob and Esau and the story of Joseph and his brothers, the rejected brother, the "other brother," is the one in whose face the grace of God brightly shines.

Today: Pray, "God, help me see your face shining in people who are rejected, disrespected, and considered outsiders and outcasts."

DAY FOUR: *Reflect the Face of God*

The stories from Genesis we have been considering pulsate with some of the most powerful and radical themes of the Bible. Blessing, power, or favor is not given for privilege over others, but for service for the benefit of others. The weaker brother or sister, the one who is deemed ugly or dull or disfavored or illegitimate, is always beloved by God. From Abel to Ishmael to Hagar to Esau to Leah to Joseph, God keeps showing up, not in the victors who have defeated or exploited or rejected a weaker rival, but in the weaker ones who have been defeated or rejected.

These same themes are the heartbeat of two of Jesus's greatest parables. In the parable of the prodigal son, the father who runs out to welcome his runaway younger son behaves exactly as Esau did—running to him, embracing him, kissing him, showing grace rather than retaliation. And he acts just as Joseph did, as well, not making the runaway grovel as a slave, but welcoming him as a beloved member of the family. And in the parable of the good Samaritan, it is the disfavored Samaritan, not the high-status priest or Levite, who models the love of God.

As in Genesis, life today is full of rivalries and conflicts. We all experience wrongs, hurts, and injustices through the actions of others—and we all inflict wrongs, hurts, and injustices upon others. If we want to reflect the image of God, we will choose grace over hostility, reconciliation over revenge, and equality over rivalry. When we make that choice, we encounter God in the faces of our former rivals and enemies. And as we are humbled, surrendering to God and seeking to be reconciled with others, our faces, too, reflect the face of God. We come alive as God's image bearers indeed.

Today: Imagine what it would be like for others to see God's face reflected in your face.

WEEK NINE

FREEDOM!

Scripture Readings

> Exodus 1:1–14; 3:1–15
> John 8:1–11
> Galatians 5:1, 13–15

Key Verses—Galatians 5:13–15

For you were called to freedom, brothers and sisters; only do not use your freedom as an opportunity for self-indulgence, but through love become slaves to one another. For the whole law is summed up in a single commandment, "You shall love your neighbor as yourself." If, however, you bite and devour one another, take care that you are not consumed by one another.

DAY ONE: *A Common Reality*

Slavery was a sad and common reality in the ancient world. There were at least four ways that people became slaves. First, when people suffered a terrible misfortune like sickness, accident, flood, debt, theft, or famine, they could quickly find themselves in danger of death by starvation or homelessness. In that desperate situation, they might be forced to sell themselves into slavery, under the simple reasoning that being a live slave was better than being a dead nonslave. Second, when nations won a war, they often killed off all of their vanquished enemies. But some nations decided to keep their defeated foes alive as slaves instead of killing them. Third, refugees or other vulnerable minorities might be enslaved by the dominant majority. Finally, babies born to slaves were destined to be slaves.

That was what happened to the descendants of Abraham between the end of Genesis and the beginning of Exodus in the Bible. As Genesis ended, Joseph had welcomed his brothers into Egypt as refugees to escape a famine in their land to the north. Finding refuge solved the famine problem, but refugee and minority status made them vulnerable to enslavement.

As Exodus begins, the Hebrews, as Abraham's descendants were then called, have been enslaved. And they have also grown in numbers, so much so that the Egyptians have begun to fear that they might rebel. In response, the Egyptian ruler, the Pharaoh, calls for a gradual genocide by decreeing that all the male babies born to the Israelite slaves be thrown into the Nile River to drown. You can see how this strategy would leave the next generation of Hebrew women either barren or vulnerable to sexual enslavement by Egyptian men. After one generation, no more "pure" Hebrews would be born.

Today: Lament how genocide and slavery have been tragic parts of human history, and pray that we will never let them be part of our future.

DAY TWO: *Get Involved*

Often in the Bible, when there is a big problem, God prepares a person or people to act as God's partners or agents in solving it. In other words, God gets involved by challenging us to get involved. In this case, God prepared a man named Moses.

Moses was one of the babies whom the Pharaoh required to be drowned in the Nile. His mother came up with a creative way to save his life. She placed him in the Nile River as required, but first she put baby Moses in a little raft of reeds. His raft floated downstream, where it was found by one of Pharaoh's daughters. She felt sorry for the little baby and decided to raise him as her own. So this vulnerable slave boy was adopted into the privileged household of Pharaoh—and to top it off, Moses's own mother was hired to be the wet nurse. Quite a turn of events! Now Moses could live happily ever after, right? Not quite.

Today: Keep your heart open for ways God might challenge you to get involved as God's agent or partner in helping someone in need, solving some problem, or addressing some injustice.

DAY THREE: *Happiness Delayed Again*

The good news was that Moses survived. The bad news? Moses grew up with an identity crisis. He was an Israelite by birth but an Egyptian by culture. So a huge question was hanging over him as he matured: On whose side would he stand when he came of age? As a young man, his moment of decision came when he saw an Egyptian beating up an Israelite. He stood up for the Israelite and killed the Egyptian oppressor. Now he had made his choice. But to his surprise, his kinfolk didn't welcome him as a hero. Instead, when he tried to intervene in a quarrel between two Israelites, they distrusted him. So he went from belonging to both sides to being considered an outsider by both sides.

In disgrace, he ran away from Egypt and came to an oasis in the desert. There, he saw a group of male shepherds drive away some girls from a well. Now, sensitized to the victims of oppression, he stood up for the girls. Their father was so grateful he welcomed Moses into his family, and Moses married one of the daughters he had helped protect.

Finally Moses had a place to belong, right? Now he could settle down and be happy, right? They lived happily ever after, right? Not quite.

Today: Remind yourself that whatever is going on in your life right now is not the end of the story.

DAY FOUR: *Mission Reluctantly Accepted*

Imagine the scene: Moses is out tending sheep one day and something strange catches his attention: A bush is on fire, but it's not burning up. When Moses comes closer to check it out, he hears a voice calling his name. It's God—and God is telling him to go back to Egypt, confront Pharaoh about his exploitation of the Israelites, and lead them on a long road to freedom.

Moses feels he has already failed at helping the Israelites, so it takes some persuasion for him to agree to accept this mission. But finally he goes, supported by his older brother, Aaron. They confront Pharaoh with the message: "God says, 'Let my people go!'" Predictably, Pharaoh refuses. So God sends plagues as pressure on Pharaoh, as if to say, "Oppressing others may seem like the easy road to riches, power, and comfort, but there are high costs to following that road." After that cost is dramatized ten times through ten plagues, Pharaoh relents and tells the people they can leave. Now everything will be fine, right? Happily ever after, right?

Not quite.

Today: Was there ever a time you had a "burning bush" experience—a time when God felt especially real and near or that you felt you were given a job to do?

DAY FIVE: *God in Our Troubles*

Soon after saying yes to Moses, Pharaoh has second thoughts and sends his army to pursue the Israelites and bring them back into slavery.

So Moses and the Israelites find themselves trapped between the Egyptian army and a huge body of water. At the last minute, God opens up a path through the water, and the Israelites escape. When Pharaoh's army follows, the path closes and they all drown. The fate they had planned for the Israelite babies now becomes their own fate.

Surely now there will be a happy ending for the former slaves, right? Not quite. If you're looking for a thirty-minute story with a happy ending every time, it's hard to find in the Bible—just as it is in real life. Instead, we discover the presence of God with us in our troubles, helping us deal with them, helping us discover solutions to them, helping us deal with the new problems inevitably created by those solutions, and so on. Through it all, we discover God's faithful desire to help the downtrodden, the oppressed, the exploited, and the forgotten.

Today: In what ways do you feel trapped between "Pharaoh's angry army and a sea that shows no signs of parting"? Trust God to make a way where no way is currently visible.

DAY SIX: *A Better Future Can Come*

We're all like Moses in a lot of ways. We all have choices to make: who we will become, whose side we'll stand on, whether we'll give up after our failures and frustrations, whether we'll have the faith to get up and keep moving forward when we sense God's call. Life may not be easy—but it sure can be an exciting path to walk, if we go through life with God!

The story of Moses and the escape, or exodus, from Egypt glows at the core of the whole biblical story. It makes one of history's most audacious and unprecedented claims: *God is on the side of slaves, not slave owners!* God doesn't uphold an unjust status quo but works to destabilize it so a better future can come. That revolutionary message is still unknown or rejected in much of the world today. If you believe it, you will live one way. If you don't, you'll live another way.

Today: Consider the audacious claim of the Exodus story: that God is willing to upset the status quo to help those who are oppressed and in need. How will believing this claim affect your way of life?

DAY SEVEN: *Seeing God and Others*

Jesus, as one of the descendants of the Hebrew slaves of Exodus, was formed in this story of liberation. Every year he gathered around a table to remember these events and to situate his life in the ongoing march from slavery and into freedom. All who ate that Passover meal, as it was called, were demonstrating they were not part of the slave-owning economy but were among those seeking freedom from it. They wanted God's judgment to pass over them—which is the source of the meal's name, *Passover*—so they could pass over from slavery to freedom. As part of this community, united in this meal, Jesus learned a profound way of seeing God and others. Where others used their gods to defend an unjust status quo, Jesus believed in the God of justice and liberation. Where others saw a worthless slave, an exploitable asset, a damnable sinner, a disgusting outsider, Jesus saw someone to set free.

The night before his crucifixion, Jesus and his disciples were celebrating the Passover meal. He urged his disciples to keep doing so—not just annually, but frequently, and not just in memory of Moses in ancient Egypt but also in memory of his life and message. That's why followers of Jesus continue to gather around a simple meal of bread and wine today. By participating in that meal, we are making the same choice Moses made—and the same choice Jesus made: to join God in the ongoing struggle to be free and to set others free. That's what it means to be alive in God's story of creation and nonviolent liberation. It's a road into the wild, a road we make by walking.

Today: Pray, "God, may I join you in your great work of liberation! Set me free so I can help others be set free, too!"

WEEK TEN

GETTING SLAVERY OUT OF THE PEOPLE

Scripture Readings

Exodus 20:1–21
Matthew 22:34–40
Hebrews 10:1–18

Key Verses—Matthew 22:36–40

"Teacher, which commandment in the law is the greatest?" He said to him, "'You shall love the Lord your God with all your heart, and with all your soul, and with all your mind.' This is the greatest and first commandment. And a second is like it: 'You shall love your neighbor as yourself.' On these two commandments hang all the law and the prophets."

DAY ONE: *A Journey to Freedom*

Most of us spend a lot of our lives trying to get out of something old and confining and into something new and free. That's why we so easily identify with Moses and the freed Hebrew slaves on their journey through the wild wasteland known as the wilderness.

The truth is that we're all on a wilderness journey out of some form of slavery. On a personal level, we know what it is to be enslaved to fear, alcohol, food, rage, worry, lust, shame, inferiority, or control. On a social level, in today's version of Pharaoh's economy, millions at the bottom of the pyramid work like slaves from before dawn to after dark and still never get ahead. And even those at the top of the pyramid don't feel free. They wake up each day driven by the need to acquire what others desire, and they fear the lash of their own inner slave drivers: greed, debt, competition, expectation, and a desperate, addictive craving for more, more, more.

From top to bottom, the whole system survives by plundering the planet, purchasing this generation's luxuries at the expense of future generations' necessities. Exiting from today's personal and social slavery won't be easy. It will require something like a wilderness journey into the unknown. We know who we have been: slaves. We know who we're going to be: free men and women, experiencing aliveness as God intended. And right now, we're a little bit of both, in need of the identity transformation that comes as we walk the road to freedom.

Today: In what ways are you "a little bit of both"—still enslaved in some ways, walking free in others?

DAY TWO: *Just Enough for Today*

We have much to learn from the stories of Moses and his companions. We, too, must remember that the road to freedom doesn't follow a straight line from point A to point B. Instead, it zigzags and backtracks through a discomfort zone of lack, delay, distress, and strain. In those wild places, character is formed—the personal and social character needed for people to enjoy freedom and aliveness. Like those who have walked before us, we need to know that grumbling and complaining can be more dangerous than poisonous snakes or the hot desert sun. Like them, we must be forewarned about the danger of catastrophizing the present and romanticizing the past. Like them, we must remember that going forward may be difficult, but going back is disastrous.

As they made a road through the wilderness, Moses and his fellow travelers received a mysterious food that fell from the sky each morning like dew. They called it *manna*, which in Hebrew, somewhat humorously, meant, "What is this stuff?" Like them, we will receive what we need for each day, too—often in mysterious and sometimes even humorous ways, just enough for today, provided one day at a time. And like them, we will learn that we can't survive on bread alone: We also need moral guidance, spiritual nourishment, manna for the soul.

Today: In what ways might your current difficulties help you to grow in character?

DAY THREE: *Ten Commandments*

Along with bread for their bodies, God gave the travelers inner nourishment in the form of ten commands that would become the moral basis for their lives in freedom.

1. Put the God of liberation first, not the gods of slavery.
2. Don't reduce God to the manageable size of an idol— certainly not one made of wood and stone by human hands, and not one made by human minds of rituals and words, either, and certainly not one in whose name people are enslaved, dehumanized, or killed!
3. Do not use God for your own agendas by throwing around God's holy name. If you make a vow in God's name, keep it!
4. Honor the God of liberation by taking and giving everyone a day off. Don't keep the old 24/7 slave economy going.
5. Turn from self-centeredness by honoring your parents. (After all, honor is the basis of freedom.)
6. Don't kill people, and don't do the things that frequently incite violence, including:
7. Don't cheat with others' spouses,
8. Don't steal others' possessions, and
9. Don't lie about others' behaviors or characters.
10. In fact, if you really want to avoid the violence of the old slave economy, deal with its root source—in the drama of desire. Don't let the competitive desire to acquire tempt you off the road of freedom.

Today: Reread these ten commandments several times, and ponder how they could give us wisdom for today's challenges in our personal and social lives.

DAY FOUR: *Gather Around the Family Table*

Through the ten plagues, we might say, God got the people out of slavery. Through the ten commands, God got the slavery out of the people. God also gave them a set of additional practices—rituals, holidays, and so on—to help them develop and deepen the character of free people. One of those practices was setting aside a special holy place. They started with a simple "tent of meeting" that was replaced by a larger, more elaborate gathering place called the Tabernacle. That holy space in the center of their encampment reminded them that the God of liberation was journeying with them—not only above them, visualized as a cloud of smoke and fire, but among them, walking with them in the desert dust as they made the road to freedom.

In that central holy space the people offered sacrifices. Animal sacrifice had already replaced more primitive and brutal rituals of human sacrifice. But the whole idea of appeasing God through blood shedding of any kind was gradually being replaced with the idea of communing with God over a meal. So sacrifices were seen increasingly as gifts of food, as if to say, "God is calling us to gather around the family table." At certain times of the year, and at special moments when the people realized they had done something horrible, they would come to God's big tent. They would bring the makings of a feast, as if to say, "God, we're sorry for our wrongs. We want to have our family meal again—reconciling with you and with one another. So here's some food to express our desire to sit down at the table of fellowship. We won't turn back. We'll keep walking this long road to freedom…together."

Of course, Jesus gathered his companions around a table one night and encouraged them to do the same. We call it a meal of communion. We could also call it a meal of liberation and reconciliation. Around this table, we remember where we've been, where we are, whom we're with, and where we're headed, as we make a new road by walking…together.

Today: When you pause for a meal, say a prayer of thanks, and consider God a welcome companion at your table.

DAY FIVE: *Make the Road by Walking*

The wilderness journey is always difficult and seems to last forever. Like kids on a car ride, we keep whining, "Aren't we there yet?" But the truth is, if we arrive before we've learned the lessons of the wilderness, we won't be able to enjoy the freedom that awaits us in the promised land beyond it. There is wisdom we will need there that we can gain only right here. There are strength and skill we will need in the future that we can develop only here and now, on the wilderness road. There is moral muscle we will need then that we can exercise and strengthen only through our struggles on this road, here and now. There is a depth of connection with God that will be there when we need it in the future—if we learn to trust and follow God now, on the long, wild road to freedom.

The struggles will make us either bitter or better. The trials will lead to either breakdown or breakthrough. We will often be tempted to return to our old lives, but in that tension between a backward pull and a forward call, we will discover unexplainable sustenance (like manna) and unexpected refreshment (like springs in the desert). Against all odds, walking by faith, we will survive, and more: We will learn what it means to be alive.

There are no shortcuts. The road cannot be made by wishing, by whining, or by talking. It can be made only by walking, day after day, step by step, struggle by struggle. It's easier, it turns out, to get people out of slavery than it is to get slavery out of people. So, people, let us walk the road—right through the middle of the desert.

Today: Repeat this little rhyme: Not by wishing, not by whining, not by talking. We make the road by walking!

FROM UGLINESS, A BEAUTY EMERGES

Scripture Readings

> Deuteronomy 7:1–11
> Psalm 137:1–9; 149:1–9
> Matthew 15:21–39

Key Verses—Psalm 149:1

> *Praise the Lord!*
> *Sing to the Lord a new song,*
> > *his praise in the assembly of the faithful.*

DAY ONE: *The Question of Violence*

We've come a long way in our story already. We've discovered...

>   *Creation*—God brings into being this beautiful, evolving world of wonders.
>
>   *Crisis*—We step out of the dance and enter into rivalry with God and our fellow creatures, throwing this planet into disarray.
>
>   *Calling*—God calls people to join in a global conspiracy of goodness and blessing, to heal and restore whatever human evil destroys.
>
>   *Captivity*—The people who have joined God's global conspiracy of goodness experience the horrors of slavery, but God eventually leads them by the wilderness road out of captivity toward freedom.

And now we come to a fifth major episode. It's the story of *conquest*, as the Israelites finally reach the land their ancestors had inhabited four centuries earlier. There's just one problem: Others have moved into the land and made it their home for many generations. To possess the land, the Israelites will have to displace these current residents through a war of invasion and conquest. Wars like these are the most bloody and difficult of all, but the Israelites trust that their God will give them victory.

This episode in the biblical story, more than any other, forces us to deal with one of life's most problematic questions: the question of violence. By violence, we mean an act that intends to violate the well-being of a person or people. To help some, is God willing to harm others? Is God part of the violence in the world, and is violence part of God?

Today: Simply hold in your heart the question in the previous sentence. Let it stay with you, and trouble you, throughout this day.

DAY TWO: *Before We Condemn*

Today, as in the ancient world, many people sincerely believe that God loves *us* and wants peace for *us* so much that God has no trouble harming or destroying *them* for our benefit. We find a lot of that kind of thinking in the Bible, giving God credit and praise for *our* victories and *their* defeats. Before we go too far in condemning ancient people for that exclusive way of thinking, we should realize how easy it is for us to do the same—when we create a superior *us* that looks down on *them* for thinking so exclusively!

We should also notice that where we see this kind of thinking embedded in the Bible, we also find important qualifications. For example, God's favor toward *the insiders* is dependent on the insiders living good and humble lives. If the insiders become oppressors, they should not expect God's help. And God gives the freed slaves the right to conquer just enough land for themselves, just one time. They are never given a license to create an empire, expanding to enslave others as they had previously been enslaved.

Even as they prepare for war, they are told again and again that after the conquest ends, they must treat "aliens and strangers" as neighbors, with honor and respect, remembering that they once were "aliens and strangers" themselves in Egypt. Their ultimate dream is to be farmers, not warriors—so that swords can be beaten into plowshares and spears into pruning hooks, as soon as possible.

Today: Ponder this sentence: "Their ultimate dream is to be farmers, not warriors."

DAY THREE: *No Difference*

We can't ignore the brutality found in many Bible passages. From Deuteronomy 7 to Leviticus 25 to I Samuel 15 to Psalm 137 and 149, we hear claims that "God" or "the Lord" actively commands or blesses actions that we would call crimes against humanity. Many religious scholars have assumed that because the Bible makes these claims, we must defend them as true and good. That approach, however, is morally unacceptable for growing numbers of us, and fortunately, we have another option.

We can acknowledge that in the minds of the originators of these stories, God as they understood God did indeed command these things. We can acknowledge that in their way of thinking, divine involvement in war was to be expected. We can allow that they were telling the truth as they best understood it when they found comfort and reassurance in a vision of a God who would harm or kill *them* to defend, help, or avenge *us*. We can try to empathize, remembering that when human beings suffer indignity, injustice, dehumanization, and violence, they naturally pray for revenge and dream of retribution against those who harm them. Without condoning, we can at least understand why they saw God as they did, knowing that if we had walked in their sandals, we would have been no different.

But we don't have to stop there. We can then turn to other voices in the biblical library who, in different circumstances, told competing stories to give a different—and we would say *better*—vision of God.

Today: Try to empathize with people from history—and today—who suffer indignity, injustice, dehumanization, and violence. Understand why they would naturally pray for revenge and dream of retribution. But then, make room in your heart for a better response.

DAY FOUR: *Show Mercy*

Consider two competing stories. First, in Deuteronomy 7, you'll find a passage where God commands Joshua to slaughter the seven Canaanite nations who occupy the land he wants to settle. They must be shown no mercy. Even their little girls must be seen as a threat. Then consider a story from Matthew's gospel that offers itself as a response to the earlier passage. There, we meet a woman who is identified by Matthew as a Canaanite. This identification is significant, since Canaanites no longer existed as an identifiable culture in Jesus's day. Calling this woman a Canaanite would be like calling someone a Viking or Aztec today. She asks for the one thing that had been denied her ancestors: *mercy*...mercy for her daughter, who is in great need.

Up until this point, Jesus has understood his mission only in relation to his own people. After all, they're pretty lost, and they need a lot of help. So he hesitates. How can he extend himself to this Canaanite? But how can he refuse her? In her persistence, he senses genuine faith, and he hears God's call to extend mercy even to her. So he says yes to the mother, and the daughter is healed. From there, Jesus goes to an area to the northwest of the Sea of Galilee. He teaches and heals a large crowd of people there who, like the woman and her daughter, are not members of his own religion and culture. Their non-Jewish identity is clear in their response to Jesus's kindness: "And they praised the God of Israel." What was an exception yesterday is now the new rule: *Don't kill the other. Show mercy to them.*

Today: Pray, "God, help us to move beyond killing, hating, and fearing people of other religions. Help us to show mercy, to understand, to love one another across our differences."

DAY FIVE: *A Higher Mission*

There's a fascinating ending to the story of Jesus serving people of another religion and culture in Matthew's gospel. He repeats a miracle for these outsiders that he had done previously for his fellow Jews, multiplying loaves and fish so they can eat. In the previous miracle, there were twelve baskets left over, suggesting the twelve tribes of Israel—the descendants, that is, of Jacob and his twelve sons. In this miracle, there are seven baskets left over—suggesting, it seems quite clear, the seven Canaanite nations that Jesus's ancestors had been commanded to destroy.

Matthew's version of this story makes a confession: *Our ancestors, led by Moses and Joshua, believed God sent them into the world in conquest, to show no mercy to their enemies, to defeat and kill them. But now, following Christ, we hear God giving us a higher mission. Now we believe God sends us into the world in compassion, to show mercy, to heal, to feed—to nurture and protect life rather than take it.*

Today: What kind of confessions do we need to make about ways our religion has been used in the past to harm others? What kind of actions do we need to make now, to show that our hearts have changed?

DAY SIX: *Tell New Stories*

In our ancient history, before the time of the Bible, people believed there were many warring gods, all of whom were violent and capricious. In much of the Bible, we advanced to a vision of a single God who uses violence against *them* in the service of justice for *us*. Eventually, through the biblical library, we find a beautiful new vision of God being revealed. God desires justice for all, not just for *us*. God is leading both *us* and *them* out of injustice and violence into a new way of reconciliation and peace. God loves everyone, everywhere, no exceptions.

Violence, like slavery and racism, was normative in our past, and it is still all too common in the present. How will we tell the stories of our past in ways that make our future less violent? We must not defend those stories or give them the final word. Nor can we cover them up, hiding them like a loaded gun in a drawer that can be found and used to harm. Instead, we must expose these violent stories to the light of day. And then we must tell new stories beside them, stories so beautiful and good that they will turn us toward a better vision of kindness, reconciliation, and peace for our future and for our children's future.

The stories of Jesus's life and teaching, wisely told, can help us imagine and create a more peaceful future. They help us see the glory of God shining in the face of a kind, forgiving, gentle, and nonviolent man, and in the smiles and tears, words and deeds of those who radiate his love.

Today: Pray, "God, may my smiles and tears, my words and deeds radiate your love to others, and may we tell stories that turn us toward a better future for ourselves and our children."

WEEK TWELVE

STORIES THAT SHAPE US

Scripture Readings

>2 Kings 2:1–15
>Psalm 23
>Acts 1:1–11

Key Verses—Acts 1:6–8

>*So when they had come together, they asked him, "Lord, is this the time when you will restore the kingdom to Israel?" He replied, "It is not for you to know the times or periods that the Father has set by his own authority. But you will receive power when the Holy Spirit has come upon you; and you will be my witnesses in Jerusalem, in all Judea and Samaria, and to the ends of the earth."*

DAY ONE: *The Interpretive Community*

A little girl once asked her mother if the Bible story of Elijah flying to heaven on a chariot of fire was "real or pretend." How would you have answered her question?

You might try to explain that sometimes a "pretend" story can tell more truth and do more good than a "real" one—as Jesus's parables exemplify so powerfully. You might explain how real stories often are embellished with pretend elements. Or you might respond as that little girl's wise mother did: "That's a great question! Some stories are real, some are pretend, and some of the very best ones use a mix of both reality and make-believe to tell us something important. What do you think about the Elijah story?" The mother's answer didn't tell the little girl *what* to think. It invited her *to* think—as a bona fide member of the interpretive community.

Whenever we engage with the stories of the Bible, we become members of the interpretive community. And that's a big responsibility, especially when we remember how stories from the Bible have been used to promote both great good and great harm. We might say that good interpretation begins with three elements: science, art, and heart. First, we need *critical or scientific research* into history, language, anthropology, and sociology to wisely interpret the Bible. Second, since the Bible is a literary and therefore an artistic collection, we need an *artist's eye and ear* to wisely draw meaning from ancient stories. But at every step, we also must be guided by a *humble, teachable heart* that listens for the voice of the Spirit.

Today: Think of yourself as a member of the interpretive community, using science, art, and heart to wisely understand and apply the Bible's message to your life.

DAY TWO: *Engaging Our Interpretive Imagination*

The Elijah story addresses an urgent question: *What happens when a great leader dies?* Typically, a blaze of glory surrounds the hero's departure—symbolized by the fiery chariot and horses in the story. After the leader is gone, the actual life and message of the leader are forgotten, obscured by the blaze of fame and glory. People become fans of the leader's reputation but not followers of his example. That's why the old mentor Elijah puts his young apprentice, Elisha, through many trials and warns him about the spectacle surrounding his departure. The fireworks are not the point, Elijah explains; they're a distraction, a temptation to be overcome. If the apprentice resists that distraction and remains resolutely focused on the mentor himself, a double portion of the mentor's spirit will rest on him.

We see something very similar in the story of Jesus's departure. Will his followers look up at the sky and speculate about their departed leader with their heads in the clouds? Will they be fans instead of followers? Or will they get down to work and stay focused on living and sharing Jesus's down-to-earth way of life, empowered with his Spirit?

Like young Elisha, interpreters today must remember that it's easy to miss the point of ancient stories. Those stories didn't merely aim, like a modern textbook, to pass on factual *information*. They sought people's *formation* by engaging their interpretive *imagination*.

Today: Pray, "God, help me not to miss the point of the stories in the Bible. Help me stay focused on living and sharing Jesus's down-to-earth way of life, empowered with his Spirit."

DAY THREE: *Wisely Interpreting Bible Stories*

As a first step in wisely interpreting Bible stories with science, art, and heart, we need to put each story in its intended historical context and get a sense for the big narrative in which each story is nested. Roughly speaking, we can locate the stories of Abraham and Sarah somewhere around 2000–1700 BC. We can place the stories of Moses and the exodus around 1400 BC. We can locate the conquest of the Canaanites around 1300 BC, after which the Hebrew tribes formed a loose confederacy under a series of leaders who are somewhat misleadingly called *judges* in the Bible. *Tribal leaders* or even *warlords* might be more accurate names.

Those were violent times, and some of the stories from those times are bone-chilling, especially regarding the appallingly low status of women and the appallingly violent behavior of men. For example, the Book of Judges ends with the account of a brutal gang rape, murder, and dismemberment of a young woman, followed by a horrific aftermath of intertribal retaliation and kidnapping of innocent young women. Interestingly, in the very next story in the biblical library, the Book of Ruth, we find the polar opposite—the poignant tale of two kind and courageous women, Ruth and Naomi. They forged a resilient life of dignity and beauty in the midst of brutality. Where the men failed, the women prevailed.

Today: Ponder this statement, and look for examples of it in today's world: "Where the men failed, the women prevailed."

DAY FOUR: *The Story of David*

Around 1050 BC, pressured by aggressive nations around them and brutality among them, the twelve tribes formed a stronger alliance. They united under a king named Saul. Saul turned out to be a disappointment, but in his shadow a more heroic figure named David appeared. The story of David's gradual rise from shepherd boy to king unfolds in great detail, each episode revealing Saul as less strong and noble, and David as more clever and charismatic. When Saul was killed in battle, David established his throne in Jerusalem, inaugurating what is still remembered as Israel's golden age.

David was heroic, but far from perfect, and the Bible doesn't cover up his serious failings—including those of a sexual nature. When David wanted to build a temple to honor God, God said no: A place of worship should not be associated with a man of bloodshed. David's son Solomon was not a warrior, so he was allowed to fulfill his father's dream by building a temple. But Solomon used slave labor to build that temple—a tragic irony in light of God's identity as the liberator of slaves.

Today: Look for examples of tragic irony in the world of politics and religion, like a king building a temple with slave labor to honor the God who liberates slaves.

DAY FIVE: *A Dream Was Born*

After Solomon's death, around 930 BC, the kingdom split in two. Ten of the original twelve tribes who lived in the northern region broke away from the two tribes who lived to their south. From that time, the Kingdom of Israel in the north, with its capital in Samaria, was governed by its own line of kings. And the Kingdom of Judah in the south continued under the rule of David's descendants in Jerusalem. Nearly all the kings of both nations were corrupt, ineffective, and faithful only to their own agendas of gaining and maintaining power at any cost.

Those darker times made the memory of David's reign seem all the more bright. A dream was born in many hearts: that a descendant of David would one day arise and come to the throne, inaugurating a new kingdom, a new golden age, a new day. The old dream of a promised land now was replaced by a new dream—for a promised *time*, a time when the peace, unity, freedom, and prosperity of David's reign would return. This expectation kept hope alive in difficult times, but it also created an unintended byproduct: a sense of pious complacency, as people accepted the status quo in hopes that someday God would swoop in and fix everything.

Today: Ponder how the dream of a better day can both sustain hope and create complacency.

DAY SIX: *Living by a Different Interpretation*

About ten centuries after King David, when Jesus came on the scene, many were still waiting for a "son of David," a militant Messiah, to swoop in someday, fix everything, and usher in Golden Age 2.0. They expected this warrior king to raise a revolutionary army, overthrow their oppressors, and restore civil law and religious order. In anticipation of the warrior king's arrival, some were sharpening daggers and swords. But Jesus was living by a different interpretation of the old stories, so he refused to conform to their expectations. Instead of arming his followers with daggers, swords, spears, chariots, and warhorses, he armed them with faith, hope, service, forgiveness, and love. When he healed people, he didn't tell them, "I will save you!" or "My faith will save you!" but "Your faith has saved you." Working from a fresh interpretation of the past, he freed them from both passive, pious complacency and desperate, violent action. His fresh interpretation empowered them for something better: faithful, peaceful action.

Today: How might we need "a fresh interpretation of the past" in our day?

DAY SEVEN: *Shaped by Our Stories*

Consider our huge challenges today. How will we deal with political and economic systems that are destroying the planet, privileging the super-elite, and churning out weapons of unprecedented destruction at an unprecedented rate? How will we deal with religious systems that often have violent extremists on one wing and complacent bureaucrats on the other? How will we grapple with complex forces that break down family and community cohesion and leave vulnerable people at great risk—especially women, and especially the very young and the very old? How will we face our personal demons—of greed, lust, anxiety, depression, anger, and addiction—especially when people are spending billions to stimulate those demons so we will buy their products?

These aren't pretend problems. To find real-world solutions, we need to be wise interpreters of our past. Like Elijah's apprentice, Elisha, we must stay focused on the substance at the center, undistracted by all the surrounding fireworks, because the meaning we shape from the stories we interpret will, in turn, shape us.

Today: Look for evidence of the "huge challenges" described in today's reading.

WEEK THIRTEEN

THE GREAT CONVERSATION

Scripture Readings

    Isaiah 1:1–2:5
    Romans 15:1–13
    Matthew 9:10–17

Key Verses—Isaiah 1:18

Come now, let us argue it out,
    says the Lord:
though your sins are like scarlet,
    they shall be like snow;
though they are red like crimson,
    they shall become like wool.

DAY ONE: *Bigger Trouble Brewing*

It was about 800 BC. The Israelites and Judeans had already survived so much. In addition to all the trouble within their respective borders—much of it caused by corrupt leaders—even bigger trouble was brewing outside. The two tiny nations were dwarfed by superpower neighbors, each of which had desires to expand. To the north and east were the Assyrians. To the east were the Babylonians, and to their east, the Persians. To the south were the Egyptians, and to the West, the Mediterranean Sea. How could Israel and Judah, each smaller than present-day Jamaica, Qatar, or Connecticut, hope to survive, surrounded in this way?

The northern Kingdom of Israel fell first. In 722 BC, the Assyrians invaded and deported many of the Israelites into Assyria. These displaced Israelites eventually intermarried and lost their distinct identity as children of Abraham. They're remembered today as "the ten lost tribes of Israel." The Assyrians quickly repopulated the conquered kingdom with large numbers of their own, who then intermarried with the remaining Israelites. The mixed descendants, later known as Samaritans, would experience a long-standing tension with the "pure" descendants of Abraham in Judah to the south.

Judah resisted conquest for just over another century, during which Assyrian power declined and Babylonian power increased. Finally, around 587 BC, Judah was conquered by the Babylonians. Jerusalem and its temple were destroyed. The nation's "brightest and best" were deported as exiles to the Babylonian capital. The peasants were left to till the land and "share" their harvest with the occupying regime. For about seventy years, this sorry state of affairs continued.

Today: How does this description of Bible times correspond with political realities in today's world?

DAY TWO: *Interpreting Their Plight*

While Babylon was oppressing Judea to the west, it was being pressured by its neighbor to the east, the Persians. Soon the Persians conquered the Babylonians. They had a more lenient policy for managing the nations under their power, so, in 538, they allowed the exiled Judeans to return and rebuild their capital city. But even with this increased freedom, the people remained under the heel of foreigners. They had survived, but they still felt defeated.

How should they interpret their plight? Some feared that God had failed or abandoned them. Others blamed themselves for displeasing God in some way. Those who felt abandoned by God expressed their devastation in heart-rending poetry. Those who felt they had displeased God tried to identify their offenses, assign blame, and call for repentance. It was during this devastating period of exile and return that much of the oral tradition known to us as the Old Testament was either written down for the first time or reedited and compiled. No wonder, arising in such times of turmoil and tumult, the Bible is such a dynamic collection!

Today: Consider why, during times of turmoil and tumult, people would begin compiling their sacred literature.

DAY THREE: *Changing and Evolving*

As the Jewish people changed and evolved, their understanding of God changed and evolved. For example, when they were nomadic wanderers in the desert, they envisioned God as a pillar of cloud and fire, cooling them by day and warming them by night. When they were involved in conquest, God was the Lord of Hosts, the commander of armies. When they were being pursued by enemies, God was pictured as a hiding place in the rocks. When they became a unified kingdom, God was their ultimate king. When they returned to their land and felt more secure, more gentle images of God took center stage—God as their shepherd, for example. When they suffered defeat, they saw God as their avenger. When they suffered injustice, God was the judge who would convict their oppressors and restore justice. When they felt abandoned and alone in a foreign land, they imagined God as a loving mother who could never forget her nursing child.

Today: Ask yourself what images for God are most important and meaningful for you in this period of your life.

DAY FOUR: *Human Affairs*

Not only do we see the Jewish understanding of God evolve under evolving circumstances, we also see their understanding of human affairs mature. For example, to immature minds, there are two kinds of leaders: those who have been set in place by God and those who haven't. The former deserve absolute obedience, since to disobey them would be to disobey God. But in the Bible, we see this simplistic thinking challenged. Moses, for example, was a God-anointed leader, and people were indeed urged to obey him, and they were punished when they didn't. Yet when Moses made mistakes of his own, he got no special treatment. The same with Saul and the same even with David. All leaders are accountable, and none can claim absolute authority.

Today: Consider the importance of respecting leaders while holding them accountable and withholding absolute authority from them.

DAY FIVE: *Moral Reasoning*

As the Jewish understanding of human affairs matured, their moral reasoning matured as well. In the Garden of Eden story, Adam and Eve wanted to grasp the fruit of knowing good and evil, as if that were a simple thing. But as the biblical story unfolded, first it became clear that the line between good and evil didn't run between groups of *us* and *them*. There were good guys among *them*—including people like Melchizedek, Abimelech, Jethro, Rahab, and Ruth. And there were plenty of bad guys among *us*—including most of the kings of Israel and Judah. It became clear that the dividing line doesn't simply run between good and bad individuals, as many people today still believe. Some of the Bible's best "good guys"—like David and Solomon—did really bad things. So the Bible presents a morally complex and dynamic world where the best of us can do wrong and the worst of us can do right. The line between good and evil runs—and moves—within each of us.

Today: Notice the tendency in yourself and others to be immature in our moral reasoning, as if good and evil were not intertwined in all of us.

DAY SIX: *Irreconcilable Viewpoints*

The Bible often leads us deeper into moral wisdom by drawing a third option from two irreconcilable viewpoints on an issue. For example, some biblical voices interpreted the move from an alliance of tribes to a kingdom as a tragic sign that the people had rejected God as their king. Others saw the monarchy as a gift from God, a big improvement over the previous chaos. When both sets of voices are heard, it's clear that each had some of the truth: A strong central government can be both a curse and a blessing, not just one or the other.

Similarly, some biblical voices argued that God required animals to be slaughtered so their blood could be offered as a sacrifice. Without sacrifice, they believed, sins could not be forgiven, so they gave detailed instructions for sacrifice that, they claimed, were dictated by God. Other voices said no, that God never really desired bloody sacrifices, but instead wanted another kind of holy gift from humanity: contrite and compassionate hearts, and justice, kindness, and humility. When we give both sets of voices a fair hearing, we can agree that sacrifices fulfilled a necessary function for the people at one point in their development, even though ultimately sacrifices weren't an absolute and eternal necessity.

Meanwhile, many voices claimed that Abraham's descendants were God's only chosen and favored people. Others countered that God created and loves all people and has chosen and guided all nations for various purposes. If we listen to both claims, we can conclude that just as a little girl feels she is uniquely loved by her parents, even as her little brother feels the same way, each nation is intended to feel it is special to God—not to the exclusion of others, but along with others.

Today: Listen for opposing viewpoints, and see if you can derive wisdom from both and in this way find a third option or third way forward.

DAY SEVEN: *Seek Wisdom from Conversation*

From Genesis to Job, the Bible is full of conversations in which differing voices make their case, point and counterpoint, statement and counter-statement. Sadly, throughout history people have often quoted one side or the other to prove that their view alone is "biblical." That's why it's important for us to remain humble as we read the Bible, not to seek ammunition for the side of an argument we already stand on, but to seek the wisdom that comes when we listen humbly to all the different voices arising in the biblical library. Wisdom emerges from the conversation among these voices, voices we could arrange in five broad categories.

First, there are the voices of the *priests*, who emphasize keeping the law, maintaining order, offering sacrifices, and faithfully maintaining traditions and taboos. Then there are the voices of the *prophets*, often in tension with the priests, who emphasize social justice, care for the poor, and the condition of the heart. Next are the *poets*, who express the full range of human emotion and opinion—the good, the bad, and the ugly. Then come the *sages*, who, in proverb, essay, and creative fiction, record their theories, observations, questions, and doubts. And linking them together are *storytellers*, each with varying agendas, who try to tell the stories of the people who look back to Abraham as their father, Moses as their liberator, David as their greatest king, and God as their Creator and faithful companion. To be alive is to seek wisdom in this great con-versation...and to keep it going today.

Could it be that we are doing just that, here and now, walking this road in conversation together?

Today: Pray, "God, help me learn wisdom from the great conversation among priests, poets, prophets, sages, and storytellers. And help me con-tinue the conversation today."

II

ALIVE IN THE
ADVENTURE OF JESUS

In Part I, we explored what it means to be alive in the story of creation...a story that includes crisis, calling, captivity, conquest, and conversation. Into that conversation comes a man named Jesus, a man whose character, words, and example changed history. In Part II, we will explore what it means to be alive in the adventure of Jesus.

We begin with the story of his birth (traditionally celebrated during the seasons of Advent and Christmas), and then we follow him through childhood to adulthood, as the light of God shines brightly through him (celebrated during the season of Epiphany). Our exploration will lead to this life-changing choice: Will we identify ourselves as honest and sincere followers of Jesus today?

PROMISED LAND, PROMISED TIME

Scripture Readings

Daniel 7:9–28
Isaiah 40:9–11
Luke 1:67–79

Key Verses—Luke 1:76–79

And you, child, will be called the prophet of the Most High;
for you will go before the Lord to prepare his ways,
to give knowledge of salvation to his people
by the forgiveness of their sins.
By the tender mercy of our God,
the dawn from on high will break upon us,
to give light to those who sit in darkness and in the shadow of death,
to guide our feet into the way of peace.

DAY ONE: *Lives Are Shaped by Hope*

To be alive is to desire, to hope, and to dream, and the Bible is a book about desires, hopes, and dreams. The story begins with God's desire for a good and beautiful world, of which we are a part. Soon, some of us desire the power to kill, enslave, or oppress others. Enslaved and oppressed people hope for liberation. Wilderness wanderers desire a promised land where they can settle. Settled people dream of a promised time when they won't be torn apart by internal factions, ruled by corrupt elites, or dominated by stronger nations nearby.

Desires, hopes, and dreams inspire action, and that's what makes them so different from a wish. Wishing is a substitute for action. Wishing creates a kind of passive optimism that can paralyze people in a happy fog of complacency: "Everything will turn out fine. Why work, struggle, sacrifice, or plan?" Guess what happens to people who never work, struggle, sacrifice, or plan? Things don't normally turn out the way they wish!

In contrast, our desires, hopes, and dreams for the future guide us in how to act now. If a girl hopes to be a doctor someday, she'll study hard and prepare for medical school. If a boy dreams of being a marine biologist someday, he'll spend time around the sea and learn to snorkel and scuba dive. Their hope for the future guides them in how to act now. They align their lives by their hope, and in that way, their lives are shaped by hope. Without action, they would be wishing, not hoping.

Today: Notice the difference between passive wishing and active hoping.

DAY TWO: *The Book of Isaiah*

Prophets in the Bible have a fascinating role as custodians of the best hopes, desires, and dreams of their society. They challenge people to act in ways consistent with those hopes, desires, and dreams. And when they see people behaving in harmful ways, they warn them by picturing the future to which that harmful behavior will lead.

One of the most important prophetic compositions was the Book of Isaiah. Most scholars today agree that at least three people contributed to the book over a long period of time, but their combined work has traditionally been attributed to one author. The first thirty-nine chapters of Isaiah were situated in the southern Kingdom of Judah, just before the northern Kingdom of Israel was invaded and colonized by the Assyrians. The prophet saw deep spiritual corruption and complacency among his people and warned them that this kind of behavior would lead to decline and defeat.

That defeat came in 587 BC at the hand of the Babylonians. After the invasion, many survivors were taken as exiles to Babylon. Chapters 40 to 55, often called Second Isaiah, addressed those Judean exiles, inspiring hope that they would someday return to their homeland and rebuild it. That soon happened, beginning in 538 BC under the leadership of Ezra and Nehemiah. That era of rebuilding was the setting for Third Isaiah, chapters 56 to 66.

Today: Corruption and complacency, leading to defeat, exile, and longing, followed by a new beginning and time of rebuilding—look for this pattern in your life and in the world around you today.

DAY THREE: *A Rich Recipe for Hope*

For readers in later generations, ingredients from the experiences of corruption, exile, and rebuilding blend into one rich recipe for hope, full of imagery that still energizes our imagination today.

> *They shall beat their swords into plowshares,*
> *and their spears into pruning-hooks.*
> *Nation shall not lift up sword against nation,*
> *neither shall they learn war any more. (2:4)*

> *A shoot shall come out from the stump of [David's father] Jesse,*
> *and a branch shall grow out of his roots.*
> *The Spirit of the Lord shall rest on him . . .*
> *The wolf shall live with the lamb,*
> *the leopard shall lie down with the kid,*
> *the calf and the lion and the fatling together,*
> *and a little child shall lead them . . . .*
> *They will not hurt or destroy*
> *on all my holy mountain;*
> *for the Earth will be full of the knowledge of the Lord*
> *as the waters cover the sea. (11:1–2, 6, 9)*

> *Here is my servant, whom I uphold,*
> *my chosen, in whom my soul delights;*
> *I have put my spirit upon him;*
> *he will bring forth justice to the nations.*
> *He will not cry or lift up his voice,*
> *or make it heard in the street;*
> *a bruised reed he will not break,*
> *and a dimly burning wick he will not quench;*
> *he will faithfully bring forth justice. (42:1–3)*

Today: Take two lines from Isaiah's poetry above, commit them to memory, and repeat them to yourself throughout the day.

DAY FOUR: *The Prophetic Vision*

Isaiah's descriptions of a beautiful possible future were so inspiring that Jesus and his early followers quoted Isaiah more than any other writer. But many other prophets added their own colors to this beautiful vision of hope. In Ezekiel's vision, people's hearts of stone will be replaced with hearts of flesh. For Malachi, the hearts of parents would turn to their children, and children to their parents. Joel describes the Spirit of God being poured out on all humanity—young and old, men and women, Jew and Gentile. Amos paints the vivid scene of justice rolling down like a river, filling all the lowest places. And Daniel envisioned the world's beastlike empires of violence being overcome by a simple unarmed human being, a new generation of humanity.

Today: Choose an image from Ezekiel, Malachi, Joel, Amos, or Daniel and bring it to life in your imagination today, whenever you have a free moment.

DAY FIVE: *Translate Hope into Action*

In the centuries between the time of the prophets and the birth of Jesus, these prophetic dreams never completely died. But they were never completely fulfilled, either. Yes, conditions for the Jews improved during the Persian occupation, but things still weren't as good as the prophets promised. Next the Greek and Seleucid empires took control of the region, and for a time, the Jews threw off their oppressors. But their independence was brief, and the full dream of the prophets remained unfulfilled. Next the Romans seized power, subjugating and humiliating the Jews and testing their hope as never before. Yet their dream lived on. It remained alive in people like Elizabeth and Zechariah, Mary and Joseph, and Anna and Simeon, and even among humble shepherds who lived at the margins of society.

To be alive in the adventure of Jesus is to have a desire, a dream, a hope for the future. It is to translate that hope for the future into action in the present and to keep acting in light of it, no matter the disappointments, no matter the setbacks and delays.

Today: Pray, "Living God, help me walk this day in the light of hope rather than the shadow of disappointment."

WEEK FIFTEEN

WOMEN ON THE EDGE

Scripture Readings

Luke 1:5–55
Isaiah 7:14, 9:2–7
Romans 12:1–2

Key Verses—Luke 1:38

Then Mary said, "Here am I, the servant of the Lord; let it be with me according to your word." Then the angel departed from her.

DAY ONE: *Why Pray Now?*

Imagine a woman in the ancient world who all her life longed to have children. She married young, maybe around the age of fifteen. At sixteen, still no pregnancy. At twenty, still no pregnancy. At twenty-five, imagine how she prayed. By thirty, imagine her anxiety as her prayers were mixed with tears of shame and disappointment—for herself, for her husband. At forty, imagine hope slipping away as she wondered if it even made sense to pray anymore. Imagine her sense of loss and regret at age fifty. Why pray now?

Of course, this was the story of Abraham's wife, Sarah, back in the book of Genesis. That ancient story was echoed in the gospel of Luke. Luke tells us of a woman named Elizabeth who was married to a priest named Zechariah. They prayed for a child, but none came, year after year. One day as Zechariah was doing his priestly duties, he had a vision of an angelic messenger from God. Zechariah's prayers for a son would be answered, the messenger said. When Elizabeth gave birth, they should name their child John. Zechariah found this impossible to believe. "I'm an old man," he said, "and Elizabeth is past her prime as well!" The messenger told him that because of his skepticism, he would not be able to speak until the promised baby was born.

Today: Ask yourself, "What dream or hope is slipping away from me?"

DAY TWO: *Waiting for the Impossible*

In a way, the stories of Sarah and Elizabeth are a picture of the experience of the Jewish people. The prophets had inspired them to dream of a better day. Their prophecies echoed the first promise to Abraham: that everyone everywhere would be blessed through Abraham's descendants. But those promises and prophecies had been delayed and frustrated and delayed again, until it seemed ridiculous to keep the dream alive.

All of us experience this sense of frustration, disappointment, impatience, and despair at times. We all feel that we have the capacity to give birth to something beautiful and good and needed and wonderful in the world. But our potential goes unfulfilled, or our promising hopes miscarry. So we live on one side and then on the other of the border of despair.

And then the impossible happens.

Today: Pray, "God, help me to avoid limiting myself by the word *impossible*."

DAY THREE: *Nothing Is Impossible with God*

Elizabeth had a young relative named Mary. Mary was engaged but not yet married. Significantly, she was a descendant of King David, whose memory inspired the hope of a David-like king who would bring the better days long hoped for among her people. When Elizabeth was about six months pregnant, an angelic messenger—the same one who appeared to Zechariah, it turns out—now appeared to Mary. "Greetings, favored one!" he said. "The Lord is with you!" Mary felt, as any of us would, amazed and confused by this greeting.

The messenger said, "Don't be afraid, Mary. You will conceive and bear a son..." The messenger's words echoed the promises of the prophets from centuries past—promises of a leader who would bring the people into the promised time. Mary asked, "How can this be, since I am a virgin?" The angel replied that the Holy Spirit would come upon her, so the child would be conceived by the power of God. He added that Elizabeth, her old and barren relative, was also pregnant. "Nothing will be impossible with God," he said.

Today: Hold these three angelic messages in your heart: *Do not be afraid! The Lord is with you! Nothing will be impossible with God.*

DAY FOUR: *Impossible Possibilities*

Many people today will suspect that Luke made up this story about Mary to echo Isaiah's prophecy about a son being born to a virgin, just as he invented the story of Elizabeth conceiving in old age to echo the story of Sarah. It's tempting to quickly assign both stories to the category of primitive, prescientific legend and be done with them. After all, both stories are, to scientific minds, simply impossible.

But what if that's the point? What if their purpose is to challenge us to blur the line between what we think is possible and what we think is impossible? Could we ever come to a time when swords would be beaten into plowshares? When the predatory people in power—the lions—would lie down in peace with the vulnerable and the poor—the lambs? When God's justice would flow like a river—to the lowest and most "godforsaken" places on Earth? When the brokenhearted would be comforted and the poor would receive good news? If you think, *Never— it's impossible,* then maybe you need to think again. Maybe it's not too late for something beautiful to be born. Maybe it's not too soon, either. Maybe the present moment is pregnant with possibilities we can't see or even imagine.

In this light, the *actual* point of these pregnancy stories—however we interpret their *factual* status—is a challenge to us all: to dare to hope, like Elizabeth and Mary, that the seemingly impossible is possible. They challenge us to align our lives around the "impossible possibilities" hidden in this present, pregnant moment.

Today: Say to yourself, "Maybe the present moment is pregnant with possibilities I can't yet see or even imagine."

DAY FIVE: *A Different Kind of Leader*

What meaning might people in the first century have attributed to a story of a virgin birth? The leaders of ancient empires typically presented themselves as divine-human hybrids with superpowers. Pharaohs and caesars were "sons of gods." In them, the violent power of the gods was fused with the violent power of humans to create superhuman superviolence—which allowed them to create superpower nations. But here is God gently inviting—not coercing—a young woman to produce a child who will be known not for his violence but for his kindness. This is a different kind of leader entirely—one who doesn't rule with the masculine power of swords and spears, but with a mother's sense of justice and compassion.

Today: Look for evidence of "superhuman supermasculine superviolence" strutting its stuff, and also look for the quieter, gentler, nonviolent power embodied in mothers.

DAY SIX: *Through the "Weaker Sex"*

In Luke's telling of the birth of Jesus, God aligns with the creative feminine power of womanhood rather than the violent masculine power of statehood. The doctrine of the virgin birth, it turns out, isn't about bypassing sex but about subverting violence. The violent power of top-down patriarchy is subverted not by revolutionary counterviolence but by the creative power of pregnancy. It is through what proud men have considered "the weaker sex" that God's true power enters and changes the world. That, it turns out, is exactly what Mary understood the messenger to be saying:

> *God has looked with favor on the lowliness of his servant...scattered the proud...brought down the powerful...lifted up the lowly...filled the hungry with good things, and sent the rich away empty. (Luke 1:48, 51, 52, 53)*

Today: Pray, "God, help me to shift my trust from the violent masculine power of statehood and coercion to the creative feminine power of motherhood and creativity."

DAY SEVEN: *Present Ourselves to God*

Mary presents herself to the Holy Spirit to receive and cooperate with God's creative power. She surrenders and receives, she nurtures and gives her all...because she dares to believe the impossible is possible. Her son Jesus will consistently model her self-surrender and receptivity to God, and he will consistently prefer the insightful kindness of motherhood to the violent blindness of statehood.

That's what it means to be alive in the adventure of Jesus. We present ourselves to God—our bodies, our stories, our futures, our possibilities, even our limitations. "Here I am," we say with Mary, "the Lord's servant. Let it be with me according to your will."

So in this Advent season—this season of awaiting and pondering the coming of God in Christ—let us light a candle for Mary. And let us, in our own hearts, dare to believe the impossible by surrendering ourselves to God, courageously cooperating with God's creative, pregnant power—in us, for us, and through us. If we do, then we, like Mary, will become pregnant with holy aliveness.

Today: Picture yourself "pregnant with holy aliveness."

KEEP HEROD IN CHRISTMAS

Scripture Readings

> Jeremiah 32:31–35
> Micah 5:2–5a
> Matthew 1:18–2:15

Key Verses—Micah 5:2

> *But you, O Bethlehem of Ephrathah,*
> > *who are one of the little clans of Judah,*
> *from you shall come forth for me*
> > *one who is to rule in Israel,*
> *whose origin is from of old,*
> > *from ancient days.*

DAY ONE: *Herod the Great*

Right in the middle of Matthew's version of the Christmas story comes a shock. It is disturbing, terrifying, and horrific. And it is essential to understanding the adventure and mission of Jesus.

King Herod, or Herod the Great, ruled over Judea in the years leading up to Jesus's birth. Although he rebuilt the Temple in Jerusalem—a sign of his Jewish identity—he was a puppet king who also depended on the Roman empire for his status. He was, like many biblical characters—and like many of us, too—a man with an identity crisis. Cruel and ruthless, he used slave labor for his huge building projects. He had a reputation for assassinating anyone he considered a threat—including his wife and two of his own sons. Late in his reign, he began hearing rumors, rumors that the long-awaited liberator prophesied by Isaiah and others had been born. While a pious man might have greeted this news with hope and joy, Herod only saw it as a threat—a threat to political stability and to his own status as king.

In previous years, there had been a lot of resistance, unrest, and revolt in Jerusalem, so Rome wasn't in a tolerant frame of mind. Any talk of rebellion, Herod knew, would bring crushing retaliation against the city. Herod inquired of the religious scholars to find out if the holy texts gave any indication of where this long-anticipated child would be born. Their answer came from the Book of Micah: Bethlehem.

Herod did what any desperate, ruthless dictator would do. First, he tried to enlist as spies some foreign mystics, known to us as "the wise men from the East." He wanted them to discover the child's identity and whereabouts so he could have the child killed. But the wise men were warned of his deceit in a dream and so avoided becoming his unwitting accomplices. Realizing that his "Plan A" had failed, Herod launched "Plan B." He sent his henchmen to find and kill any young boy living in the area of Bethlehem. But the particular boy he sought had already been removed from Bethlehem and taken elsewhere.

The result? A slaughter of innocent children in Bethlehem.

Today: Consider how children (and their mothers) often suffer most from the insecurity and desperation of ruthless men.

DAY TWO: *How Will We Manage Power?*

In his slaughter of innocent children, King Herod emulated the horrible behavior of Pharaoh centuries before, in the days of Moses. A descendant of the slaves behaved like the ancient slave master. The story of Herod tells us once again that the world can't be simply divided between the good guys—*us*—and the bad guys—*them*—because, like Herod, members of *us* will behave no differently from *them*, given the power and provocation. So all people face the same profound questions: *How will we manage power? How will we deal with violence?*

Herod—and Pharaoh before him—model one way: Violence is simply one tool, used in varying degrees, to gain or maintain power.

The baby whom Herod seeks to kill will model another way. His tool will be service, not violence. And his goal will not be gaining and maintaining power, but using his power to heal and empower others. He will reveal a vision of God that is reflected more in the vulnerability of children than in the violence of men, more in the caring of mothers than in the cruelty of kings.

Today: Notice how people—including you—use power: to gain and maintain for themselves, or to serve and empower others?

DAY THREE: *Sad Music Played Again*

The next war—whoever wages it—will most likely resemble every war in the past. It will be planned by powerful older men in their comfortable headquarters, and it will be fought on the ground by people the age of their children and grandchildren. Most of the casualties will probably be between eighteen and twenty-two years old—in some places, much younger. So the old, sad music of the ancient story of Herod and the slaughter of the children will be replayed again. And again, the tears of mothers will fall.

Today: Look for signs of "the old, sad music of the ancient story" being replayed today.

DAY FOUR: *What We Believe Matters*

The sacrifice of children for the well-being and security of adults has a long history among human beings. For example, in the ancient Middle East there was a religion dedicated to an idol named Molech. Faithful adherents would sacrifice infants to Molech every year, a horrible display of twisted religiosity to appease their god's wrath and earn his favor. In contrast, beginning with the story of Abraham and Isaac, we gradually discover that the true God doesn't require appeasement at all. In fact, God exemplifies true, loving, mature parenthood…self-giving for the sake of one's children, not sacrificing children for one's own selfish interests.

This is why it matters so much for us to grapple with what we believe about God. Does God promote or demand violence? Does God favor the sacrifice of children for the well-being of adults? Is God best reflected in the image of powerful old men who send the young and vulnerable to die on their behalf? Or is God best seen in the image of a helpless baby, identifying with the victims, sharing their vulnerability, full of fragile but limitless promise?

Today: Ponder God being seen in the image of a helpless and vulnerable baby.

DAY FIVE: *Light a Candle*

We do not live in an ideal world. To be alive in the adventure of Jesus is to face at every turn the destructive reality of violence. To be alive in the adventure of Jesus is to side with vulnerable children in defiance of the adults who see them as expendable. To walk the road with Jesus is to withhold consent and cooperation from the powerful and to invest it instead with the vulnerable. It is to refuse to bow to all the Herods and all their ruthless regimes—and to reserve our loyalty for a better king and a better kingdom.

Jesus has truly come, but each year during the Advent season, we acknowledge that the dream for which he gave his all has not yet fully come true. As long as elites plot violence, as long as children pay the price, and as long as mothers weep, we cannot be satisfied.

So let us light a candle for the children who suffer in our world because of greedy, power-hungry, and insecure elites. Let us light a candle for grieving mothers who weep for lost sons and daughters, throughout history and today. Let us light a candle for all people everywhere to hear their weeping. In the Advent season, we dare to believe that God feels their pain and comes near to bring comfort. If we believe that is true, then of course we must join God and come near, too. That is why we must keep Herod and the ugliness of his mass murder in the beautiful Christmas story.

Today: Find a quiet place. Light a candle, and reread today's reading. If your heart moves you, write a poem or prayer.

WEEK SEVENTEEN

SURPRISING PEOPLE

Scripture Readings

Psalm 34:1–18
Matthew 1:1–17
Luke 2:8–20

Key Verses—Luke 2:8–10

In that region there were shepherds living in the fields, keeping watch over their flock by night. Then an angel of the Lord stood before them, and the glory of the Lord shone around them, and they were terrified. But the angel said to them, "Do not be afraid; for see—I am bringing you good news of great joy for all the people."

DAY ONE: *Luke's Ancestor Lists*

And Abraham was the father of Isaac, and Isaac the father of Jacob, and Jacob... To modern readers, the ancestor lists that are so common in the Bible seem pretty tedious and pointless. But to ancient people, they were full of meaning. They were shorthand ways of showing connections, helping people remember how they were related, and reminding them of the story that they found themselves in.

Both Matthew's and Luke's gospels give us ancestor lists for Jesus. Although they are very different lists, both agree on two essential points. First, Jesus was a descendant of Sarah and Abraham. That reminded people of God's original promise to Abraham and Sarah—that through their lineage, all nations of the world would be blessed. Second, Jesus was a descendant of King David. That brought to mind all the nostalgia for the golden age of David's reign, together with all the hope from the prophets about a promised time under the benevolent reign of a descendant of David.

Today: Whenever you check the news, try to put today's headlines in context of the sweep of history over decades, centuries, and millennia.

DAY TWO: *Distinct Treasures*

The ancestor lists of Luke and Matthew offer distinct treasures. Luke's gospel starts with the present and goes back, all the way to Abraham, and then all the way to Adam, the original human in the Genesis story: "son of Enoch, son of Jared, son of Mahalaleel, son of Cainan, son of Enos, son of Seth, son of Adam, son of God." That use of that phrase "son of God" is fascinating. It suggests a primary meaning of the term: to be *the son of* is to "find your origin in." It also suggests that Jesus, as the son of Adam, is in some way a new beginning for the human race—a new genesis, we might say. Just as Adam bore the image of God as the original human, Jesus will now reflect the image of God. We might say he is Adam 2.0.

That understanding is reinforced by what comes immediately before Luke's ancestor list: A voice comes from heaven and says, "You are my Son, the Beloved; with you I am well pleased." Just as *Son of David* prepares us to expect Jesus to model leadership, and just as *Son of Abraham* prepares us to expect Jesus to model blessing and promise for all, *Son of God* sets us up to expect Jesus to model true humanity as Adam did.

Matthew's version, which starts in the distant past and moves to the present, holds lots of treasures, too. Most surprising is his inclusion of five women. In the ancient world, people were unaware of the existence of the human egg and assumed that a man provided the only seed of a new life. So ancestor lists naturally focused on men. It's surprising enough for Matthew to include women at all, but the women he selects are quite astonishing.

First, there is Tamar. She had once posed as a prostitute in a web of sexual and family intrigue. Then there is Rahab—a Gentile of Jericho who actually was a prostitute. Then there is Ruth, another Gentile who entered into a sexual liaison with a wealthy Jew named Boaz. Then there is Bathsheba, who was married to a foreigner—Uriah the Hittite—and with whom King David committed adultery. Finally there is Mary, who claims to be pregnant without the help of Joseph. These are not the kind of women whose names were typically included in ancestor lists of the past!

But that, of course, must be Matthew's point. Jesus isn't entering into a pristine story of ideal people. He is part of the story of Gentiles as well as Jews, broken and messy families as well as noble ones, normal folks as well as kings and priests and heroes. We might say that Jesus isn't entering humanity from the top with a kind of trickle-down grace, but rather from the bottom, with grace that rises from the grass roots up.

Today: Keep in mind the contrast between "trickle-down grace" and "grassroots grace."

DAY THREE: *Unsung Heroes*

Consider the unsung heroes of Luke's Christmas story: shepherds. They're the ones who, along with Joseph and Mary, have a front-row seat to welcome the "good news of great joy for all the people." They're the down-to-earth people who hear the celestial announcement from angelic messengers.

Shepherds were marginal people in society—a lot like Tamar, Rahab, Ruth, Bathsheba, and Mary. They weren't normal "family men," because they lived outdoors most of the time, guarding sheep from wolves and thieves and guiding sheep to suitable pasture. A younger son, for whom there was no hope of inheriting the family farm, might become a shepherd, as would a man who for some reason was not suitable for marriage. It was among poor men like these that Jesus's birth was first celebrated.

Today: The Apostle Paul once said, "Associate with the lowly" (Romans 12:16). Today, look for an opportunity to associate with and show uncommon respect to some down-to-earth people who many would consider "beneath" them.

DAY FOUR: *The Special Place of the Poor*

The poor, of course, have a special place in the Bible. The priests and prophets of Israel agreed that God had a special concern for the poor. God commanded all right-living people to be generous to them. Provision was made for the landless to be able to glean from the fields of the prosperous. According to Proverbs, those who exploited the poor—or simply didn't care about them—would not prosper, and those who were good to the poor would be blessed.

The poor were especially central to the life and ministry of Jesus. Jesus understood himself to be empowered by the Spirit to bring good news to the poor. In Jesus's parables, God cared for the poor and confronted the rich who showed the poor no compassion. Jesus taught rich people to give generously to the poor, and even though others considered the poor to be cursed, Jesus pronounced the poor and those who are in solidarity with them to be blessed. When Jesus said, "The poor you will always have with you," he was echoing Deuteronomy 15:4 (NLT), which says, "There should be no poor among you," for there is actually enough in God's world for everyone.

Although much has changed from Jesus's day to ours, this has not: a small percentage of the world's population lives in luxury, and the majority live in poverty. For example, about half the people in today's world struggle to survive on less than $2.50 per day. Those who subsist on $1.25 per day make up over a billion of the world's seven billion people. About half of the people in sub-Saharan Africa and more than 35 percent of people in Southeast Asia fit in this category. They are today's shepherds, working the rice fields, streaming into slums, sleeping on sidewalks, struggling to survive.

Today: Try to estimate how much money you spend today—not just in stores, but on your rent or mortgage, utilities, transport, insurance, etc. Compare your daily expense to the statistics in today's reading.

DAY FIVE: *God's Light Came Shining*

Do you remember how the whole biblical story begins? "In the..." And do you remember the first creation that is spoken into being? "Let there be..."

In the stories of Jesus's birth, we celebrate a new *beginning*. We welcome the dawning of a new *light*.

A new day begins with sunrise. A new year begins with lengthening days. A new life begins with infant eyes taking in their first view of a world bathed in light. And a new era in human history began when God's light came shining into our world through Jesus.

The Fourth Gospel tells us that what came into being through Jesus was not merely a new religion, a new theology, or a new set of principles or teachings—although all these things did indeed happen. The real point of it all, according to John, was *life*, vitality, *aliveness*—and now that Jesus has come, that radiant aliveness is here to enlighten all people everywhere.

Some people don't see it yet. Some don't want to see it. They've got some shady plans that they want to preserve undercover, in darkness. From pickpockets to corrupt politicians, from human traffickers to exploitive business sharks, from terrorists plotting in hidden cells to racists spreading messages of hate, they don't welcome the light, because transparency exposes their plans and deeds for what they are: evil. So they prefer darkness.

But others welcome the light. They receive it as a gift, and in that receiving, they let God's holy, radiant aliveness stream into their lives. They become portals of light in our world, and they start living as members of God's family—which means they're related to all of God's creation. That relatedness is the essence of enlightenment.

Today: Pray, "God, I open my heart, my mind, my whole being to receive your light and your aliveness."

DAY SIX: *A New Understanding of Aliveness*

What do we mean when we say Jesus is the light? Just as a glow on the eastern horizon tells us that a long night is almost over, Jesus's birth signals the beginning of the end for the dark night of fear, hostility, violence, and greed that has descended on our world. Jesus's birth signals the start of a new day, a new way, a new understanding of what it means to be alive.

Aliveness, he will teach, is a gift available to all by God's grace. It flows not from taking but from giving, not from fear but from faith, not from conflict but from reconciliation, not from domination but from service. It isn't found in the outward trappings of religion—rules and rituals, controversies and scruples, temples and traditions. No, it springs up from our innermost being like a fountain of living water. It intoxicates us like the best wine ever and so turns life from a disappointment into a banquet. This new light of aliveness and love opens us up to rethink everything—to go back and become like little children again. Then we can rediscover the world with a fresh, childlike wonder—seeing the world in a new light, the light of Christ.

Today: Cultivate childlike wonder by stopping to notice and enjoy whatever sparks your curiosity.

DAY SEVEN: *Kneel at the Manger*

Picture a silent, holy night long ago when Luke tells us of a young and very pregnant woman and weary man walking beside her. They had traveled more than eighty miles, a journey of several days, from Nazareth in the province of Galilee to Bethlehem in the province of Judea. Mary went into labor, and because nobody could provide them with a normal bed in a normal house, she had to give birth in a stable. We can imagine oxen and donkeys and cattle filling the air with their sounds and scent as Mary wrapped the baby in rags and laid him in a manger, a food trough for farm animals. On that dark night, in such a humble place, enfleshed in a tiny, vulnerable, homeless, helpless baby...God's light began to glow.

Politicians compete for the highest offices. Business tycoons scramble for a bigger and bigger piece of the pie. Armies march and scientists study and philosophers philosophize and preachers preach and laborers sweat. But in that silent baby, lying in that humble manger, there pulses more potential power and wisdom and grace and aliveness than all the rest of us can imagine.

To be alive in the adventure of Jesus is to kneel at the manger and gaze upon that little baby who is radiant with so much promise for our world today.

So let us light a candle for the Christ child, for the infant Jesus, the Word made flesh. Let our hearts glow with that light that was in him, so that we become candles through which his light shines still. Christmas is not just for one day a year. It is a process as well as an event. Your heart and mine can become the little town, the stable, the manger...even now. Let a new day, a new creation, a new you, and new me, begin. Let there be light.

Today: Find a quiet place. Light a candle. Read the last paragraph of this reflection aloud. See what kind of prayer or poetry arises in your heart.

WEEK EIGHTEEN

SHARING GIFTS

Scripture Readings

> Psalm 117
> Matthew 2:1–12
> Luke 2:25–32

Key Verses—Matthew 2:9–11

When they had heard the king, they set out; and there, ahead of them, went the star that they had seen at its rising, until it stopped over the place where the child was. When they saw that the star had stopped, they were overwhelmed with joy. On entering the house, they saw the child with Mary his mother; and they knelt down and paid him homage. Then, opening their treasure chests, they offered him gifts of gold, frankincense, and myrrh.

DAY ONE: *"Better to Give Than to Receive"*

They were called Magi...we know them as wise men. They were astrologers, holy men of a foreign religion. They had observed a strange celestial phenomenon, which they interpreted to mean that a new king had been born in Judea. According to Matthew's gospel, they traveled to honor him, bringing valuable treasures of gold, frankincense, and myrrh—precious gifts indeed.

In their giving of gifts they were wiser than they realized. Gift-giving, it turns out, was at the heart of all Jesus would say and do. God is like a parent, Jesus would teach, who loves to shower sons and daughters with good gifts. The kingdom or commonwealth of God that Jesus constantly proclaimed was characterized by an abundant, gracious, extravagant economy of grace, of generosity, of gift-giving. "It is better to give than to receive," Jesus taught, and his followers came to understand Jesus himself as a gift expressing God's love to the whole world.

So, in memory of the wise men's gift-giving to Jesus, in honor of Jesus's teaching and example of giving, and as an echo of God's self-giving in Jesus, we joyfully give one another gifts when we celebrate the birth of Jesus. Sometimes we get distracted by the rush and commerce, but, rightly understood, it is a fitting tradition.

Today: Surprise someone with an unexpected gift, just because.

DAY TWO: *A Better Way*

Not everyone felt generosity in response to the birth of Jesus. King Herod was furious about anyone who might unsettle the status quo. When he deployed troops to the Bethlehem region with orders to kill all infant boys, Joseph was warned in a dream to escape. So the family fled south to Egypt, where Jesus spent part of his childhood as a refugee.

How meaningful it is that members of other religions—the Magi from the east and the Egyptians to the south—help save Jesus's life. Could their role in the Christmas story be a gift to us today? Could they be telling us that God has a better way for people of different religions to relate to one another?

Through the centuries, religions have repeatedly divided people. Religions—including the Christian religion—have too often spread fear, prejudice, hate, and violence in our world. But in the Magi's offering of gifts to honor the infant Jesus, and in the Egyptians' protective hospitality for Jesus and his refugee family, we can see a better way, a way Jesus himself embodied and taught as a man. They remind us that members of Earth's religions don't need to see their counterparts as competitors or enemies. Instead, we can approach one another with the spirit of gift-giving and honor, as exemplified by the Magi. We can be there to welcome and protect one another, as exemplified by the Egyptians.

Instead of looking for faults and errors by which other religions can be discredited, insulted, and excluded, we can ask other questions: *What good can be discovered in this religion? Let us honor it. What treasures have they been given to share with us? Let us warmly welcome them. What dangers do they face? Let us protect them. What gifts do we have to share with them? Let us generously offer them.*

Today: If possible, have a meal or cup of tea with a member of another religion. Explain why you wanted to do so. Use the questions above to guide you.

DAY THREE: *A Highly Cherished Identity*

According to Matthew, when King Herod died, Joseph had another dream telling him it was safe to return to his homeland. But Herod's son still ruled Judea, the region around Bethlehem, so the family went farther north to another region, Galilee. They resettled in Nazareth, Galilee—which would be Jesus's address throughout the rest of his childhood and young adulthood.

So, having been protected by the Magi and the Egyptians, Jesus grew up as a Galilean Jew. The Jews were the descendants of the Judeans who had survived the Babylonian invasion more than five centuries earlier. They had not lost their identity while living under exile in Babylon. Nor had they lost that identity over the following centuries, when they survived occupation and oppression by the Persians, Greeks, and Romans. Because the Jews had so courageously survived oppression and mistreatment by others, and because they believed God had given them special blessings to enjoy and share with everyone, no wonder Jewish identity was highly cherished. No wonder it was repeatedly affirmed and celebrated through holidays like Passover and rites of passage like circumcision.

Today: Remember the story of your ancestry and your childhood.

DAY FOUR: *A Gift for Everyone*

Luke's gospel doesn't tell us about the Magi or the Egyptians. For Luke, the next big event after Jesus's birth came eight days later, when Jesus's parents took him to the Temple in Jerusalem to be circumcised, a primary sign of Jewish identity for every newborn son. You can imagine his parents' surprise when an old man, a perfect stranger named Simeon, came up to them in the Temple and took Jesus from their arms and began praising God. "This child will be a light for revelation to the Gentiles, and a glory to God's people, Israel," Simeon said. He was seeing in Jesus a gift for *us* and for *them* both, not one against the other or one without the other.

Old Simeon the Jew in Luke's gospel and the non-Jewish Magi from the East in Matthew's gospel agree: This child is special. He is worthy of honor. He has gifts that will bring blessing to his own people, and to all people everywhere.

To be alive in the adventure of Jesus is to know ourselves as part of a tradition and, through that tradition, to have a history and an identity to enjoy, preserve, and to share. And to be alive in the adventure of Jesus is to see others as part of their unique traditions, too, with their own history, identity, and gifts. Like the Magi, like the Egyptians, like old Simeon…we don't have to see people of other religions in terms of *us* versus *them*. We can see people of other religions as beloved neighbors, us with them, them with us, with gifts to share.

May we who follow Jesus discover the gifts of our tradition and share them generously, and may we joyfully receive the gifts that others bring as well. For every good gift and every perfect gift comes from God.

Today: Pray, "God, help me cherish my own tradition, and help me to honor and respect the traditions of others, which are as precious (and maybe problematic) to them as mine is to me."

WEEK NINETEEN

JESUS COMING OF AGE

Scripture Readings

> I Kings 3:1–28
> Luke 2:39–3:14; 3:21–22
> I Timothy 4:6–16

Key Verses—Luke 3:21–22

Now when all the people were baptized, and when Jesus also had been baptized and was praying, the heaven was opened, and the Holy Spirit descended upon him in bodily form like a dove. And a voice came from heaven, "You are my Son, the Beloved; with you I am well pleased."

DAY ONE: *God's Child*

What were you like when you were twelve? In what ways are you the same today? How have you changed?

We have only this one glimpse into Jesus's childhood. Jesus was twelve, when boys came of age in ancient Jewish culture. He joined his family on their annual pilgrimage south to Jerusalem for the Passover holiday. This was a journey of more than sixty miles—not a short trip on foot, maybe taking four or five days each way. This year, as at each Passover holiday, the Jewish people would celebrate the story of God liberating their ancestors from slavery in Egypt. Because the Romans now ruled over them, making them feel like slaves again, the holiday kept alive the hopes that a new Moses might arise among them and lead them to expel the Romans. Like every good holiday, then, this Passover was to be about both the past and the present.

People traveled to and from the Passover festival in large groups, so Mary and Joseph assumed that Jesus was among their fellow travelers when they began the long trek home. When Jesus couldn't be found, they rushed back to Jerusalem, where they looked for him for three long days. Finally they came to the Temple, and there Jesus sat, a twelve-year-old boy among the religious scholars and teachers. He was asking questions of them and answering questions they posed in return. Everyone was amazed at this young spiritual prodigy. He was like a modern-day Solomon, King David's son who was famous for his wisdom.

His mother pulled him aside and gave him exactly the lecture you would expect. "Child!" she began, as if to remind this young adolescent that he wasn't grown up yet. "Why have you treated us like this? Listen! Your father and I have been worried sick. We've been looking everywhere for you!" Jesus replied, "Didn't you know that it was necessary for me to be in my Father's house?"

The reply tells us a lot about Jesus. By the age of twelve, he saw God in tender, fatherly terms. He saw himself as God's child. He was already deeply curious—demonstrated by his questions to the religious scholars. And he was deeply thoughtful—demonstrated by his wise answers to their questions. Like most parents of teenagers, of course, Mary and Joseph were completely baffled by his behavior and his explanation of it. He went back to Nazareth with them, and the next eighteen years were summarized by Luke in these fourteen words: "Jesus matured in wisdom and years, and in favor with God and with people."

Today: Think back to when you were twelve, just coming of age, and try to empathize with Jesus when he was at that same stage of life.

DAY TWO: *John Bursts onto the Scene*

As Jesus was maturing in Nazareth, his relative John, son of Elizabeth and Zechariah, was coming of age back in Jerusalem. As the son of a priest, he would have lived the comfortable, privileged life of the upper classes. We would expect him to follow in his father's footsteps at the Temple in Jerusalem, offering sacrifices, officiating at festivals, and performing ritual cleansings called baptisms.

Baptisms were essential, because pilgrims who came from distant lands to the Temple were understood to be "unclean" as a result of their contact with people of other religions and cultures. Several special baths had been constructed around the Temple so that worshipers could ceremonially wash off that contamination and present themselves to God as "clean people" again. It was another way to preserve religious identity during a time of occupation and domination by "unclean foreigners."

Can you imagine how shocking it was for Zechariah's son to burst onto the scene, preaching and performing baptisms—not in Jerusalem, but more than eighty miles to the north and east? Can you imagine the disruption of him performing ritual cleansing—not in the private, holy baths near the Temple, but in public, out in the countryside, along the banks of the Jordan River? Can you imagine the gossip about his choice to trade the luxurious robes of the priesthood for the rough garments of a beggar and the high-class menu of Jerusalem for the subsistence fare of the wilderness? What would such actions have meant?

Today: Ponder the ways John the Baptist was similar to and different from his father, and think about ways your life is similar to and different from the lives of your parents.

DAY THREE: *Rethink Everything*

John's departure from both family and Temple suggested that John was protesting against the religious establishment his father faithfully served. Jerusalem's Temple was not all it was held up to be, he would have been saying. A new kind of baptism—with a radical new meaning—was needed. Traveling to a special city and an opulent building could not make people clean and holy. What they needed most was not a change in location, but a change in orientation, a change in heart. People needed a different kind of cleanness—one that couldn't come through a conventional ceremonial bath in a holy temple.

According to John, the identity that mattered most wasn't one you could inherit through tribe, nationality, or religion—as descendants of Abraham, for example. The identity that mattered most was one you created through your actions…by sharing your wealth, possessions, and food with those in need, by refusing to participate in the corruption so common in government and business, by treating others fairly and respectfully, and by not being driven by greed. One word summarized John's message: *repent*, which meant "rethink everything," or "question your assumptions," or "have a deep turnaround in your thinking and values." His baptism of repentance symbolized being immersed in a flowing river of love, in solidarity not just with the clean, privileged, superior *us*—but with everyone, everywhere.

Today: Ponder the message, "Rethink everything!" and let it unsettle and challenge you.

DAY FOUR: *Preparing the Way*

Like prophets of old, John issued a powerful warning: God would soon intervene to confront wrong and set things right, and the status quo would soon come to an end. Crowds started streaming out to the countryside to be baptized by John. His protest movement grew, and with it, expectation and hope. Maybe John would be the long-awaited liberator, the people whispered—like Moses and Joshua, leading people to freedom; like David, instituting a new reign and a new golden age. John quickly squelched those expectations. "I'm not the one you're waiting for," he said. "I'm preparing the way for someone who is coming after me. He will really clean things up. He will bring the change we need."

John kept thundering out his message of warning and hope, week after week, month after month. He dared to confront the powerful and name their hypocrisy. (Herod Antipas, the son of the Herod who tried to kill Jesus, couldn't withstand the agitation of John's protest movement, so he ultimately had John arrested and, eventually, beheaded.)

Today: Consider the ways that powerful elites try to stamp out messages that challenge their position. Consider the courage it takes to speak truth to power.

DAY FIVE: *A Dove, a Lamb, a Beloved Child*

Among the crowds coming to be baptized one day was a young man about John's age. By receiving John's baptism, this young man identified himself with this growing protest movement in the Galilean countryside. As he came out of the water, people heard a sound, as if the sky was cracking open with a rumble of thunder. They saw something descending from the sky...it looked like a dove landing on his head. Some claimed to hear the voice of God saying, "You are my Son, whom I dearly love. In you I find pleasure" (Mark 1:11, author's paraphrase).

What Jesus had said about God at the age of twelve in the Temple, God now echoed about Jesus at age thirty at the riverside: they shared a special parent-child relationship, a deep connection of love and joy. And in that relationship, there was an invitation for us all, because Jesus taught that all of us could enter into that warm and secure parent-child relationship with God.

That dove is full of meaning as well. Jesus came, not under the sign of the lion or tiger, not under the sign of the bull or bear, not under the sign of the hawk or eagle or viper...but under the sign of the dove—a sign of peace and nonviolence. Similarly, when John first saw Jesus, he didn't say, "Behold the Lion of God, come to avenge our enemies," but rather "Behold the Lamb of God, who takes away the sin of the world." To remove sin rather than get revenge for it—that was an agenda of peace indeed.

So now Jesus had come of age and stepped onto the stage: a man with a dovelike spirit, a man with the gentleness of a lamb, a man of peace whose identity was rooted in this profound reality: *God's beloved child*.

When we awaken within that deep relationship of mutual love and pleasure, we are ready to join in God's peace movement today—an adventure of protest, hope, and creative, nonviolent, world-transforming change.

Today: Pray, "God, may I live under the sign of the dove, the sign of the lamb, the banner of the beloved child of God."

JOIN THE ADVENTURE!

Scripture Readings

> Isaiah 61:1–4
> Luke 4:1–30; 5:1–11
> 2 Timothy 2:1–9

Key Verses—Luke 5:10b

> *Then Jesus said to Simon, "Do not be afraid; from now on you will be catching people."*

DAY ONE: *Facing Our Inner Demons*

To never be given a chance to succeed—that's a tragedy. But in some ways it's even worse to have your chance and not be ready for it. That's why in almost every story of a great hero, there is an ordeal or a test that must be passed before the hero's adventure can begin.

That was the case with Jesus. Before he could begin his public adventure, Jesus felt the Holy Spirit leading him away from the crowds, away from the cities, and away from the fertile Jordan Valley, out into the solitude of the harsh, dry, barren Judean desert.

By saying Jesus fasted in the desert for forty days, Luke's gospel is inviting us to remember Moses who, before becoming the liberator of the Hebrew slaves, spent forty years in the wilderness, where he eventually encountered God in the burning bush. Luke's gospel is also inviting us to remember the story of the newly liberated Hebrew slaves who, after leaving Egypt, were tested for forty years in the wilderness before they were prepared to enter the promised land. Once again the gospel writers present Jesus as mirroring the experience of his ancestral people.

Luke describes Jesus's testing in the vivid language of an encounter with the devil. Some take this language literally. Others see the devil as a literary figure who developed over time among ancient storytellers to personify all that is dark, evil, deceitful, and violent in human nature and human culture.

"Turn these stones into bread," the devil says in his first temptation. In other words, *Who needs the character formation and self-control that come from spiritual disciplines like fasting? That's a long, hard process. You can have it all, right now—public influence and private self-indulgence—if you just use your miraculous powers to acquire whatever you desire!* In the second temptation, Jesus is offered the chance to get on the fast track to power by acknowledging that self-seeking power, not self-giving love, reigns supreme: "You can rule over all the kingdoms of the world—if you'll simply worship me!" In the third temptation, the devil tells him, "Prove yourself as God's beloved child by throwing yourself off the Temple!" This seemingly suicidal move, with angelic intervention at the last moment before impact, would provide just the kind of public-relations spectacle that showmen love. But Jesus is not a showman, and he isn't interested in shortcuts. Besides, he doesn't need to prove he is God's beloved child. He knows that already.

So he will not use his power for personal comfort and pleasure. He will refuse unscrupulous means to achieve just and peaceful ends. He will not reach for spectacle over substance. And so Jesus sets the course for the great work before him—not driven by a human lust for pleasure, power, or prestige, but empowered by the Spirit. Of course, if we want to join Jesus in his great work, we must face our own inner demons and discover the same Spirit-empowerment.

Today: Ponder this question: if you were the protagonist in the story, what three temptations would be most likely to defeat you?

DAY TWO: *Deep Rethinking and Radical Adjustment*

Imagine Jesus, ready to launch his public ministry, returning to his hometown, Nazareth. Like any good Jewish man, he goes to the synagogue on the Sabbath day. There is a time in the synagogue gathering where men can read a passage of Scripture and offer comment upon it. So on this day, Jesus stands and asks for the scroll of the prophet Isaiah. He unrolls the scroll until he comes to the passage that speaks of the Spirit anointing someone to bring good news to the poor, release to the captives, healing to the blind, freedom to the oppressed.

By quoting these words, Jesus stirs the hopes of his people—hopes for the time Isaiah and other prophets had urged the people to wait for, pray for, and prepare for. Then he sits—a teacher's customary posture in those days. He offers this amazing commentary—notable for its brevity and even more for its astonishing claim: "Today this Scripture has been fulfilled in your hearing."

If he had said, "Someday this Scripture will be fulfilled," everyone would have felt it was a good, comforting sermon. If he had said, "This Scripture is already fulfilled in some ways, not yet in others," that would also have been interesting and acceptable. But either commentary would postpone until the future any need for real change in his hearers' lives. For Jesus to say the promised time was here already, fulfilled, today...that was astonishing. That required deep rethinking and radical adjustment.

The same is true for us today.

Today: Treat this day as the day of opportunity, the day of decision, the day that deep dreams can be fulfilled.

DAY THREE: *Facing Domestication and Intimidation*

Imagine if a prophet arose today in Panama, Sierra Leone, or Sri Lanka. In an interview on the BBC or Al Jazeera he says, "Now is the time! It's time to dismantle the military-industrial complex and reconcile with enemies! It's time for CEOs to slash their mammoth salaries and give generous raises to all their lowest-paid employees! It's time for criminals, militias, weapons factories, and armies to turn in their bullets and guns so they can be melted down and recast as trumpets, swing sets, and garden tools. It's time to stop plundering the Earth for quick corporate profit and to start healing the Earth for long-term universal benefit. Don't say 'someday' or 'tomorrow.' The time is today!" Imagine how the talking heads would spin!

The Nazareth crowd is impressed that their hometown boy is so articulate and intelligent and bold. But Jesus won't let them simply be impressed or appreciative for long. He quickly reminds them of two stories from the Scriptures, one involving a Sidonian widow in the time of Elijah and one involving a Syrian general in the time of Elisha. God bypassed many needy people of our religion and nation, Jesus says, to help those foreigners, those Gentiles, those outsiders. You can almost hear the snap as people are jolted by this unexpected turn.

Clearly, the good news proclaimed by the hometown prophet is for *them* as well as *us*, for *all humankind* and not just for *our kind*. Somehow, that seems disloyal to the Nazarenes. That seems like a betrayal of their unique and hard-won identity. In just a few minutes, the crowd quickly flips from proud to concerned to disturbed to furious. They are transformed by their fury from a congregation into a lynch mob, and they push Jesus out the door and over to the edge of a cliff. They're ready to execute this heretical traitor.

Again, imagine if a pope, a patriarch, or a famous Protestant TV preacher today were to declare that God is just as devoted to Muslims, Hindus, and atheists as to Christians. They might not be thrown off a cliff, but one can easily imagine tense brows and grave voices advocating for them to be thrown out of office or taken off the air!

No wonder Jesus needed that time of preparation in the wilderness. He needed to get his mission clear in his own heart so that he wouldn't be captivated by the expectations of adoring fans or intimidated by the threats of furious critics. If we dare to follow Jesus and proclaim the radical dimensions of God's good news as he did, we will face the same twin dangers of domestication and intimidation.

Today: Ponder the courage of Jesus to speak truths that people didn't want to hear, and ask yourself what truths people today need to hear, but resist.

DAY FOUR: *Rediscovering Discipleship*

Jesus managed to avoid execution after his "Nazareth Manifesto." But he knew it wouldn't be his last brush with hostile opposition. Soon he began inviting select individuals to become his followers. As with aspiring musicians who are invited to become the students of a master musician, this was a momentous decision for them. To become disciples of a rabbi meant entering a rigorous program of transformation, learning a new way of life, a new set of values, a new set of skills. It meant leaving behind the comforts of home and facing a new set of dangers on the road. Once they were thoroughly apprenticed as disciples, they would then be sent out as apostles to spread the rabbi's controversial and challenging message everywhere. One did not say *yes* to discipleship lightly.

The word *Christian* is more familiar to us today than the word *disciple*. These days, *Christian* often seems to apply more to the kinds of people who would push Jesus off a cliff than it does to his true followers. Perhaps the time has come to rediscover the power and challenge of that earlier, more primary word *disciple*. The word *disciple* occurs more than 250 times in the New Testament, in contrast to the word *Christian*, which occurs only three times. Maybe those statistics are trying to tell us something.

To be alive in the adventure of Jesus is to hear that challenging good news of *today*, and to receive that thrilling invitation to follow him…and to take the first intrepid step on the road as a *disciple*.

Today: Pray, "Living God, I want to be a disciple of Jesus today."

WEEK TWENTY-ONE

SIGNIFICANT AND
WONDERFUL

Scripture Readings

2 Samuel 11:26–12:15
John 2:1–12
Mark 1:21–28

Key Verses—John 2:9–11

When the steward tasted the water that had become wine, and did not know where it came from (though the servants who had drawn the water knew), the steward called the bridegroom and said to him, "Everyone serves the good wine first, and then the inferior wine after the guests have become drunk. But you have kept the good wine until now." Jesus did this, the first of his signs, in Cana of Galilee, and revealed his glory; and his disciples believed in him.

DAY ONE: *The Problem with Miracles*

You can't go many pages in the gospels without encountering a miracle. Some of us find it easy and exciting to believe in miracles. Others of us find them highly problematic.

If you find it easy to believe in miracles, the gospels are a treasure of inspiration. But you still have to deal with one big problem: The miracles in the gospels easily stir hopes that are almost always dashed in people's lives today. For example, in Matthew 9 you read about a little girl being raised from the dead, but since that time how many millions of faithful, praying parents have grieved lost children without miraculous happy endings? In Matthew 14, you read about fish and bread being multiplied to feed the hungry, but since that day, how many millions of faithful, praying people have slowly starved, and no miracle came? Doesn't the possibility of miracles only make our suffering worse when God could grant them but doesn't? It's all so much worse if accusatory people then blame the victim for not having enough faith.

Today: Consider the problem of miracles described in today's reading.

DAY TWO: *Imagine Miracles Happening*

If you are skeptical about miracles in the Bible, you avoid some problems. But you have another problem, no less significant: If you're not careful, you can be left with a reduced world, a disenchanted, mechanistic world where the impossible is always and forever impossible. You may judge the miracle stories in the gospels as silly legends, childish make-believe, false advertising, or deceitful propaganda. But in banishing what you regard as superstition, you may also banish meaning and hope. If you lock out miracles, you can easily lock yourself in—into a closed mechanistic system, a small box where God's existence doesn't seem to make much difference.

There is a third alternative, a response to the question of miracles that is open to both skeptics and believers in miracles alike. Instead of "Yes, the miracle stories actually happened," or "No, they didn't really happen," we could ask another question: What happens to us when we imagine miracles happening? In other words, perhaps the story of a miracle is intended to do more than inform us about an event that supposedly happened in the past, an event that, if you were to believe it, might prove something else.

Perhaps a miracle story is meant to shake up our normal assumptions, inspire our imagination about the present and the future, and make it possible for us to see something we couldn't see before. Perhaps the miracle that really counts isn't one that happened to *them* back then but one that could happen in *us* right now as we reflect upon the story.

Perhaps, by challenging us to consider impossible possibilities, these stories can stretch our imagination, and·in so doing, can empower us to play a catalytic role in cocreating new possibilities for the world of tomorrow. Doesn't that sound rather...miraculous?

Today: Whether or not you find it easy to believe that miracles were historical facts, ponder the understanding of miracles presented in today's reading.

DAY THREE: *Let's Do Some Wondering*

Consider Jesus's first miracle in the Fourth Gospel. The story begins, "On the third day there was a wedding in Cana of Galilee." Jesus's mother notices that the wedding host has run out of wine, and she nudges Jesus to do something about it. Jesus resists, but Mary doubts his resistance. She tells the servants to get ready to do whatever Jesus instructs.

Jesus points them to some nearby stone containers—six of them, used to hold water for ceremonial cleansing. These cleansings express the intention to live as "clean people," in contrast to "unclean people." The containers are huge—potentially holding twenty or thirty gallons each. But they are empty. "Fill them with water," Jesus says. So the servants get to work drawing 120 to 180 gallons of water and filling the huge containers. Jesus instructs them to draw out a sample to give to the banquet master. He takes a taste. He's amazed! "You've saved the best wine until last!" he says.

John says this was the first of the signs by which Jesus revealed his glory. That word *signs* is important. Signs point. They signify. They mean something. Often, the word *signs* is linked with *wonders*—which make you wonder and astonish you with awe. So having warmed up our imagination by picturing a story about a faraway place in a long-ago time, let's now apply our inspired imagination to our lives, our world, here and now. Let's consider the significance of the sign. Let's do some wondering.

In what ways are our lives—and our religions, and our cultures—like a wedding banquet that is running out of wine? What are we running out of? What are the stone containers in our day—huge but empty vessels used for religious purposes? What would it mean for those empty containers to be filled—with wine? And why so much wine? Can you imagine what 180 gallons of wine would mean in a small Galilean village? What might that superabundance signify? What might it mean for Jesus to repurpose containers used to separate the clean from the unclean? And what might it mean for God to save the best for last?

Questions like these show us a way of engaging with the miracle stories as signs and wonders, without reducing them to the level of "mere facts" on the one hand or "mere superstition" on the other. They stir us to imagine new ways of seeing, leading to new ways of acting, leading to new ways of being alive.

Today: Reflect on one or more of the questions about the water-into-wine miracle raised in today's reading.

DAY FOUR: *Question for Our Own Times*

In Mark's gospel, the first miracle is very different from John's story set in Cana. It happens in Capernaum, Jesus's home base, in the synagogue on the Sabbath day. The people have gathered, and Jesus is teaching with his trademark authority. Suddenly, a man "with an unclean spirit" screams: "What do you want with us, Jesus of Nazareth? Have you come to destroy us? I know who you are—the Holy One of God!" Jesus tells the spirit to be quiet and leave the man, and the spirit shakes the man violently and leaves.

Today, we would probably diagnose the man as being mentally or emotionally unwell, anxiety-ridden, maybe even paranoid. Instead of being possessed by a demon, we would understand him to be possessed by a chemical imbalance, a psychiatric disorder, a neurological malady, or a powerful delirium. But even with our difference in diagnosing and understanding human behavior, we can imagine how we would respond to seeing Jesus return this man to mental well-being with one impromptu therapy session lasting less than ten seconds!

Again, the story stimulates us to ask questions about our own lives, our own times. What unhealthy, polluting spirits are troubling us as individuals and as a people? What fears, false beliefs, and emotional imbalances reside within us and distort our behavior? What unclean or unhealthy thought patterns, value systems, and ideologies inhabit, oppress, and possess us as a community or culture? What in us feels threatened and intimidated by the presence of a supremely "clean" or "holy" spirit or presence, like the one in Jesus? In what way might this individual symbolize our whole society? In what ways might our society lose its health, its balance, its sanity, its "clean spirit," to something unclean or unhealthy?

What would it mean for faith in the power of God to liberate us from these unhealthy, imbalanced, self-destructive disorders? Dare we believe that we could be set free? Dare we trust that we could be restored to health? Dare we have faith that such a miracle could happen to us—today?

Today: Reflect on one or more of the questions about the miracle in Capernaum raised in today's reading.

DAY FIVE: *Conversation about Meaning*

There is a time and place for arguments about whether this or that miracle story literally happened. But when we take a literary approach rather than a literalistic approach, we turn from arguments about history to conversations about meaning. We accept that miracle stories intentionally stand on the line between believable and dismissible. In so doing, they throw us off balance so that we see, think, imagine, and feel in a new way.

After people met Jesus, they started telling wild, inspiring stories like these...stories full of gritty detail, profound meaning, and audacious hope. They felt their emptiness being filled to overflowing. They watched as their lifelong obsession with *clean* and *unclean* was replaced with a superabundant, super-celebrative joy. They felt their anxiety and paranoia fade, and in their place faith and courage grew. They experienced their blindness ending, and they began to see everything in a new light. That was why these stories had to be told. And that's why they have to be told today. You may or may not believe in literal miracles, but faith still works wonders.

Today: Pray, "God, help me grow a dynamic faith that works wonders."

WEEK TWENTY-TWO

JESUS THE TEACHER

Scripture Readings

Proverbs 3:1–26
Jeremiah 31:31–34
Mark 4:1–34

Key Verses—Jeremiah 31:31–33

The days are surely coming, says the Lord, when I will make a new covenant with the house of Israel and the house of Judah. It will not be like the covenant that I made with their ancestors when I took them by the hand to bring them out of the land of Egypt—a covenant that they broke, though I was their husband, says the Lord. But this is the covenant that I will make with the house of Israel after those days, says the Lord: I will put my law within them, and I will write it on their hearts; and I will be their God, and they shall be my people.

DAY ONE: *The Ways Jesus Taught*

Who was Jesus? People in his day would have given many answers—a healer, a troublemaker, a liberator, a threat to law and order, a heretic, a prophet, a community organizer. His friends and foes would have agreed on this: He was a powerful teacher. When we scan the pages of the gospels, we find Jesus teaching in many different ways.

First, he instructed through signs and wonders. By healing blindness, for example, Jesus dramatized God's desire to heal our distorted vision of life. By healing paralysis, he showed how God's reign empowers people who are weak or trapped. By calming a storm, he displayed God's desire to bring peace. And by casting out unclean spirits, he conveyed God's commitment to liberate people from occupying and oppressive forces—whether those forces were military, political, economic, social, or personal.

Second, he gave what we might call public lectures. Crowds would gather for a mass teach-in on a hillside near the Sea of Galilee. Whole neighborhoods might jam into a single house, and then spread around the open doors and windows, eager to catch even a few words. People came to hear him at weekly synagogue gatherings. Or they might catch word that he was down at the beach, sitting in a boat, his voice rising above the sounds of lapping waves and calling gulls to engage the minds and hearts of thousands standing on the sand.

Third, he taught at surprising, unplanned, impromptu moments—in transit from here to there, at a well along a road, at a dinner party when an uninvited guest showed up, in some public place when a group of his critics tried to ambush him with a "gotcha" question. You always needed to pay attention, because with Jesus, any moment could become a teaching moment.

Fourth, he saved much of his most important teaching for private retreats and field trips with his disciples. He worked hard to break away from the crowds so he could mentor those who would carry on his work. Certain places seemed the ideal setting for certain lessons.

Fifth, Jesus taught through what we might call public demonstrations.

For example, he once led a protest march into Jerusalem, performing a kind of guerrilla theater dramatization of a royal entry, while denouncing with tears the city's ignorance of what makes for peace. Once he staged an act of civil disobedience in the Temple, stopping business as usual and dramatically delivering some important words of instruction and warning. Once he demonstrated an alternative economy based on generosity rather than greed, inspired by a small boy's fish-sandwich donation.

Sixth, Jesus loved to teach through finely crafted works of short fiction called parables. He often introduced these parables with these words: "Whoever has ears to hear, let him hear." He knew that most adults quickly sort messages into either/or categories—agree/disagree, like/dislike, familiar/strange. In so doing, they react and argue without actually hearing and thinking about what is being said. His parables drew his hearers into deeper thought by engaging their imagination and by inviting interpretation instead of reaction and argument. In this way, parables put people in the position of children who are more attracted to stories than to arguments. Faced with a parable, listeners were invited to give matters a second thought. They could then ask questions, stay curious, and seek something deeper than agreement or disagreement—namely, *meaning*.

Today: Imagine yourself enrolling in a college or graduate program with Jesus as your teacher, and think of questions you would like to ask him.

DAY TWO: *Jesus's Most Radical Teaching*

Jesus truly was a master rabbi, capable of transforming people's lives with a message of unfathomed depth and unexpected imagination. But what was the substance of his message? What was his point? Sooner or later, anyone who came to listen to Jesus would hear one phrase repeated again and again: *the kingdom of God,* or *the kingdom of heaven.* Sadly, people today hear these words and frequently have no idea what they originally meant. Or even worse, they misunderstand the phrase with complete and unquestioning certainty.

For example, many think *kingdom of God* or *kingdom of heaven* means "where righteous people go when they die," or "the perfect new world God will create after destroying this hopeless mess." But for Jesus, the kingdom of heaven wasn't a place we *go up to someday*; it was a reality we pray to *come down here now*. It wasn't a distant future reality. It was *at hand*, or within reach, today. To better understand this pregnant term, we have to realize that kingdoms were the dominant social, political, and economic reality of Jesus's day. Contemporary concepts like *nation, state, government, society, economic system, culture, superpower, empire,* and *civilization* all resonate in that one word: *kingdom*.

The kingdom, or empire, of Rome in which Jesus lived and died was a top-down power structure in which the few on top maintained order and control over the many at the bottom. They did so with a mix of rewards and punishments. The punishments included imprisonment, banishment, torture, and execution. And the ultimate form of torture and execution, reserved for rebels who dared to challenge the authority of the regime, was crucifixion. It was through his crucifixion at the hands of the Roman empire that Jesus did his most radical teaching of all.

Yes, he taught great truths through signs and wonders, public lectures, impromptu teachings, special retreats and field trips, public demonstrations, and parables. But when he mounted Rome's most powerful weapon, he taught his most powerful lesson.

Today: Ponder this sentence: It was through his crucifixion at the hands of the Roman empire that Jesus did his most radical teaching of all.

DAY THREE: *God's Nonviolent Noncompliance*

By being crucified, Jesus exposed the heartless violence and illegitimacy of the whole top-down, fear-based dictatorship that nearly everyone assumed was humanity's best or only option. He demonstrated the revolutionary truth that God's kingdom wins, not through shedding the blood of its enemies, but through gracious self-giving on behalf of its enemies. He taught that God's kingdom grows through apparent weakness rather than conquest. It expands through reconciliation rather than humiliation and intimidation. It triumphs through a willingness to suffer rather than a readiness to inflict suffering. In short, on the cross Jesus demonstrated God's nonviolent noncompliance with the world's brutal powers-that-be. He showed God to be a different kind of king, and God's kingdom to be a different kind of kingdom.

Today: Ask yourself how ready you are to have your thinking about life turned upside down.

DAY FOUR: *A Dynamic New Vision*

How would we translate Jesus's radical and dynamic understanding of *the kingdom of God* into our context today?

Perhaps a term like *global commonwealth of God* comes close—not a world divided up and ruled by nations, corporations, and privileged individuals, but a world with enough abundance for everyone to share. Maybe *God's regenerative economy* would work—challenging our economies based on competition, greed, and extraction. Maybe *God's beloved community* or *God's holy ecosystem* could help—suggesting a reverent connectedness in dynamic and creative harmony. Or perhaps *God's sustainable society* or *God's movement for mutual liberation* could communicate the dynamism of this radical new vision of life, freedom, and community.

Today: Choose one of these renderings of "kingdom of God" and reflect on it throughout the day. If you can, compose one of your own!

DAY FIVE: *Seek First the Kingdom of God*

Today as in Jesus's day, not everybody seems interested in the good news that Jesus taught. Some are more interested in revenge or isolation or gaining a competitive advantage over others. Some are obsessed with sex or a drug or another addiction. Many are desperate for fame or wealth. Still others can think of nothing more than relief from the pain that plagues them at the moment. But underneath even the ugliest of these desires, we can often discern a spark of something pure, something good, something holy—a primal desire for aliveness, which may well be a portal into the kingdom of God.

Interestingly, when the Gospel of John was written some years after its three counterparts, the term *kingdom of God* was usually translated into other terms: *life, life of the ages, life to the full*—clearly resonant with this word *aliveness.* However we name it—kingdom of God, life to the full, global commonwealth of God, God's sustainable society, or holy aliveness—it is the one thing most worth seeking in life, because in seeking it, we will find everything else worth having.

To be alive in the adventure of Jesus is to seek first the kingdom and justice of God…to become a student of the one great subject Jesus came to teach in many creative ways.

Today: Pray, "Living God, may I be an enthusiastic learner in your school of aliveness."

WEEK TWENTY-THREE

JESUS AND THE MULTITUDES

Scripture Readings

Ezekiel 34:1–31
Luke 5:17–32; 18:15–19:9

Key Verses—Ezekiel 34:1–4

The word of the Lord came to me: Mortal, prophesy against the shepherds of Israel: prophesy, and say to them—to the shepherds: Thus says the Lord God: Ah, you shepherds of Israel who have been feeding yourselves! Should not shepherds feed the sheep? You eat the fat, you clothe yourselves with the wool, you slaughter the fatlings; but you do not feed the sheep. You have not strengthened the weak, you have not healed the sick, you have not bound up the injured, you have not brought back the strayed, you have not sought the lost, but with force and harshness you have ruled them.

DAY ONE: *The Great Social Divide*

Most human societies are divided between the elites and the masses. The elites are the 1 or 3 or 5 percent at the top that have and hoard the most money, weapons, power, influence, and opportunities. They make the rules and usually rig the game to protect their interests. They forge alliances across sectors—in government, business, religion, media, the arts, science, and the military. As a result, they have loyal allies across all sectors of a society, and they reward those allies to keep them loyal.

Down at the bottom, we find the masses—commonly called "the multitude" in the gospels. They provide cheap labor in the system run by the elites. They work with little pay, little security, little prestige, and little notice. They live in geographically distant regions or in socially distant slums. So to the elites, the multitudes can remain surprisingly invisible and insignificant most of the time.

In the middle, between the elites and the multitudes, we find those loyal allies who function as mediators between the few above them and the many below them. As such, they make a little more money than the masses, and they live in hope that they or their children can climb up the pyramid, closer to the elites. But those above them generally don't want too much competition from below, so they make sure the pyramid isn't too easy to climb.

These dynamics were at work in Jesus's day, and he was well aware of them. In his parables, he constantly made heroes of people from the multitudes: day laborers, small farmers, women working in the home, slaves, and children. He captured the dilemma of what we would call middle management—the stewards, tax collectors, and their associates who extracted income from the poor and powerless below them for the sake of the rich and powerful above them. And he exposed the duplicity and greed of those at the top—especially the religious leaders who enjoyed a cozy, lucrative alliance with the rich elites.

Today: Notice the elites, the masses, and those in the middle, and open yourself to seeing these social and economic realities in new ways.

DAY TWO: *Turning the Dominance Period on Its Head*

In addressing the social realities of his day, Jesus constantly turned the normal dominance pyramid on its head, confusing even his disciples.

Take, for example, the time a group of parents brought their little children to Jesus to be blessed (Mark 10:13–16). Their great teacher had important places to go and important people to see, so the disciples tried to send them away. But Jesus rebuked them. "Let those little children come to me," he said. "For of such is God's kingdom."

Or take the time Jesus and his disciples were passing through Samaria, a region that "proper folks" hated to pass through because its inhabitants were considered religiously and culturally "unclean" (John 4:4–42). Jesus decided to wait outside the city while his companions went into town to buy lunch. When they returned, Jesus was sitting by a well, deep in a spiritual and theological conversation with a Samaritan woman...and one with a sketchy reputation at that. The sight of Jesus and this woman talking respectfully was a triple shock to the disciples: Men didn't normally speak with women as peers, Jews didn't normally associate with Samaritans, and "clean" people didn't normally interact with those they considered morally stained.

Or take the time Jesus and his disciples, accompanied by a large crowd, passed a blind man along the road (Mark 10:46–52). The man seemed marginal and insignificant, just another beggar, and the people around told him to quiet down when he started crying out for mercy. But to Jesus, he mattered. The same thing happened when Jesus was on his way to heal the daughter of a synagogue official named Jairus (Mark 5:21–43). Along the way, Jesus was touched by a woman with an embarrassing "female problem" that rendered her "unclean." She didn't even think she was important enough to ask for Jesus's help. Jesus healed her, publicly affirmed her value, and then he healed the official's little girl. Little children, a Samaritan, a man who might today be classified as "disabled" and "unemployed," a frightened and "unclean" woman, a little girl...they all mattered to Jesus.

Today: Keep your eyes open for people in life who you normally ignore or consider insignificant, and seek to see them with the eyes and heart of Christ.

DAY THREE: *Value in the Notorious and Sinful*

It wasn't just weak or vulnerable people whom Jesus considered important. Even more scandalous, he saw value in those considered by everyone to be notorious and sinful. Once, for example, Jesus and his companions were invited to a formal banquet (Luke 7:36–50). Imagine their shock when a woman known to be a prostitute snuck into the gathering uninvited. Imagine their disgust when she came and honored Jesus by washing his feet with her tears and drying them with her hair. When the host indulged in predictably judgmental thinking about both the woman and Jesus, Jesus turned the tables and held her up as an example for all at the banquet to follow.

That host was a member of the Pharisees, a religious reform movement in Jesus's day. The Pharisees were pious, fastidious, and religiously knowledgeable. They maintained a close association with "the scribes," or religious scholars. Today some might call them "hyperorthodox" or "fundamentalist." But back then, most would have considered them pure and faithful people, the moral backbone of society.

Today: Picture the scene of Jesus and the other guests sitting at the Pharisee's table as this woman washes Jesus's feet with her tears. Imagine you are one of the guests watching the story unfold. Then imagine you are the woman, then the Pharisee, then Jesus.

DAY FOUR: *A Strange Fascination*

From the start, the Pharisees seemed strangely fascinated with Jesus. When Jesus once claimed his disciples needed a moral rightness that surpassed that of the Pharisees, they must have been unsettled. How could anyone possibly be more upright than they? He further troubled them by his refusal to follow their practice of monitoring every action of every person as clean or unclean, biblical or unbiblical, legal or illegal. To make matters worse, he not only associated with "unclean" people— he seemed to enjoy their company! The Pharisees just didn't know what to do with a man like this. So they kept throwing questions at him, hoping to trap him in some misstatement.

Once they criticized Jesus for healing someone on the Sabbath, their name for the seventh day of the week when no work was supposed to be done (Luke 14:1–6). Jesus asked them a question: *If your son—or even your ox—falls in a hole on the Sabbath, will you wait until the next day to rescue it?* By appealing to their basic humanity—kindness to their own children, if not their own beasts of burden—he implied that God must possess at least that level of "humanity." In so doing, Jesus proposed that basic human kindness and compassion are more absolute than religious rules and laws. "The Sabbath was made for human beings," Jesus said in another debate with the Pharisees (Mark 2:27). "Human beings weren't made for the Sabbath."

Jesus often turned the condemning language of the Pharisees back on them (Matthew 23). "You travel over land and sea to make a single convert," he said, "and convert him into twice the son of hell he was before you converted him! You wash the outside of the cup but leave the inside filthy and putrid. You are like those who make beautiful tombs...slapping lots of white paint on the outside, only to hide rot and death inside!"

Today: Ponder this question: Why did Jesus bother the Pharisees so much, and why did they bother him?

DAY FIVE: *Stand with the Multitudes*

The contrast between Jesus and the Pharisees was nowhere clearer than in their attitude toward the multitudes. The Pharisees once looked at the multitudes and said, "This crowd doesn't know the Scriptures—damn them all" (John 7:49). But when Jesus looked at the multitudes, "he had compassion for them, because they were harassed and helpless, like sheep without a shepherd" (Matthew 9:36).

With a few exceptions, the Pharisees in the gospels come out looking ugly. Their portrait in the gospels bears no resemblance to the honorable and wise Pharisees depicted in Jewish history from the historical period just after the gospels were written. Whether or not the gospel portraits were accurate, Christians in later centuries used their negative depiction of the Pharisees to stereotype and vilify all Jews. The consequences were horrible beyond words. Those Christians who did this anti-Semitic stereotyping ended up resembling nobody more than the hypocritical and judgmental Pharisees as depicted in the gospels.

There are always multitudes at the bottom being marginalized, scapegoated, shunned, ignored, and forgotten by elites at the top. And there are always those in the middle torn between the two. To be alive in the adventure of Jesus is to stand with the multitudes, even if doing so means being marginalized, criticized, and misunderstood right along with them.

Today: Pray, "Lord, help me to stand with the multitudes. Help me to see them as Jesus did, as oppressed and disempowered, like 'sheep without a shepherd.'"

WEEK TWENTY-FOUR

JESUS AND HELL

Scripture Readings

Jonah 4:1–11
Luke 16:19–31
Matthew 25:31–40

Key Verses—Luke 16:19–23

There was a rich man who was dressed in purple and fine linen and who feasted sumptuously every day. And at his gate lay a poor man named Lazarus, covered with sores, who longed to satisfy his hunger with what fell from the rich man's table; even the dogs would come and lick his sores. The poor man died and was carried away by the angels to be with Abraham. The rich man also died and was buried. In Hades, where he was being tormented, he looked up and saw Abraham far away with Lazarus by his side.

DAY ONE: *The Language of Fire and Brimstone*

Jesus was boring, if you go by the tame and uninteresting caricature many of us were given. He was a quiet, gentle, excessively nice, somewhat fragile guy on whose lap children liked to sit. He walked around in flowing robes in pastel colors, never dirty, always freshly washed and pressed. He liked to hold a small sheep in one arm and raise the other as if hailing a taxi. Or he was like an *x* or *n*—an abstract part of a mathematical equation, not important primarily because of what he said or how he lived, but only because he filled a role in the cosmic calculus of damnation and forgiveness.

The real Jesus was far more complex and interesting than any of these caricatures. And nowhere was he more defiant, subversive, courageous, and creative than when he took the language of fire and brimstone from his greatest critics and used it for a very different purpose.

Today: Consider Jesus as "complex and interesting... defiant, subversive, courageous, and creative."

DAY TWO: *Overturning Conventional Understanding*

Jesus believed there was an afterlife. Death was not the end for Jesus. But one of the most striking facets of his life and ministry was the way he took popular understandings of the afterlife and turned them upside down.

Who was going to hell? Rich and successful people who lived in fancy houses and stepped over their destitute neighbors who slept in the gutters outside their gates. Proud people who judged, insulted, excluded, avoided, and accused others. Fastidious hypocrites who strained out gnats and swallowed camels. The condemnation that the religious elite so freely pronounced on the marginalized, Jesus turned back on them.

And who, according to Jesus, was going to heaven? The very people whom the religious elite despised, deprived, avoided, excluded, and condemned. Heaven's gates opened wide for the poor and destitute who shared in few of life's blessings; the sinners, the sick, and the homeless who felt superior to nobody and who therefore appreciated God's grace and forgiveness all the more; even the prostitutes and tax collectors. Imagine how this overturning of the conventional understanding of hell must have shocked everyone—multitudes and religious elite alike.

Today: Ask yourself, "What conventional religious understandings might Jesus overturn today?"

DAY THREE: *A Transformative Vision of God*

Again and again, Jesus took conventional language and imagery for hell and reversed it. We might say he wasn't so much teaching about hell as he was un-teaching about hell. In so doing, he wasn't simply arguing for a different understanding of the afterlife. He was doing something far more important and radical: proclaiming a transformative vision of God. God is not the one who punishes some with poverty and sickness, nor is God the one who favors the rich and righteous. God is the one who loves everyone, including the people the rest of us think don't count. Those fire-and-brimstone passages that countless preachers have used to scare people about hell, it turns out, weren't intended to teach us about hell: Jesus overturned conventional notions of hell to teach us a radical new vision of God!

Today: Remember times people have tried to use scare tactics on you. How effective were they? How did you respond?

DAY FOUR: *Violence Won't Produce Peace*

Jesus used fire-and-brimstone language to warn his countrymen about the catastrophe they faced if they followed their current path—a wide and smooth highway leading to another violent uprising against the Romans. Violence won't produce peace, he warned; it will produce only more violence. If his countrymen persisted in their current path, Jesus warned, the Romans would get revenge on them by taking their greatest pride—the Temple—and reducing it to ashes and rubble. The Babylonians had done it once, and the Romans could do it again. That was why he advocated a different path—a "rough and narrow path" of nonviolent social change instead of the familiar broad highway of hate and violence.

Today: Ask yourself, "Who in the world today seems most eager to fight a war? What might Jesus say to them?"

DAY FIVE: *Waking Up Complacent People*

The actual purpose of Jesus's fire-and-brimstone language was not to predict the destruction of the universe or to make absolute for all eternity the insider-outsider categories of *us* and *them*. Its purpose was to wake up complacent people, to warn them of the danger of their current path, and to challenge them to change—using the strongest language and imagery available. As in the ancient story of Jonah, God's intent was not to destroy but to save. Neither a great big fish nor a great big fire gets the last word, but rather God's great big love and grace.

Sadly, many religious people still use the imagery of hell more in the conventional way Jesus sought to reverse. Like Jonah, they seem disappointed that God's grace might get the final word. If more of us would reexamine this fascinating dimension of Jesus's teaching and come to a deeper understanding of it, we would see what a courageous, subversive, and fascinating leader he was, pointing us to a radically different way of seeing God, life, and being alive.

Today: Pray, "God, help me to believe that your 'great big love and grace' will get the last word!"

JESUS, VIOLENCE, AND POWER

Scripture Readings

Isaiah 42:1–9; 53:1–12
Matthew 16:13–17:9

Key Verses—Matthew 16:13–16

Now when Jesus came into the district of Caesarea Philippi, he asked his disciples, "Who do people say that the Son of Man is?" And they said, "Some say John the Baptist, but others Elijah, and still others Jeremiah or one of the prophets." He said to them, "But who do you say that I am?" Simon Peter answered, "You are the Messiah, the Son of the living God."

DAY ONE: *Caesarea Philippi*

Once Jesus took his disciples on a field trip. There was something he wanted them to learn, and there was a perfect place for them to learn it. So he led them on a twenty-five-mile trek north from their base in Galilee to a city called Caesarea Philippi, a regional center of the Roman empire.

The city was built beside a dramatic escarpment or cliff face. A famous spring emerged from the base of the cliff. Before Roman occupation, the spring had been known as Panias, because it was a center for worship of the Canaanite god Baal, and later for the Greek god Pan. Worshipers carved elaborate niches, still visible today, into the cliff face. There they placed statues of Pan and other Greek deities. Panias also had a reputation as the site of a devastating military defeat. At Panias, invading armies affiliated with Alexander the Great took the whole region for the Greek empire.

Eventually the Romans replaced the Greeks, and when their regional ruler Herod the Great died, his son Herod Philip was given control of the region around Panias. He changed the name to Caesarea Philippi. By the first name he honored Caesar Augustus, the Roman emperor. By the second name, he honored himself and distinguished the city from another city named Caesarea Maritima—on the coast. The city was, in effect, Philip's Caesarville.

Today: Imagine going on a field trip with Jesus to a city like Washington, New York, Los Angeles, or Chicago, or imagine going to the site of the latest mass shooting, environmental catastrophe, or terrorist attack. Imagine what he might teach you in settings like these.

DAY TWO: *The Son of Man*

Imagine what it would be like to enter Caesarville with Jesus and his team. Today, we might imagine a Jewish leader bringing his followers to Auschwitz, a Japanese leader to Hiroshima, a Native American leader to Wounded Knee, or a Palestinian leader to the wall of separation. There, in the shadow of the cliff face with its idols set into their finely carved niches, in the presence of all these terrible associations, Jesus asks his disciples a carefully crafted question: "Who do people say the Son of Man is?"

We can imagine that an awkward silence might follow this rather strange and self-conscious question. But soon the answers flow. "Some people say you're John the Baptist raised from the dead; others say Elijah; and still others, Jeremiah or one of the prophets."

Jesus sharpens the question: "What about you? Who do you say I am?" Another silence, and then Peter, a leader among them, speaks: "You are the Christ, the Son of the living God."

Today: Ask yourself, "Why would Jesus ask this specific question at this specific location?"

DAY THREE: *King Jesus*

It may sound like Peter is making a theological claim with these words. But in this setting, they're as much a political statement as a theological one. *Christ* is the Greek translation for the Hebrew term *Messiah*, which means "the one anointed as liberating king." To say "liberating king" anywhere in the Roman empire is dangerous, even more so in a city bearing Caesar's name. By evoking the term *Christ*, Peter is saying, "You are the liberator promised by God long ago, the one for whom we have long waited. You are King Jesus, who will liberate us from King Caesar."

Similarly, *son of the living God* takes on an incandescent glow in this setting. Caesars called themselves "sons of the gods," but Peter's confession asserts that their false, idolatrous claim is now trumped by Jesus's true identity as one with authority from the true and living God. The Greek and Roman gods in their little niches in the cliff face may be called on to support the dominating rule of the caesars. But the true and living God stands behind the liberating authority of Jesus.

Today: Where might Jesus take us today on a field trip to ask us the same question about who we believe him to be?

DAY FOUR: *Back Down to Earth*

Jesus says that God has blessed Peter with this revelation. He speaks in dazzling terms of Peter's foundational role in Jesus's mission. "The gates of hell" will not prevail against their joint project, Jesus says, using a phrase that could aptly be paraphrased "the authority structures and control centers of evil." Again, imagine the impact of those words in this politically charged setting.

Surely this Caesarville field trip has raised the disciples' hopes and expectations about Jesus to sky-high levels. But Jesus quickly brings them back down to earth. Soon, he says, he will travel south to Jerusalem. There he will be captured, imprisoned, tortured, and killed by the religious and political establishment of their nation, after which, he will be raised. Peter appears not to hear the happy ending, only the horrible middle. So he responds just as we would have, with shock and denial: "Never, Lord! This shall never happen to you!" (Matt. 16:22). Do you feel Peter's confusion?

Today: Imagine you are Peter, asking this question and receiving this answer, and try to feel Peter's confusion.

DAY FIVE: *"Get Behind Me, Satan!"*

Jesus just said that Peter "gets it"—that Jesus is indeed the liberating king, the revolutionary leader anointed and authorized by the living God to set oppressed people free. If that's true, then the one thing Jesus can*not* do is be defeated. He must conquer and capture, not *be* conquered and captured. He must torture and kill his enemies, not *be* tortured and killed by them. So Peter corrects Jesus: "Stop talking this nonsense! This could never happen!"

At that moment, Jesus turns to Peter in one of the most dramatic cases of conceptual whiplash ever recorded in literature anywhere. "Get behind me, Satan!" Jesus says. It's a stunning reversal. Jesus has just identified Peter as the blessed recipient of divine revelation. Now he identifies Peter as a mouthpiece of the dark side. Jesus has just named Peter as a foundational leader in a movement that will defeat the gates of hell. Now he claims Peter is working on the side of hell. Do you feel the agony of this moment?

Today: Put in your own words why this is a dramatic case of "conceptual whiplash."

DAY SIX: *God's Way is Different*

Like most of his countrymen, Peter knows with unquestioned certainty that God will send a Messiah to lead an armed uprising to defeat and expel the occupying Roman regime and all who collaborate with it. But no, Jesus says. That way of thinking is human, Satanic, the opposite of God's plan. Since the beginning, Jesus has taught that the nonviolent will inherit the Earth. Violence cannot defeat violence. Hate cannot defeat hate. Fear cannot defeat fear. Domination cannot defeat domination. God's way is different. God must achieve victory through defeat, glory through shame, strength through weakness, leadership through servanthood, and life through death. The finely constructed mental architecture in which Peter has lived his whole adult life is threatened by this paradoxical message. It's not the kind of change of perspective that happens quickly or easily.

Today: It's easy to say words like "hate cannot defeat hate" or "violence cannot defeat violence." Ask yourself, "How much, honestly, do I really believe there is an alternative to hate and violence?"

DAY SEVEN: *Let's Keep Walking*

Why does a master teacher take students on a field trip? By removing students from familiar surroundings, the teacher can dislodge them from conventional thinking. By taking them to a new place, the teacher can help them see from a new vantage point, a new perspective.

It was less than a week later that Jesus took three of his disciples on another field trip, this time to the top of a mountain. There they had a vision of Jesus, shining in glory, conversing with two of the greatest leaders in Jewish history. Again, Peter was bold to speak up, offering to make three shrines to the three great men, elevating Jesus to the same elite level as the great liberator Moses and the great prophet Elijah. This time, God's own voice rebuked Peter, as if to say, "Moses and Elijah were fine for their time, but my beloved son Jesus is on another level entirely, revealing my true heart in a unique and unprecedented way. Listen to him!"

Moses the lawgiver and Elijah the prophet, great as they were, differed from Jesus in one important way: They had both engaged in violence in God's name. But in God's name Jesus will undergo violence, and in so doing, he will overcome it. And that was why, as they came down the mountain, Jesus once again spoke of suffering, death, and resurrection—a different kind of strategy for a different kind of victory.

In many ways, we're all like Peter. We speak with great insight one minute and we make complete fools of ourselves the next. We're clueless about how many of our pious and popular assumptions are actually illusions. We don't know how little we know, and we have no idea how many of our ideas are wrong. Like Peter, we may use the right words to describe Jesus—*Christ, son of the living God*. But we still don't understand his heart, his wisdom, his way. But that's okay. Peter was still learning, and so are we. After all, life with Jesus is one big field trip that we're taking together. So let's keep walking.

Today: Pray, "God, I don't know how little I know. But I want to learn. I want to keep walking with you on the road of discipleship."

WEEK TWENTY-SIX

MAKING IT REAL

Scripture Readings

Mark 2:1–19
Hebrews 11:1–8
I John 1:1–2:6

Key Verses—Hebrews 11:1–3

Now faith is the assurance of things hoped for, the conviction of things not seen. Indeed, by faith our ancestors received approval. By faith we understand that the worlds were prepared by the word of God, so that what is seen was made from things that are not visible.

DAY ONE: *We May Be Poor, But We Are Not Stupid*

Imagine a house in Capernaum, near the Sea of Galilee. A crowd has completely filled the house. An even bigger crowd surrounds it, with people crammed around every open window and door. Imagine asking a woman on the edge of the crowd about what's going on inside. She whispers that inside the house is a rabbi everyone wants to hear. "I will be glad to tell you what I know about him."

She leads us a distance away from the house where she can speak without disturbing anyone. She explains that the rabbi inside is the son of a tradesman from Nazareth. He has no credentials or status, no army or weapons, no nobility or wealth. He travels from village to village with a dozen of his friends plus a substantial number of supportive women, teaching deep truths to the peasants of Galilee.

"Look around at us," she says. "We are poor. Many of us are unemployed, and some are homeless. See how many of us are disabled, and how many are, like me, women. Few of us can afford an education. But to be uneducated is not the same as being stupid. Stupid people cannot survive in times like these. So we are hungry to learn. And wherever this rabbi goes, it is like a free school for everyone—even women like me. Do you see why we love him?"

Today: Imagine what a surprise it was for a famous rabbi to open a "free school" for anyone who wanted to listen and learn.

DAY TWO: *Starting a New Religion?*

Imagine you are in a small town called Capernaum. You meet a woman who has come to hear Jesus teach. You ask her, "Do you think this man is starting a new religion?"

She thinks for a moment and whispers, "I think Rabbi Jesus is doing something far more dangerous than starting a new religion. He says he is announcing a new kingdom."

We continue, "So he is a rebel?"

"His kingdom is not like the regimes of this world that take up daggers, swords, and spears," she says. "He heals the sick, teaches the unschooled, and inspires the downtrodden with hope. So no, I would not say that he is a rebel. Nor would I say that this is a revolution. I would call it an uprising, an uprising of learning and hope."

Today: Think of the way of Jesus, not as a religion, but as an uprising of learning and hope.

DAY THREE: *Faith Makes It Real*

Again, imagine yourself in conversation with a woman in a crowd who has been listening to Jesus. "According to Rabbi Jesus," she says, "you cannot point to this land or that region and say, 'The kingdom of God is located here,' because it exists in us, among us. It does not come crashing in like an army, he says. It grows slowly, quietly, under the surface, like the roots of a tree, like yeast in dough, like seeds in soil. Our faith waters the seed and makes it grow. Do you see this? When people trust it is true, they act upon it, and it becomes true. Our faith unlocks its potential. Our faith makes it real. You can see why this message is unlike anything people around here have ever heard."

Today: Ponder this description of faith as that which makes possibilities real.

DAY FOUR: *What Is Crazy?*

In Jesus's day, some people were dreaming about a holy war against Rome and Rome's puppets in Jerusalem. Even little boys were sharpening their knives and talking of war. But to others, this talk of war was foolish. They had seen too many die already in failed revolutions. "There must be another way," they said hopefully. "Another kind of uprising. An uprising of peace."

Jesus, a few dared to hope, might lead that kind of uprising.

To others, his message was the crazy dream of poets and artists, the fantasy of children at play or old men who drink too much. But others asked themselves, "What other message could possibly change the world?" Perhaps what was truly crazy was what they were doing instead—thinking that a little more hate might conquer hate, a little more war might cure war, a little more pride might overcome pride, a little more revenge might end revenge, a little more gold would cure greed, or a little more division could create cohesion.

Today: Look for signs of the craziness described in today's reading—hate curing hate, war curing war, revenge ending revenge.

DAY FIVE: *Trust? Follow!*

When the subject of Jesus comes up, we might ask, "Do you believe this or that about him?" But in Jesus's day, the real question was more practical: "Do you trust him?" It was a question about confidence, which leads to commitment. The call to trust Jesus was inseparable from the call to follow him. It's the same for us today. If we truly trust him, we will follow him on the road, imitate him, learn from his example, live by his way. Because his message was and is so radical on so many levels, believing and following can't be treated lightly. Commitment is costly. It requires us to rethink everything. It changes the course of our lives. Let's face it: Many people are happy to be called Christians and believe certain things about Jesus. But having the confidence to actually follow his way of life? That's another story.

Today: Ponder the degree to which you actually trust or have confidence in Jesus—that he was right, that he was good, that he deserves to be followed.

DAY SIX: *Moving Again*

Picture that house surrounded by a crowd in Capernaum, near the Sea of Galilee. You can't see inside, but the crowd is buzzing about a paralyzed man being healed. They recount the story of what happened.

"Jesus said to him, 'Your faith has healed you,'" they say. "And it was true. The man got up and walked! His faith made it real!"

Faith is a powerful force, indeed. If we don't trust, if we don't have confidence, we won't act, and we won't make what is possible real. But if we do have faith, what was impossible becomes possible. We may be paralyzed and stuck now, but faith can get us moving again.

Today: Pray, "God, help me have faith so what is possible can become real."

DAY SEVEN: *Make It So*

Imagine that you have been paralyzed for many years, and that your friends have brought you to Jesus. "Your faith has made you well," he says, and suddenly you feel strength returning to your body. You sit up, then rise to your feet, and take a step, then another, then another.

Imagine your joy at being set free from your paralysis!

Now ask yourself where you are currently stuck in your life, paralyzed by fear, bogged down by failure, discouraged by setbacks, defeated and going nowhere. Do you see that if you believe there's no hope, your faith will make it so? And do you see that if you dare to believe you can break free, your faith can make it so?

Today: Remind yourself, "Faith can make it so."

III

ALIVE IN A GLOBAL UPRISING

Joining the adventure of Jesus is a starting line, not a finish line. It leads us into a lifetime of learning and action. It challenges us to stand up against the way things have been and the way things are, to help create new possibilities for the way things can and should be. It enlists us as contemplative activists in an ongoing uprising of peace, freedom, justice, and compassion. In Part III, we focus on what it means for us to join in his adventure.

A NEW IDENTITY

Scripture Readings

Matthew 5:1–16

Key Verses—Matthew 5:1–3a

When Jesus saw the crowds, he went up the mountain; and after he sat down, his disciples came to him. Then he began to speak, and taught them, saying: Blessed are the poor in spirit...

DAY ONE: *Pay Attention*

Imagine yourself in Galilee, on a windswept hillside near a little fishing town called Capernaum. Flocks of birds circle and land. Wildflowers bloom among the grasses between rock outcroppings. The Sea of Galilee glistens blue below us, reflecting the clear midday sky above.

A small group of disciples circles around a young man who appears to be about thirty. He is sitting, as rabbis in this time and culture normally do. Huge crowds extend beyond the inner circle of disciples, in a sense eavesdropping on what he is teaching them. This is the day they've been waiting for. This is the day Jesus is going to pass on to them the heart of his message.

Jesus begins in a fascinating way. He uses the term *blessed* to address the question of identity, the question of who we want to be. In Jesus's day, to say "Blessed are these people" is to say "Pay attention: these are the people you should aspire to be like. This is the group you want to belong to." It's the opposite of saying "Woe to those people" or "Cursed are those people," which means, "Take note: you definitely don't want to be like those people or counted among their number." His words no doubt surprise everyone, because we normally play by these rules of the game:

> Do everything you can to be rich and powerful.
> Toughen up and harden yourself against all feelings of loss.
> Measure your success by how much of the time you are
>   thinking only of yourself and your own happiness.
> Be independent and aggressive, hungry and thirsty for higher
>   status in the social pecking order.
> Strike back quickly when others strike you, and guard your
>   image so you'll always be popular.

Today: Look for people who are living by these "normal rules of the game."

DAY TWO: *Who Is Blessed?*

Jesus defines success and well-being in a profoundly different way. Who are blessed? What kinds of people should we seek to be identified with?

> The poor and those in solidarity with them.
>
> Those who mourn, who feel grief and loss.
>
> The nonviolent and gentle.
>
> Those who hunger and thirst for the common good and aren't satisfied with the status quo.
>
> The merciful and compassionate.
>
> Those characterized by openness, sincerity, and unadulterated motives.
>
> Those who work for peace and reconciliation.
>
> Those who keep seeking justice even when they're misunderstood and misjudged.
>
> Those who stand for justice as the prophets did, who refuse to back down or quiet down when they are slandered, mocked, misrepresented, threatened, and harmed.

Today: Choose at least two of the statements above, commit them to memory, and remind yourself of them through the day.

DAY THREE: *Upside Down*

Only a few sentences into his Sermon on the Mount, Jesus has already turned our normal status ladders and social pyramids upside down. He advocates an identity characterized by solidarity, sensitivity, and nonviolence. He celebrates those who long for justice, embody compassion, and manifest integrity and nonduplicity. He creates a new kind of hero: not warriors, corporate executives, or politicians, but brave and determined activists for preemptive peace, willing to suffer with him in the prophetic tradition of justice.

Our choice is clear from the start: If we want to be his disciples, we won't be able to simply coast along and conform to the norms of our society. We must choose a different definition of well-being, a different model of success, a new identity with a new set of values.

Jesus promises we will pay a price for making that choice. But he also promises we will discover many priceless rewards.

Today: Pray, "Lord, I don't want to coast along and conform to the norms of society. I want a new identity and a new way of life."

DAY FOUR: *A New Identity*

If we seek the kind of unconventional blessedness Jesus proposes, we will experience the true aliveness of God's kingdom, the warmth of God's comfort, the enjoyment of the gift of this Earth, the satisfaction at seeing God's restorative justice come more fully, the joy of receiving mercy, the direct experience of God's presence, the honor of association with God and of being in league with the prophets of old. That is the identity he invites us to seek.

That identity will give us a very important role in the world. As creative nonconformists, we will be difference makers, aliveness activists, catalysts for change. Like salt that brings out the best flavors in food, we will bring out the best in our community and society. Also like salt, we will have a preservative function—opposing corruption and decay. Like light that penetrates and eradicates darkness, we will radiate health, goodness, and well-being to warm and enlighten those around us. Simply by being who we are—living boldly and freely in this new identity as salt and light—we will make a difference, as long as we don't lose our "saltiness" or try to hide our light.

Today: Picture yourself as "salt that brings out the best in your community and society," or as "light that radiates health, goodness and well-being" to others.

DAY FIVE: *Who We Are*

Every day we're tempted to let ourselves be tamed, toned down, shut up, and glossed over. But Jesus means for us to stand *apart* from the status quo, to stand *up* for what matters, and to stand *out* as part of the solution rather than part of the problem. He means for our lives to overcome the blandness and darkness of evil with the salt and light of good works. Instead of drawing attention to ourselves, those good works will point toward God. "Wow," people will say, "when I see the goodness and kindness in your life, I can believe there's a good and kind God out there, too."

The way Jesus phrases these memorable lines tells us something important about him. Like all great leaders, he isn't preoccupied with himself. He puts others—us—in the spotlight when he says, "*You* are the salt of the Earth. *You* are the light of the world." Yes, there's a place and time for him to declare who *he* is, but he begins by declaring who *we* are.

Imagine people listening to these words in the Galilean sunshine. Notice how they're hanging on Jesus's every word. They can tell something profound and life-changing is happening within them and among them. Jesus is not simply trying to restore their religion to some ideal state in the past. Nor is he agitating unrest to start a new religion to compete with the old one. No, it's abundantly clear that he's here to start something bigger, deeper, and more subversive: a global uprising that can spread to and through every religion and culture. This uprising begins with a new identity. So he spurs his hearers into reflection about who they are, who they want to be, what kind of people they will become, what they want to make of their lives.

As we consider Jesus's message today, we join those people on that hillside, grappling with the question of who we are now and who we want to become in the future. Some of us are young, with our whole lives ahead of us. Some of us are further along, with a lot of hopes left and not a lot of time to fulfill them. As we listen to Jesus, each of us knows, deep inside: *If I accept this new identity, everything will change for me. Everything will change.*

Today: Calculate how many years you have left if you are going to live to be eighty-five (or, if you prefer, a hundred). Then ask, "What kind of person do I want to be for my remaining years?"

WEEK TWENTY-EIGHT

A NEW PATH TO ALIVENESS

Scripture Readings

Matthew 5:17–48

Key Verses—Matthew 5:17–18; 48

"Do not think that I have come to abolish the law or the prophets; I have come not to abolish but to fulfill. For truly I tell you, until heaven and earth pass away, not one letter, not one stroke of a letter, will pass from the law until all is accomplished.

"Be perfect, therefore, as your heavenly Father is perfect."

DAY ONE: *The Highest Intent of Tradition*

There was tension in the air. Many people present that day would have felt it. Many in the crowd stuck to the familiar road of tradition, playing by the rules, leading conservative, conventional, and respectable lives. They were worried that Jesus was too...different, too noncompliant. Others ran on a very different road. Unfettered by tradition, they gladly bent any rule that got in their way. They were worried that Jesus wasn't different and defiant enough.

According to Jesus, neither group was on the road to true aliveness.

When Jesus said, "Do not think that I have come to abolish the law or the prophets," you can imagine the traditionalists in the crowd felt relieved, because that was just what they feared he was about to do. When he added, "I have come not to abolish but to fulfill," they must have tensed up again, wondering what he could possibly mean by "fulfill." Then, when he said, "Unless your righteousness *exceeds* that of the scribes and Pharisees, you will never enter the kingdom of heaven," the nontraditionalists would have looked dismayed. How could anyone be more righteous than that fastidious crowd?

As Jesus continued, it became clear he was proposing a third way that neither the compliant nor the noncompliant had ever considered before. Aliveness won't come through unthinking conformity to tradition, he tells them. And it won't come from defying tradition, either. It will come only if we discern and fulfill the highest intent of tradition—even if doing so means breaking with the details of tradition in the process.

If tradition could be compared to a road that began in the distant past and continues to the present, Jesus dares to propose that the road isn't finished yet. To extend the road of tradition into the future—to fulfill its potential—we must first look back to discern its general direction. Then, informed by the past, we must look forward and dare to step beyond where the road currently ends, venturing off the map, so to speak, into new territory. To stop where the road of tradition currently ends, Jesus realizes, would actually end the adventure and bring the tradition to a standstill. So faithfulness doesn't simply allow us to extend the tradition and seek to fulfill its unexplored potential; it *requires* us to do so.

But what does it mean to fulfill the tradition? Jesus answers that question with a series of examples. Each example begins, "You have heard that it was said…," which introduces what the tradition has taught. Then Jesus dares to say, "But I say…" This is not, as his critics will claim, an act of abolishment or destruction. His "but I say" will creatively fulfill the intent of the tradition.

Today: Whenever you see a rule, try to discern its intent.

DAY TWO: *A Right Relationship*

The tradition said, "Don't murder." That was a good start. However, the tradition didn't want us to stop merely at the point of avoiding murder. So as a first step beyond what the tradition required, Jesus calls us to root out the anger that precedes the physical violence that leads to murder. As a second step, he calls us to deal with the verbal violence of name-calling that precedes the physical violence that leads to murder. As a third step, he urges us to engage in preemptive reconciliation. In other words, whenever we detect a breach in a relationship, we don't need to determine who is at fault. The intent of tradition isn't merely to be "in the right"; the goal is to be in a right relationship. We are to deal with the breach quickly and proactively, seeking true reconciliation. Being in a right relationship—not merely avoiding murder—was the intent of the tradition all along.

That kind of preemptive reconciliation, Jesus teaches, will help us avoid the chain reactions of offense, revenge, and counteroffense that lead to murder and that keep our court systems busy and our prison systems full.

Today: Concentrate on staying in right relationship with each person who crosses your path today.

DAY THREE: *Transforming Our Deeper Desires*

After discerning the intent of the law in relation to violence, Jesus moves to four more issues, each deeply important both to individuals and societies: sexuality, marriage, oaths, and revenge. In each case, conventional religious morality—which Jesus calls the righteousness of the scribes and Pharisees—focuses on *not doing external wrong*: not murdering, not committing adultery, not committing illegal divorce, not breaking sacred oaths, not getting revenge. For Jesus, true aliveness focuses on *transforming our deeper desires.*

So, regarding sexuality, the tradition requires you to avoid adultery. But Jesus says to extend the road, to go further and deeper by learning to manage your internal lustful desires. Regarding divorce, you can try to "make it legal" in the eyes of society as the tradition requires. But Jesus challenges you to go further and deeper by desiring true fidelity in your heart. Regarding oaths, you can play a lot of silly verbal games to shade the truth. Or you can go further and deeper, desiring simple, true speech, saying what you mean and meaning what you say. And regarding retaliation against injustice, you can react in ways that play right into unjust systems. Or you can go further and deeper, transcending those systems entirely.

Today: Choose at least one—monitoring your internal desires, desiring true fidelity in your heart, or desiring to speak true—and make it your focus this day.

DAY FOUR: *Turn the Other Cheek*

As people living under Roman occupation, Jesus's hearers were used to getting shoved around. It was not uncommon for a Roman soldier to give one of them a backhand slap—the insulting whack of a superior to an inferior. When this happened, some would skulk away in humiliation or beg the bully not to hit them again. But that rewarded the oppressor's violence, and it made them complicit in their own diminishment.

That was why others dreamed of retaliation, of pulling out a dagger and slitting the throat of the oppressor. But that would reduce them to the same violent level as their oppressors. Jesus offered them a creative alternative: *Stand tall and courageously turn the other cheek*, he said. In so doing, they would choose nonviolence, strength, courage, and dignity…and they would model a better way of life for their oppressors, rather than mirroring the violent example they were setting.

Today: Notice how you respond to offense, and experiment with ways to "turn the other cheek" by choosing nonviolence, strength, and dignity over retreat or revenge.

DAY FIVE: *A Creative Response*

Often, a Roman soldier would order a civilian of an occupied nation to carry his pack for a mile. If the civilian refused to do so, he would show courage and self-respect, but he would probably end up dead or in jail. Most would comply, but once again, doing so would reinforce the oppressor's sense of superiority and the civilian's own sense of humiliation. Jesus tells his disciples to surprise their oppressors by volunteering to take the pack a second mile. The first mile may be forced upon them, but the second mile they'll walk free. The first mile, they are oppressed, but the second mile they transcend their oppression and treat their oppressor as a human being, demonstrating the very human kindness that he fails to practice.

Neither the compliant nor the defiant typically imagine such creative responses. Jesus is helping their moral and social imagination come alive.

Today: Notice when you are compliant or defiant in response to an offense, and imagine a more creative response.

DAY SIX: *Love Extended*

Jesus employs his "you have heard it said…but I say…" pattern once more, perhaps the most radical example of all. Tradition always requires love and responsibility toward friends and neighbors, people we like, people like us, people "of our kind." That is a big step beyond utter selfishness and narcissism. But Jesus says that the road of tradition was never meant to end there. Love should now be extended further than before, to outsiders as well as insiders, to *them* as well as *us*, even to our enemies. We may not have walked the road that far yet, but that is God's intent for us.

Today: Repeat these two words to yourself: "Love beyond." Seek to love beyond your normal limits of family, friends, countrymen, shared religion or race or politics, etc.

DAY SEVEN: *The Third Way*

Again, using example after example, Jesus directs his disciples beyond what the tradition requires to what the Creator desires. "Be perfect, therefore, as your heavenly Father is perfect," he says. Some people might assume that by "be perfect" he means "achieve external technical perfection," which is what the scribes and Pharisees aim for. But Jesus means something far deeper and wiser. He tells them that God doesn't let rain and sunshine fall only on good people's lands, leaving bad people to starve. No, God is good to all, no exceptions. God's perfection is a compassionate and gracious perfection. It goes far beyond the traditional requirements of the scribes and Pharisees.

For us today, as for the disciples on that Galilean hillside, this is our better option—better than mere technical compliance to tradition, better than defiance of tradition. This is our third way. God is out ahead of us, calling us forward—not to stay where tradition has brought us so far, and not to defy tradition reactively, but to fulfill the highest and best intent of tradition, to make the road by walking forward together.

Today: Pray, "God, help me to become compassionate as you are. Help me to practice nondiscriminatory love, loving not because others are lovable, but because my nature becomes more perfectly loving as yours is."

WEEK TWENTY-NINE

YOUR SECRET LIFE

Scripture Readings

Matthew 6:1–18

Key Verses—Matthew 6:5–6

"And whenever you pray, do not be like the hypocrites; for they love to stand and pray in the synagogues and at the street corners, so that they may be seen by others. Truly I tell you, they have received their reward. But whenever you pray, go into your room and shut the door and pray to your Father who is in secret; and your Father who sees in secret will reward you."

DAY ONE: *Connect with God in Secret*

All of us agree: the world isn't what it should be. We all wish the world would change. But how? How can we change the world, when we can hardly change ourselves? The forces of conformity and peer pressure are so strong. We set out to change the world, and time and time again the reverse happens. Or we resist the status quo with such fury that we become bitter, cynical, angry—hardly models of a better world. That's why we aren't surprised when Jesus turns to the dynamics of change in our personal lives. He shows us how to *be* the change we want to *see* in the world.

The key concept, according to Jesus, is the opposite of what we might expect: If you want to see change in the outside world, the first step is to withdraw into your inner world. Connect with God in secret, and the results will occur "openly."

Jesus offers three specific examples of how this withdrawal process works: giving in secret, praying in secret, and fasting in secret. Giving, praying, and fasting are often called spiritual disciplines or practices: actions within our power by which we become capable of things currently beyond our power.

Today: Return to this thought: *The peace, justice, balance, and well-being we want to see in the world around us must be preceded by an ecology of harmony, balance, health, and joy inwardly.*

DAY TWO: *Practice Makes Habit*

Can you run twenty miles? If you haven't trained, no matter how well intentioned you are, you will be reduced to a quivering mass of cramps and exhaustion before you reach the finish line. But, as thousands of people have learned, you can start training. You can start running shorter distances in private and gradually increase them. A few months from now you could cross the finish line in full public view!

If through physical practice a lazy slug can end up a lean and energetic runner, then through spiritual practice an impatient and self-obsessed egotist can become a gentle, generous, and mature human being. But Jesus makes clear that not just any practices will do: We need the right practices, employed with the right motives. "Practice makes perfect," it turns out, isn't quite accurate. It's truer to say practice makes *habit*. That's why Jesus emphasizes the importance of practicing prayer, fasting, and generosity in secret. If we don't withdraw from public view, we'll habitually turn our spiritual practices into a show for others, which will sabotage their power to bring deep change in us. So, instead of seeking to appear more holy or spiritual in public than we are in private, Jesus urges us to become more holy or spiritual in private than we appear to be in public.

Today: Pray, "Lord, help me to be a better person in private than I appear to be in public."

DAY THREE: *Giving in Secret*

When it comes to *giving to the poor*, Jesus says, don't publicize your generosity like the hypocrites do. Don't let your left hand know how generous your right hand is. By giving in secret, you'll experience the true reward of giving. A lot of us have found that a good way to make secret giving habitual is to give on a regular basis, as a percentage of our income. As our income increases over time, we can increase our standard of giving and not just our standard of living. It's kind of ironic: a lot of people do ugly things in secret—they steal, lie, cheat, and so on. Jesus reverses things, urging us to plot goodness in secret, to do good and beautiful things without getting caught.

Today: Check your standard of giving. What percentage of your income would you feel great about giving away to help others? How does that compare to what you're actually giving?

DAY FOUR: *The Model Prayer*

According to Jesus, prayer can either strengthen your soul in private or raise your profile in public, but not both. So don't parrot the empty phrases of those who pray as if they were being paid by the word. A few simple words, uttered in secret, make much more sense...especially since God knows what you need before you even ask. Jesus offers a model for the kind of simple, concise, private prayer that he recommends. His model prayer consists of four simple but profound moves.

First, we orient ourselves to God. We acknowledge God as the loving parent whose infinite embrace puts us in a family relationship with all people, and with all of creation. And we acknowledge God as the glorious holy mystery whom we can name but who can never be contained by our words or concepts.

Second, we align our greatest desire with God's greatest desire. We want the world to be the kind of place where God's dreams come true, where God's justice and compassion reign.

Third, we bring to God our needs and concerns: our physical needs for things like food and shelter, and our social and spiritual needs for things like forgiveness for our wrongs and reconciliation with those who have wronged us.

Finally, we prepare ourselves for the public world into which we will soon reenter. We ask to be guided away from the trials and temptations that could ruin us, and we ask to be liberated from evil.

Immediately after the model prayer, Jesus adds a reminder that God isn't interested in creating a forgiveness market where people come and acquire cheap forgiveness for themselves. God is interested in creating a whole forgiveness economy—where forgiveness is freely received and freely given, unleashing waves of reconciliation in our world that is so ravaged by waves of resentment and revenge.

Today: Learn the four moves of prayer by heart and practice them throughout the day.

DAY FIVE: *Only in Secret*

Jesus takes us through the same pattern with the spiritual practice of *fasting*: "Whenever you...do not...but do," he says. Whenever you fast, don't try to look all sad and disheveled like those who make spirituality a performance. Instead, keep your hunger a secret. Let every minute when your stomach is growling be a moment where you affirm to God, "More than my body desires food, I desire you, Lord! More than my stomach craves fullness, I crave to be full of you! More than my tongue desires sweetness or salt, my soul desires your goodness!"

Jesus teaches, if we make our lives a show staged for others to avoid their criticism or gain their praise, we won't experience the reward of true aliveness. It's only in secret, in the presence of God alone, that we begin the journey to aliveness.

Today: Skip a meal today or tomorrow as a way to affirm that you desire to be full of God.

DAY SIX: *Who We Are in Secret*

Just as we can practice giving, prayer, and fasting for social enhancement or spiritual benefit, we can build our lives around public, external, financial wealth or a higher kind of "secret" wealth. Jesus calls this higher wealth "treasure in heaven." Not only is this hidden wealth more secure, it also recenters our lives in God's presence, and that brings a shift to our whole value system so that we see everything differently. When we see and measure everything in life in terms of money, all of life falls into a kind of dismal shadow. When we seek to be rich in generosity and kindness instead, life is full of light.

Some people shame the poor, as if the only reason poor people are poor is that they're lazy or stupid. Some shame the rich, as if the only reason they're rich is that they're selfish and greedy. Jesus doesn't shame anyone, but calls everyone to a higher kind of wealth and a deeper kind of ambition. And that ambition begins, not with how we want to appear in public, but with who we want to be in secret.

The world won't change unless we change, and we won't change unless we pull away from the world's games and pressures. In secrecy, in solitude, in God's presence, a new aliveness can, like a seed, begin to take root. And if that life takes root in us, we can be sure it will bear fruit through us...fruit that can change the world.

Today: Ask yourself, *What kind of wealth (or treasure) am I seeking?*

WEEK THIRTY

WHY WE WORRY, WHY WE JUDGE

Scripture Readings

Matthew 6:19–7:12

Key Verses—Matthew 7:7–8

> *"Ask, and it will be given you; search, and you will find; knock, and the door will be opened for you. For everyone who asks receives, and everyone who searches finds, and for everyone who knocks, the door will be opened."*

DAY ONE: *The Problem of Anxiety*

Wise parents soon learn what makes their kids cranky: not getting enough sleep, too much sugar, being hungry, not getting time alone, too much time alone, lack of stimulation, too much stimulation. Have you ever wondered what makes grown-ups cranky?

In the next section of Jesus's core teaching, he strips away layer after layer until he exposes three core problems that turn us into dismal grouches and keep us from enjoying life to the full.

Our first core problem is anxiety. Driven by anxiety, we act out scripts of destruction and cruelty rather than life and creativity. We worry about things beyond our control—and in so doing, we often miss things within our control. For example, you may fear losing someone you love. As a result, driven by your anxiety, you grasp, cling, and smother, and in that way you drive away the person you love. Do you catch the irony? If you're anxious about your life, you won't enjoy or experience your life—you'll only experience your anxiety! So to be alive is to be on guard against anxiety.

Jesus names some of the things we tend to be anxious about. First, we obsess about our bodies. Are we too fat or thin, too tall or short, or too young or old; and how is our hair? Then we obsess about our food, our drink, and our clothing. Are we eating at the best restaurants, drinking the finest wines, wearing the most enviable styles? Our anxieties show us how little we trust God: *God must be either so incompetent or uncaring that we might end up miserable or starving or naked or dead!* So we worry and worry, as if anxiety will somehow make us taller, thinner, better looking, better dressed, or more healthy!

Not only are our anxieties ridiculous and counterproductive, Jesus explains, they're also unnecessary. He points to the flowers that surround his hearers on the hillside. See how beautiful they are? Then he gestures to the flock of birds flying across the sky above them. See how alive and free they are? God knows what they need, Jesus says. God cares for them. God sustains them through the natural order of things. And God does the same for us, but we are too anxious to appreciate it.

Today: Keep your eyes open for birds. Whenever you see or hear one, remind yourself of Jesus's teaching about anxiety.

DAY TWO: *A Universal Diagnosis*

Anxiety doesn't stop its dirty work at the individual level. It makes whole communities tense and toxic. Anxiety-driven systems produce a pecking order as anxious people compete and use one another in their pursuit of more stuff to stave off their anxiety. Soon participants in such a system feel they can't trust anybody, because everyone's out for himself or herself, driven by fear. Eventually, anxiety-driven people find a vulnerable person or group to vent their anxiety upon. The result? Bullying, scapegoating, oppression, injustice. And still they will be anxious. Before long, they'll be making threats and launching wars so they can project their internal anxiety on an external enemy. No doubt, many of Jesus's original hearers would have thought, *He's describing the Romans!* But to some degree, the diagnosis applies to us all.

Today: Look for connections between anxiety and harmful behaviors in others—and yourself.

DAY THREE: *Learning from the Songbirds and Wildflowers*

Jesus advocates the opposite of an anxiety-driven system. He describes a faith-sustained system that he calls *God's kingdom and justice*. He makes this staggering promise: If we seek God's kingdom and justice first, everything that we truly need—financially, physically, or socially—will be given to us. His promise makes sense. When we each focus anxiously on our own individual well-being without concern for our neighbor, we enter into rivalry and everyone is worse off. But when we learn from the songbirds and wildflowers to live by faith in God's abundance, we collaborate and share. We watch out for each other rather than compete with each other. We bless each other rather than oppress each other. We desire what God desires—for all to be safe, for all to be truly alive—so we work for the common good. When that happens, it's easy to see how everyone will be better off. Contagious aliveness will spread across the land!

Today: Whenever you notice a songbird or a flower, remind yourself of God's abundance for all.

DAY FOUR: *Children in the Same Family*

To refrain from judging does not mean we stop discerning, as Jesus's tough words about not throwing pearls before swine make clear. Put simply, if we want to experience discerning but nonjudgmental aliveness, then in everything—with no exceptions—we will do unto all others— with no exceptions—as we would have them do to us. In these words, Jesus brings us back to the central realization that we are all connected, all children in the same family, all loved by the same parent, all precious and beloved. In this way, Jesus leads us out of an anxiety-driven and judgment-driven system, and into a faith-sustained, grace-based system that yields aliveness.

Today: Strive today to see each person as one of your relatives.

DAY FIVE: *Truly Loved*

Beneath our anxiety and judging lies an even deeper problem, according to Jesus. We do not realize how deeply we are *loved*. He invites us to imagine a child asking his mom or dad for some bread or fish. No parent would give their hungry child a stone or snake, right? If human parents, with all their faults, know how to give good gifts to their children, can't we trust the living God to be generous and compassionate to all who call out for help?

So next time you're grouchy, angry, anxious, and uptight, here is some wisdom to help you come back from being "out of your mind" to being "in your right mind" again. Try telling yourself, *My own anxiety is more dangerous to me than whatever I am anxious about. My own habit of condemning is more dangerous to me than what I condemn in others. My misery is unnecessary because I am truly, truly, truly loved.* From that wisdom, unworried, unhurried, unpressured aliveness will flow again.

Today: Say to yourself, "My own anxiety is more dangerous to me than whatever I am anxious about."

WEEK THIRTY-ONE

THE CHOICE IS YOURS

Scripture Readings

Matthew 7:13–29

Key Verses—Matthew 7:13-14; 28–29

"Enter through the narrow gate; for the gate is wide and the road is easy that leads to destruction, and there are many who take it. For the gate is narrow and the road is hard that leads to life, and there are few who find it."

When he came to the other side, to the country of the Gadarenes, two demoniacs coming out of the tombs met him. They were so fierce that no one could pass that way. Suddenly they shouted, "What have you to do with us, Son of God? Have you come here to torment us before the time?"

DAY ONE: *Desired Action*

Imagine that hillside in Galilee. Jesus is seated, surrounded by his disciples, a huge crowd circled around them. Perhaps it's the rhythm and tone of his voice. Maybe it's the pace of his words. Somehow the people know he is building toward a climax, a moment of decision. He presents a series of vivid images, all in pairs.

First, there are two gates, opening to two roads. We can't travel both. One, he says, is broad and smooth like a Roman highway. It leads to destruction. One is narrow and rocky like a mountain path. It leads to life. "Go along with the crowd," Jesus implies, "and you'll end up in disaster. But dare to be different, dare to follow a new and different path, and you'll learn what it means to be alive."

Next, there are two vines or two trees producing two different kinds of fruit, each representing aliveness. One approach to life produces thorns, briers, and thistles; another approach produces luscious fruits. Get your inner identity straight, he tells them, and your life will be fruitful.

Next, there are two groups of people, one entering Jesus's presence, the other going away. One group may boast of all its religious credentials, but Jesus isn't impressed by talk. He's looking for people he *knows*, people he recognizes—people, we might say, who "get" him and understand what he's about. We can identify them because they translate their understanding into action.

Finally, there are two builders building two houses, one on sand, one on rock. They both represent people who hear Jesus's message. They both experience falling rain, rising floodwaters, and buffeting winds. The big difference? The person who builds on the solid foundation, whose structure withstands the storm, doesn't just *hear* Jesus's message; he translates it into *action*.

Each pair of images challenges us to move beyond mere interest and agreement to commitment and action. And what is the desired action? To take everything Jesus has taught us—all we have considered as we have listened to him here on this hillside—and translate it into our way of living, our way of being alive.

Today: Be aware of the fact that your way of life is a matter of choosing, not going along with the crowd.

DAY TWO: *Who You Are*

If building our "house on the rock" means practicing Jesus's teachings, it makes sense over the next few days to go back and review the twenty core teachings of Jesus's Sermon on the Mount. The first few focus on our identity:

1. Be among the lowly in spirit, remain sensitive to pain and loss, live in the power of gentleness, hunger and thirst for true righteousness, show mercy to everyone rather than harshness, don't hide hypocrisy or duplicity in your heart, work for peace, be willing to joyfully suffer persecution and insult for doing what is right.
2. Dare to be a nonconformist by being boldly different, like salt and light in the world. Demonstrate your differentness through works of generosity and beauty.
3. Reject both mindless conformity to tradition and rebellious rejection of it. Instead, discern the true intent of tradition and pursue that intent into new territory.

Today: Keep these three core teachings in mind and seek to build your life upon them.

DAY THREE: *Going Beyond the Minimum*

Jesus's Sermon on the Mount emphasizes going beyond simply rule-keeping, as these three core teachings make clear:

4. Never hate, hold grudges, or indulge in anger, but instead, aim to be the first to reach out a hand in reconciliation.
5. Do not nurture secret fantasies to be sexually unfaithful to your spouse. Insure fidelity by monitoring your desires—the way you see (symbolized by the eye) and grasp (symbolized by the hand) for pleasure. And do not settle for maintaining the appearance of legality and propriety; aspire to true fidelity in your heart.
6. Avoid "word inflation" when making vows. Instead, practice clear, straight speech, so simple words like yes and no retain their full value.

Today: Keep these three core teachings in mind and seek to build your life upon them.

DAY FOUR: *Live Nonviolently*

Jesus's way is a way of reconciliation and revolutionary love, as you see in these two core teachings:

7. Reject revenge. Instead, pursue creative and nonviolent ways to overcome wrongs done to you.
8. Love your enemies as well as your friends, and so imitate God's big, generous heart for all creatures.

Today: Keep these two core teachings in mind and seek to build your life upon them.

DAY FIVE: *Your Inner Life*

Jesus teaches his followers to do their inner work by developing their life with God in secret, as these nine core teachings emphasize:

9. Cultivate a hidden life of goodness by giving to the poor, praying, and fasting secretly.

10. Pray in secret through four movements of your heart. First, orient yourself toward a caring yet mysterious God. Second, align your desires with God's great desire for a just and compassionate world. Third, bring to God your needs and concerns—both physical and spiritual. Finally, prepare to reenter the public world of temptation and oppression, trusting God to guide you and strengthen you.

11. Remember that God isn't setting up a forgiveness market but is building a whole forgiveness economy.

12. Don't let greed cloud your outlook on life, but store up true wealth by investing in a growing portfolio of generosity and kindness.

13. Be especially vigilant about money becoming your slave master.

14. Don't let anxiety run and ruin your life, but instead trust yourself to God's gracious and parental care, and seek first and foremost to build the just and generous society that would fulfill God's best dreams for humanity.

15. Don't develop a sharp eye for the faults and failures of others, but instead first work on your own blindness to your own faults and failures.

16. Don't push on people treasures they are not yet ready for or can't yet appreciate the value of.

17. Go to God with all your needs, and don't be discouraged if you face long delays. Remember that God loves you as

a faithful, caring parent and will come through in due time.

Today: Review these nine core teachings at least twice before you go to bed tonight.

DAY SIX: *It's Not Talk; Action Counts*

So much of our religious activity centers on talk and words. But Jesus closes the Sermon on the Mount with a call to action.

18. Do to others as you would have them do to you.
19. Realize that aliveness includes tough choices, and that thriving includes suffering.
20. Don't be misled by religious talk; what counts is actually living by Jesus's teaching.

Today: Keep these final three core teachings in mind and seek to build your life upon them.

DAY SEVEN: *If You Had Been There*

Some may claim that God is angry and needs to be appeased through sacrifice. Some may claim that God is harsh and demanding, requiring humans to earn God's favor through scrupulous religious rule keeping. Some may claim that God scrutinizes our brains and speech for perfect doctrinal correctness. But Jesus, like the prophets before him, proclaims a different vision of God. Based on what Jesus taught in his Sermon on the Mount, God is gracious and compassionate and does not need to be appeased through sacrifice. God's love is freely given and does not have to be earned. What God desires most is that we seek God's commonwealth of justice, live with generosity and kindness, and walk humbly—and secretly—with God.

Today: Ask yourself, *If I were there that day on the Galilean hillside, what would my decision have been? No doubt I would have been impressed, but would I have said yes?*

WEEK THIRTY-TWO

PASSION WEEK

Scripture Readings

Zechariah 9:9–10
Psalm 122
Luke 19:29–46

Key Verses—Zechariah 9:9–10

Rejoice greatly, O daughter Zion!
 Shout aloud, O daughter Jerusalem!
Lo, your king comes to you;
 triumphant and victorious is he,
humble and riding on a donkey,
 on a colt, the foal of a donkey.
He will cut off the chariot from Ephraim
 and the war-horse from Jerusalem;
and the battle bow shall be cut off,
 and he shall command peace to the nations;
his dominion shall be from sea to sea,
 and from the River to the ends of the earth.

DAY ONE: *The Spirit of Anticipation*

The scene opens on a mountainside outside Jerusalem, early on a Sunday morning. Jesus is sitting on a donkey, and his disciples begin walking beside him down the road that leads to Jerusalem.

At first all is quiet, with only the sound of the donkey's hooves clomping on the road. But soon they hear something up ahead. A crowd is gathering. Children are shouting. Palm branches are waving. People are taking their coats and spreading them on the dusty road to make a lavish, multicolor carpet, as if Jesus were a king being welcomed to the capital. Voices echo across the valley: "Blessings on the king who comes in the name of the Lord! Peace in heaven and glory in the highest heavens!" The air is full of anticipation.

Some religious leaders rush up to Jesus and sternly warn him that this is dangerous. They are worried that proclaiming Jesus as king will be seen as a revolutionary act, the kind that might bring the Roman soldiers riding in on their horses, swords and spears in hand, to slaughter them all in the name of law and order. But Jesus refuses to silence the crowd. "If they are silent, the rocks will start shouting!" he said.

The parade rounds a bend, and there is Jerusalem spread before them in all her beauty, the Temple glistening in the sun. A reverent silence descends upon our parade. It is a sight that has choked up many a pilgrim.

But Jesus doesn't just get choked up. He begins to weep. The crowd clusters around him as he begins to speak to Jerusalem. "If only you know on this day of all days the things that lead to peace," he says through his tears. "But you can't see. A time will come when your enemies will surround you, and you will be crushed and this whole city leveled…all because you didn't recognize the meaning of this moment of God's visitation." Imagine the shock of the crowd to see this moment shift from celebration to lament.

Today: If you were to weep in lament for your town, your state, or your nation as Jesus did for his, what might you say?

DAY TWO: *A Study in Contrasts*

People who took part in that march toward Jerusalem that day must have recalled the prophet Zechariah's words: "Rejoice greatly, Daughter Zion! Sing aloud, Daughter Jerusalem! Look, your king will come to you. He is righteous and victorious. He is humble and riding on an ass, on a colt, the offspring of a donkey. He will cut off the chariot from Ephraim and the warhorse from Jerusalem. The bow used in battle will be cut off; he will speak peace to the nations. His rule will stretch from sea to sea, and from the river to the ends of the Earth."

To feel the full drama of that moment, it is necessary to imagine another parade that frequently took place on the other side of Jerusalem, whenever King Herod rode into the city in full procession from his headquarters in Caesarea Philippi. He would enter not on a young donkey but on a mighty warhorse. He would come in the name of Caesar, not in the name of the Lord. He wasn't surrounded by a ragtag crowd holding palm branches and waving their coats. He was surrounded by chariots and uniformed soldiers with their swords and spears and bows held high. His military procession was a show of force intended to inspire fear and compliance, not hope and joy.

In that light, the meaning of this day begins to become clear to us. Caesar's kingdom, the empire of Rome, rules by fear with threats of violence, demanding submission. God's kingdom, the kingdom of heaven, rules by faith with a promise of peace, inspiring joy. Jesus's tears were trying to tell us something: He knew that the religious and political leaders would reject his message. They would respond to Caesar's violence with violence of their own, and that's why Jesus made that dire prediction.

Today: Think about how Jesus's message of peace would be evaluated by religious and political leaders today.

DAY THREE: *A Major Disruption*

Jesus led that little peace march into Jerusalem and straight to the Temple. There he caused a big disruption. He drove out the merchants who sold animals for sacrifice. He drove out those who exchanged foreign currency for the Temple currency. He was clearly challenging popular assumptions about the necessity of sacrifice and about the need for opulent temples and all they represent. This time he linked together quotes from two of the greatest prophets, Isaiah and Jeremiah. My house will be a house of prayer for all peoples, Isaiah said. But you have turned it into a hideout for crooks, Jeremiah said.

Through the dramatic events of this day, Jesus gave people much to ponder: To be alive is to learn what makes for peace. It's not more weapons, more threats, more fear. It's more faith, more freedom, more hope, more love, more joy.

Today: Let your heart echo the crowds that day: "Blessed is the one who comes in the name of the Lord!"

DAY FOUR: *A Table, a Basin, Some Food, Some Friends*

Every Passover, Jewish people everywhere pause to share a meal to commemorate the liberation of their ancestors from slavery in Egypt. They associate each element of the meal—bitter herbs, unleavened bread, a lamb, fruit, and more—with different meanings from their liberation story. On Thursday of Jesus's final week, Jesus brought his disciples together to celebrate Passover. He drew their attention not to the roast lamb but to a simple loaf of bread and a cup of wine. Near the end of the meal, Jesus lifted the bread and gave thanks for it. He said, "This is my body, given for you. Do this in remembrance of me." Then he raised a cup of wine and said, "This cup is the new covenant by my blood, which is poured out for you for the forgiveness of sins." He added, "Whenever you take this bread and drink from this cup, do so in memory of me." The words must have been haunting to the disciples, suggesting that he would soon be gone.

In the Fourth Gospel's telling of this story, the bread and wine aren't even mentioned. Instead, Jesus washes his disciples' feet, taking the role of a servant, inviting his disciples to follow his example of service and love. Both perspectives on that night have something to teach us. Jesus is announcing a new liberation. He is calling us to leave our old ways of oppression and slavery behind, and to embrace a new way of life characterized by self-giving, mutual service, and mutual love.

Later on that dramatic night, after the holy supper, after Jesus went to a garden to pray, after his disciples fell asleep, after Judas came to betray Jesus with a kiss, after Peter pulled out his sword to fight and Jesus told him to put it away, after Jesus was arrested, and after his disciples ran away, Jesus was brutally tortured by the Roman Guard. They lashed him thirty-nine times, one fewer than the forty lashes that constituted a death sentence. Imagine the contrast: at dinner, Jesus speaking of liberation and love. A few hours later, Jesus, captured and tortured.

Today: Feel the drama of that Passover meal, and feel the trauma of what came next.

DAY FIVE: *Holding Up a Mirror*

After that special dinner, just before Jesus's arrest, he asked his disciples to come to a nearby garden with him to pray. "My Father, if it is possible, take this cup of suffering away from me," he said. "However, not what I want but what you want." With tears and in great distress, he prayed a second and third time. But the thrust of his prayer shifted from what might be possible to what might not be possible: "My Father, if it is not possible that this cup be taken away unless I drink it, then let it be what you want." In the second and third prayers, he was clearly preparing to die.

But why? Why was there no other way? Why did this good man have to face torture and execution as if he were some evil monster?

We can imagine many reasons. Some are political. The Pharisees were right to be concerned on Sunday when Jesus came marching into the capital. That little parade—which the Romans would have called a rebellious mob—proclaimed Jesus as king. From there, Jesus marched into the Temple and called it a hideout for crooks, turning over the tables and causing a major disruption. Only a fool would do things like these without expecting consequences. Jesus was no fool.

We can imagine other reasons for this tragedy to unfold. People assumed that God was righteous and pure in a way that made God hate the unrighteous and impure. But Jesus said that God was pure love, so overflowing in goodness that God poured out compassion on the pure and impure alike. He not only spoke of God's unbounded compassion—he embodied day after day in the way he sat at table with everyone, in the way he was afraid to be called a "friend of sinners," in the way he touched untouchables and refused to condemn even the most notorious of sinners. He taught and embodied a very different vision of what God is like, and that's the kind of thing that can get a person killed.

Even as he was dying on that cross, Jesus was teaching, revealing, uncovering the truth. What could it mean when political leaders and religious leaders came together to mock and torture and kill this man of peace? Is this the only way religions and governments maintain order—by threatening people with pain, shame, and death if they don't comply? And is this how they unify people—by turning them into a mob that comes together in its shared hatred of the latest failure, loser, rebel, criminal, outcast…or prophet? The Romans boasted of their peace, and the priests boasted of their holiness and justice, but on that Friday, it all looked like a sham, a fraud, a con game. "What kind of world have we made?" the people must have asked. "What kind of people have we become?"

One minute the crowds were flocking to Jesus hoping for free bread and healing. The next minute they were shouting, "Crucify him!" And even his so-called disciples were no better. One minute they were eating a meal with him and he was calling them his friends. The next, they stood at a distance, unwilling to identify themselves with him and so risk what he was going through. As Jesus died, it was as if he held up a mirror to show us ourselves.

Today: Ponder what the crucifixion tells us about humanity.

DAY SIX: *Everything Must Change*

It grew strangely dark in the middle of that Friday afternoon, and in the darkness, even from a distance, Jesus's disciples could hear him pray, "Father, forgive them, for they don't know what they are doing."

Imagine what the disciples must have thought: *Forgive them? Forgive us?*

Their thoughts may have returned to the garden the night before, when Jesus asked if there could be any other way. And now it was clear. There could be no other way to show us what we are truly like: violent, corrupt, misguided, unjust, cruel, people who "do not know what they do" indeed.

And there could be no other way to show humanity what God is truly like. God is not vengeful, vindictive, and retaliatory. God is not revealed in killing and conquest...in violence and hate. Rather, God is revealed in this crucified man—giving of himself to the very last breath, giving and gracious, self-giving and forgiving.

If God is like this, and if we are like this...everything must change. Everything must change.

Today: Ask yourself, *Do I truly believe God is like that crucified man speaking words of forgiveness?*

WEEK THIRTY-THREE

THE UPRISING BEGINS

Scriptural Readings

> Ezekiel 37:1–14
> Luke 24:1–32
> Colossians 1:9–29

Key Verses—Luke 24:1–5

But on the first day of the week, at early dawn, they came to the tomb, taking the spices that they had prepared. They found the stone rolled away from the tomb, but when they went in, they did not find the body. While they were perplexed about this, suddenly two men in dazzling clothes stood beside them. The women were terrified and bowed their faces to the ground, but the men said to them, "Why do you look for the living among the dead? He is not here, but has risen."

DAY ONE: *The Men Didn't Believe Them*

A group of women claimed that at dawn on Sunday, before the sun had risen, they went to the tomb to properly wash Jesus's corpse and prepare it for its final burial. When they arrived, they had a vision involving angels. One of the women claimed that Jesus appeared to her.

Most of the men didn't buy it. *It was just the gardener,* they thought.

But Peter went running back and found the tomb empty. Empty! The burial cloths were still there, neatly folded. Who would take a naked corpse and leave the bloody cloths that it was wrapped in? Peter wondered what was going on—but he didn't have any clear theory.

Today: Imagine yourself as one of the women, telling your story. Then imagine yourself as one of the men who simply couldn't (or wouldn't) believe.

DAY TWO: *A Mysterious Stranger*

Late that same Sunday afternoon, two of Jesus's followers were deep in conversation as they walked the seven-mile road from Jerusalem to their home, a little town called Emmaus. The walk took a couple of hours. Along the way they were trying to come up with some kind of interpretation of the events that had transpired. Suddenly, a stranger approached.

"What are you folks talking about?" he asked.

One of them replied, "Are you kidding? Are you the only person in this whole region who doesn't know all that's been happening around Jerusalem recently?"

"Like what?" he asked.

They told him about Jesus, that he was clearly a prophet who said and did amazing things. They told him how the religious and political leaders came together to arrest him. They went into some detail about the horror of the crucifixion on Friday. "We had hoped," one of them said, "that this Jesus was the one who was going to turn things around for Israel, that he would set us free from the Roman occupation."

After a few steps, the other added, "And this morning was the third day since his death, and some women from our group told us that they had a vision of angels who said he was alive." It was pretty clear from the tone of this disciple's voice that the report of the women wasn't taken very seriously.

That's when the stranger interrupted. "You just don't get it, do you?" he said. "This is exactly what the prophets said would happen. They have been telling us all along that the Liberator would have to suffer and die like this before entering his glory." As they continued walking, he started explaining things to them from the Scriptures. He began with Moses, and step by step he showed them the pattern of God's work in history, culminating in what happened in Jerusalem in recent days.

Today: Reflect on how hard it is, after you have had your hopes dashed or disappointed, to have your hopes resurrected again.

DAY THREE: *A Treasure Hidden in Mystery*

The stranger explained something like this to the two disciples on the Emmaus road: *God calls someone to proclaim God's will. Resistance and rejection follow, often culminating in an expulsion or murder to silence the speaker. But this isn't a sign of defeat. This is the only way God's most important messages are ever heard—through someone on the verge of being rejected. God's word doesn't come in dominating, crushing force. It comes only in vulnerability, in weakness, in gentleness... just as you have seen over this last week.*

At that point, they realized they had reached home already, and as they slowed down, the stranger just kept walking. They asked him to stay with them since it was getting late and would soon be dark. So he came into their home and the three sat down at their table for a meal. The stranger reached to the center of the table and took a loaf of bread and gave thanks for it. He then broke it and handed a piece of it to each of them and...

It hit them both at the same instant. This wasn't a stranger... this was... it couldn't be—yes, this was Jesus! They each looked down at the fragment of bread in their hands, and when they looked back up to the stranger... he was gone!

Today: Everything about this story is mysterious: who this stranger is, where he has come from, where he is going, how he knows what he knows, how he suddenly disappears. But in the mystery, there is a treasure hidden. Open your heart to that treasure.

DAY FOUR: *Vindication!*

We can only imagine what happened after the mysterious stranger disappeared—how they felt, what they said. "When he spoke about Moses and the prophets, did you feel—?"

"—Inspired? Yes. It felt like my heart was glowing, hotter and hotter, until it was ready to ignite."

"Did this really happen, or was it just a vision?"

"*Just* a vision? Maybe a vision means seeing into what's more real than anything else."

"But it wasn't just me, right? You saw him too, right? You felt it too, right?"

"What do we do now? Shouldn't we...tell the others?"

"Yes, let's do it. Let's go back to Jerusalem, even though it's late. I could never sleep after experiencing this!"

So they packed their gear and rushed back to the city, excited and breathless. On their earlier journey, they were filled with one kind of perplexity—disappointment, confusion, sadness. Now they must have felt another kind of perplexity—wonder, awe, amazement, almost-too-good-to-be-true-ness. "Do you realize what this means?" you can imagine one of them asking, and then answering his own question: "Jesus was right after all! Everything he stood for has been vindicated!"

"Yes. And something else. We never have to fear death again."

Today: Consider what it would mean if everything Jesus had said and done had been discredited. And then consider what it means if the opposite is true.

DAY FIVE: *Christ Resurrected in Us*

We can imagine the conversation that unfolded as the two disciples rushed back to Jerusalem.

"If we don't have to fear death," one says, "we never need to fear Caesar and his forces again, either. Their only real weapon is fear, and if we lose our fear, what power do they have left? Ha! Death has lost its sting! That means we can stand tall and speak the truth, just like Jesus did."

The other replies, "If we don't need to fear death, we don't need to fear anyone or anything."

"This changes everything."

"It's not just that Jesus was resurrected. It feels like we have arisen, too. We were in a tomb of defeat and despair. But now—look at us! We're truly alive again!"

They talk as fast as they walk. Perhaps they recall Jesus's words from Thursday night about his body and blood. Perhaps they remember what happened on Friday when his body and his blood were separated from each other on the cross. Perhaps they realize that this is what crucifixion is: the slow, excruciating, public separation of body and blood.

Can we enter their conversation and join them in their wondering? Could it be that in the holy meal, when we remember Jesus, that we are making space for his body and blood to be reunited and reconstituted in us? Could our remembering him actually re-member and resurrect him in our hearts, our bodies, our lives? Could his body and blood be reunited in us, so that we become his new embodiment? Is that why the two disciples saw him and then didn't see him—because the place the Risen Christ most wanted to be seen was in their bodies—and ours, among them—and us, in them—and us?

Today: See yourself as an embodiment of the Risen Christ.

DAY SIX: *Swept Up in an Uprising*

It was dark when the two disciples reached Jerusalem. Between that Sunday's sunrise and sunset, their world had been changed forever. Everything seemed new. From now on, whenever they would break the bread and drink the wine, they would know that we were not alone. The risen Christ was with them, among them, and within them. Resurrection had begun. They had been swept up into something rare, something precious, something utterly revolutionary.

It felt like an uprising. An uprising of hope, not hate. An uprising armed with love, not weapons. An uprising that shouted a joyful promise of life and peace, not angry threats of hostility and death. It was an uprising of outstretched hands, not clenched fists. It was the "someday" they had always dreamed of, emerging in the present, rising up among them and within them.

It was so different from anything they had expected—so much better. *This is what it means to be alive, truly alive,* they thought. *This is what it means to be en route, walking the road to a new and better day.*

When they found the other disciples, they said, "The Lord is risen! He is risen, indeed!"

Today: Pray, "God, may I be part of your uprising!"

THE UPRISING OF FELLOWSHIP

Scripture Readings

Psalm 133
John 20:1–31
Acts 8:26–40

Key Verses—Psalm 133

How very good and pleasant it is
when kindred live together in unity!
It is like the precious oil on the head,
running down upon the beard,
on the beard of Aaron,
running down over the collar of his robes.
It is like the dew of Hermon,
which falls on the mountains of Zion.
For there the Lord ordained his blessing,
life forevermore.

DAY ONE: *Different Details ... on Purpose?*

Matthew, Mark, and Luke tell the story of Jesus in ways similar to one another (which is why they're often called the synoptic gospels—with a similar optic, or viewpoint). Many details differ (and the differences are quite fascinating), but it's clear the three compositions share common sources. The Fourth Gospel tells the story quite differently. These differences might disturb people who don't understand that storytelling in the ancient world was driven less by a duty to convey true details accurately and more by a desire to proclaim true meaning powerfully. The ancient editors who put the New Testament together let the differences stand as they were, so each story can convey its intended meanings in its own unique ways.

One place where details differ among all the gospels is in what happened right after the resurrection. Mark's gospel, which scholars agree was the earliest one to be written down, ends abruptly without any details about the days and weeks after the resurrection. In Luke's gospel and its sequel, the Book of Acts, Jesus explicitly tells the disciples to stay in Jerusalem. In contrast, in Matthew's gospel, the risen Jesus greets only some female disciples in Jerusalem. He tells these women to instruct the male disciples to go to Galilee, where he will appear to them later.

In the Fourth Gospel, the risen Christ appears to the disciples in Jerusalem the evening of resurrection Sunday and then again a week later. And some time after that, the disciples leave Jerusalem and go to Galilee, where he appears to them once more.

Today: Consider what meaning might Luke be trying to convey by having the risen Christ meet the disciples in Jerusalem, the capital city of their religion and nation. Consider the meaning Matthew might convey by having Jesus meet the disciples in Galilee, Jesus's hometown and the center of his ministry among the poor, the sick, and the oppressed. Ask yourself whether both meanings could be true.

DAY TWO: *Scared and Hiding*

In John's gospel, the Easter Sunday action is centered in Jerusalem, where the disciples were in real danger. If they went outside, someone might recognize them as Jesus's friends and notify the authorities. To the authorities, Jesus was nothing more than a troublemaker and rabble-rouser, and his followers were also a threat. The authorities wanted this whole uprising business to be squashed once and for all. So the disciples played it safe and stayed hidden. At any moment, temple guards or Roman soldiers might bang on the door.

There they remained, tense, jumpy, simmering with anxiety. What happened Friday had been ugly, and they didn't want it to happen to the rest of them. Every sound startled them. Suddenly, they all felt something, a presence, familiar yet…impossible. How could Jesus be among them?

"Peace be with you," he said. He showed them his scarred hands and feet. It started to dawn on them: The women's reports were not just wishful thinking—they were true, and they too were experiencing the risen Christ. "I give you my peace," he said again. And then he did three things that changed them forever.

First he said, "As the Father sent me, so I am sending you." Here they were, huddled in their little safe house like a bunch of cowards, and he was still interested in sending cowards like them to continue his mission!

Next he came close to them and breathed on them. "Welcome the Holy Spirit," he said. Of course, this reminded them all of the story in Genesis when God breathed life into Adam and Eve. It was a new beginning, he was telling them. It was a new Genesis, and they were to be the prototypes of a new kind of human community.

Next came the greatest shock of all. After what happened on Friday, anyone with scars like his would have been expected to say, "Go and get revenge on those evil beasts who did this to me." But Jesus said, "I'm sending you with the power to forgive."

Peace! Forgiveness! Those aren't the responses you expect from someone who had suffered what Jesus suffered. But in that brief moment when their locked hideout was filled with his presence, that was the message they received.

Today: Hold those three actions of Jesus in your thinking, and make them personal: sending you out, breathing the Holy Spirit into you, and commissioning you to forgive.

DAY THREE: *His Typical Skeptical Self*

Have you ever missed something big, so that your friends all say, "Wow! You should have been there!"?

That's how Thomas must have felt the days after Easter. He wasn't with the other disciples in hiding that night when Jesus had appeared. When they saw Thomas later and told him what they had experienced, he was his typical skeptical self. "I want to touch those scars with my own hands and see for myself, or I won't believe," he said. A week later, they again were all together, and this time Thomas was there, too— still skeptical, but still present. Because of the continuing threat of the authorities finding them, the doors were locked.

Just as before, Jesus's presence suddenly became real among them— visible, palpable. He spoke peace to them, and then he went straight to Thomas, inviting him to see, touch, believe. He did not criticize Thomas for doubting. He wanted to help him believe.

"My Lord and my God," Thomas replied. They couldn't help but remember back on Thursday night, when Thomas asked Jesus where he was going and what was the way to get there. Jesus replied, "I am the way." Philip then asked Jesus to show them the Father, and Jesus said, "If you have seen me, you've seen the Father." Now, ten days later, it seemed as if Thomas was beginning to understand what Jesus had meant. He saw God in a scarred man whose holy aliveness is more powerful than human cruelty.

Today: Be honest about your own doubts and skepticism, and keep showing up just as you are. No hiding is necessary.

DAY FOUR: *For Normal, Flawed People Like Us*

There's one thing you have to say about Thomas: Even though he didn't believe at first, he stayed with the group, open to the possibility that his doubt could be transformed into faith. He kept coming back. He kept showing up. If he hadn't wanted to believe, he had a week to leave for good and go back home. But he didn't. He stayed. Not believing, but wanting to believe.

The fact that Jesus made a special appearance for Thomas tells us something essential about what the uprising is all about.

It isn't just for brave people, but for scared folks like the disciples who are willing to become brave. It isn't just for believers, but for doubting folks like Thomas who want to believe in spite of their skepticism. It isn't just for good people, but for normal, flawed people like Thomas and Peter and you and me.

And it isn't just for men, either. It's no secret that men throughout human history often treat women as inferior. Even on resurrection morning, when Mary Magdalene breathlessly claimed that the Lord was risen, the men didn't offer her much in the way of respect. There were all sorts of ignorant comments about "the way women are." Looking back, we realize that by bypassing all of the male disciples and appearing first to a woman, Jesus was overcoming that discrimination. Of course, he had been treating women with uncommon respect right from the start.

Today: Picture yourself as Thomas, standing in the presence of the risen Christ with all your doubts, and see Christ seeing you as beloved and accepted and blessed.

DAY FIVE: *The Meaning of Fellowship*

The early disciples had a term for the experience of radical welcome and unconditional inclusion that they experienced together: *fellowship*. Fellowship is a kind of belonging that isn't based on status, achievement, or gender, but instead is based on a deep belief that everyone matters, everyone is welcome and everyone is loved, no conditions, no exceptions. It's not the kind of belonging you find at the top of the ladder among those who think they are the best, but at the bottom among all the rest, with all the other failures and losers who have either climbed the ladder and fallen or never gotten up enough gumption to climb in the first place.

Today: Remember times in your life when you experienced uncommon acceptance, where you felt that you were truly welcomed and you truly belonged.

DAY SIX: *You Don't Have to Hide Your Scars*

The Risen Christ showed up with his scars. He didn't hide them from the disciples.

Thomas showed up with his doubts. He didn't have to hide them from Christ or his fellow disciples.

You too can show up just as you are. Really. There is nothing you've done, nothing you've thought or questioned, nothing that's true about you that makes you unacceptable or second class.

Fellowship is for scarred people, and for scared people, and for people who want to believe but aren't sure what or how to believe. When we come together just as we are, we begin to rise again, to believe again, to hope again, to live again.

Through fellowship, the walls, floor, and ceiling are blown off our little locked room so it can become the biggest space in the world. In that expansive space of open fellowship, the Holy Spirit fills us like a deep breath of fresh air.

Today: Pray, "God, help me believe that you accept me just as I am, with my doubts and scars, my flaws and fears. Help me more deeply accept myself, too."

WEEK THIRTY-FIVE

THE UPRISING OF DISCIPLESHIP

Scripture Readings

Psalm 25
Luke 10:1–11, 17–20
John 21:1–15

Key Verses—John 21:15

When they had finished breakfast, Jesus said to Simon Peter, "Simon son of John, do you love me more than these?" He said to him, "Yes, Lord; you know that I love you." Jesus said to him, "Feed my lambs."

DAY ONE: *A Stranger on the Beach*

Imagine you are among a group of disciples some days after the resurrection. You have left the big city of Jerusalem and gone back to Galilee, your home region to the north. Thomas is there, as are Peter, Nathaniel, James, and John, plus a few more. Out of the blue, late in the day, Peter says he wants to go fishing. Fishing, of all things!

You aren't sure why, but you join him anyway. You drop the long gill net time after time through the night, reenacting an old, familiar ritual. Time after time you haul it in, hoping for something. But the net never struggles against you, never signals the weight or life of a catch.

It's dawn when you see a stranger on the shore about a hundred yards from you. He asks the question every unsuccessful fishermen dreads: "Hey, boys! Having any luck?"

"Nothing," you reply glumly.

He yells, "Drop your net over on the other side of the boat. You'll find fish there."

Today: Imagine how you'd feel if you heard those words from a stranger on the beach, and ponder areas in your life where you've been "fishing all night" and have nothing to show for it.

DAY TWO: *The Fish or the Stranger?*

There's nothing like having a stranger on the shore giving you advice after you've been fishing all night. But imagine you are among that band of disciples early that morning as the sky brightens. And imagine you decide, "We have nothing to lose. Let's do as he says."

And then it happens. You start feeling the net move, tug, pull in your hand. Not just a few fish, but a heavy, wriggling, squirming school! Most of your band of fishing brothers would be thinking about the amazing catch of fish. But one turns in his thoughts to that stranger on the shore.

"It's the Lord!" Peter cries out. He immediately throws on his shirt and swims to shore while the rest of you haul in the net. It's a wonder it hasn't torn with all that weight!

When the rest of you splash ashore, the stranger already has some bread laid out, with a charcoal fire glowing and some fish cooking. He invites you to add a few of your own fish to the meal, so Peter goes out to pull a few from the net.

"Let's have breakfast," the stranger says.

You all have this sense of who he is, so nobody asks any questions. He breaks the bread and gives it, and then the fish, to each of you. It seems strange to do something so normal—eat breakfast—under such extraordinary circumstances. But that is what you do. Later you remember how Jesus had taken the role of a servant the night before the crucifixion, washing your feet. Now, this stranger takes the same humble role, serving you a meal.

Today: Try to hold and savor the sense of wonder, the mixture of doubt and hope, the continuity and the discontinuity the disciples in this story must have felt in the presence of this stranger.

DAY THREE: *More Than These*

Imagine being on that beach eating breakfast with your fellow disciples, along with a mysterious stranger whom you suspect to be...could it be the risen Christ? You see him turn to Peter to deal with some unfinished business between them.

You recall how Peter had fallen apart that night when Jesus was arrested. You remember how when the armed guards arrived, Peter panicked, pulled out his sword, and slashed off somebody's ear. In a matter of seconds, he managed to violate half of what Jesus taught for the better part of three years. Later, Peter denied that he even knew Jesus, not once but three times, and he threw in some choice language in doing so. On the morning of the resurrection, Peter was frantic and confused, and that was just days after he had bragged about how loyal he would be. It wasn't pretty, and you could feel how Peter's colossal failure would weigh heavy on his mind, especially because Jesus had given him the nickname of "Peter the Rock."

"Simon, son of John, do you love me more than these?" the stranger asks, using Peter's original name rather than "Peter the Rock." You wouldn't be certain what Jesus means by "more than these." Does he mean more in comparison to his fellow disciples? Does he mean more than the fish, the boat, and the net—symbols of his old life before it was interrupted by Jesus?

Today: Ponder what "more than these" might refer to, and then ponder whether it matters in light of the main point of the question.

DAY FOUR: *From Failure to Love*

"Do you love me more than these?" the stranger asks.

Peter replies, "Yes, Lord. You know I love you."

"Then take care of my lambs," the stranger replies. Then, as if Peter's first reply didn't count for much, the stranger asks him again: "Simon, son of John, do you love me?" Peter replies in the same way the second time, and the stranger replies, "Shepherd my sheep." Then the question comes a third time, echoing Peter's three denials some days before. Peter replies even more strongly this time. "Lord, you know everything. Of course you know I love you!" Once again, the stranger tells him to shepherd his sheep.

And that was it. It was as if all Peter's failures melted behind us in the past, like a bad night of fishing after a great morning catch. The past and its failures didn't count anymore. What counted was love...love for Jesus, love for his flock.

Today: Have the courage to reflect on your worst failures in life. Then imagine turning from the failures of your past to a life of love in your future.

DAY FIVE: *A Chain Reaction of Love*

Like a lot of us, Peter had a way of getting it right one minute and wrong the next. Sure enough, a few minutes after telling the risen Christ of his love and receiving a commitment to love and care for Christ's flock, Peter has forgotten about love for the flock entirely and starts treating one of the other disciples as a rival, a competitor. Jesus responds forcefully: "Stop worrying about anyone else. You follow me!"

Those words remind us of how this whole adventure began for the disciples, with Jesus issuing that simple, all-or-nothing invitation: *Follow me!* Three years later, it's still about that one essential thing: following him. Of course, that's what the word *disciple* has meant all along— to be a follower, a student, an apprentice, one who learns by imitating a master.

We can imagine the honor, for uneducated fishermen like those first disciples, to sit at the feet of the greatest teacher imaginable. And we can imagine the even greater honor to be sent out to teach others, who would in turn teach and train others in this new way of life. We can imagine the chain reaction of love replicating from one generation to the next, learning and teaching, learning and teaching, spanning the centuries from that early morning beach to this very moment, right now.

This revolutionary plan of discipleship means that we must first and foremost become examples who embody the message and values of the movement Jesus launched. That doesn't mean we are perfect— just look at Peter and his amazing capacity to goof things up. But it does mean we are growing and learning, always humble and willing to get up again after we fall, always moving forward on the road we are walking.

As Jesus modeled never-ending learning and growth for us, we will model it for others, who will model it for still others. If each new generation of disciples follows this example, centuries from now, apprentices will still be learning the way of Jesus from mentors, so they can become mentors for the following generation.

Today: Understand this succession or "chain reaction" of learners and teachers, continuing from Jesus to you, learning and teaching how to live a life of love.

DAY SIX: *Tired but Resilient!*

Jesus once sent his disciples out on a kind of training mission, preparing them for the day they would carry on his work. He wouldn't let them bring anything—not even a wallet, satchel, or sandals. He sent them out in complete vulnerability—like sheep among wolves, he said. In each town, they would need to find hospitable people to shelter them and feed them—"people of peace," Jesus called them. They would become the disciples' partners, and with their support the disciples would proclaim the kingdom of God in word and deed. If people didn't respond, he told them to move on and not look back. They should look for places, like fields that are ready for harvest, where the time was right and people wanted what the disciples had to offer. The disciples returned from that training mission full of confidence and joy.

The gospels end with another sending out. Just as Jesus invited ordinary people to be his disciples, the risen Christ sends those disciples out as apostles, emissaries, or agents, to invite even more ordinary people to experience the extraordinary life of following the way of Christ. They in turn will invite still others, launching a worldwide movement of discipleship that began one morning on a beach with a handful of tired but resilient fishermen. Small beginnings with ordinary people, given lots of time and lots of faith and lots of hope and love, can change the world.

I think Jesus chose fishermen for a good reason. To be part of his uprising today, like fishermen we must be willing to fail a lot and to keep trying. We will face long, dark nights when nothing happens, but we can never give up hope. Christ caught us in his net of love, so now we go and spread the net for others. And so, fellow disciples, let's get moving. Let us walk the road with Jesus.

Today: Pray: "Many things can discourage me as I walk your path, Lord. Help me to grow stronger and more resilient through every challenge, every delay, and every disappointment!"

WEEK THIRTY-SIX

THE UPRISING OF WORSHIP

Scripture Readings

Psalm 103
Acts 2:41–47
I Corinthians 14:26–31
Colossians 3:12–17

Key Verses—Colossians 3:16–17

Let the word of Christ dwell in you richly; teach and admonish one another in all wisdom; and with gratitude in your hearts sing psalms, hymns, and spiritual songs to God. And whatever you do, in word or deed, do everything in the name of the Lord Jesus, giving thanks to God the Father through him.

DAY ONE: *Ecclesia—the Ongoing Embodiment of Christ*

For a short time after the first Easter, there were frequent reports of people seeing the risen Christ in a variety of locations. Soon, though, those reports became less frequent, until they ceased entirely. A story spread that Jesus had ascended to heaven and was now sitting at God's right hand. That fueled a lot of speculation and debate about what the disciples should expect to happen next. Some people thought God was going to stage a dramatic intervention any day. Some even stopped working in anticipation of some massive change. They just sat around waiting for Jesus to appear again.

Others would have none of this passive waiting. They interpreted the story of Jesus's ascension and enthronement to mean the time had come to get to work, living in light of what Jesus had already taught. They were convinced that what mattered now was not for Christ to appear *to* them, but for Christ to appear *in* them, *among* them, and *through* them. He wanted them to be his hands, his feet, his face, his smile, his voice... his embodiment on Earth.

They began to gather frequently as little communities they called *ecclesia*. They borrowed this term from the Roman empire, just as they "borrowed" the cross and reversed its meaning. For the Romans, the *ecclesia* was the citizens-only gathering that brought the elite from a region together to discuss the affairs of the empire. The ecclesia of Christ brought common people together around the affairs of the kingdom of God. Whenever and wherever the Roman ecclesia gathered, they honored and worshiped the emperor and the pantheon of gods that supported his regime. Whenever and wherever the early disciples gathered, they honored and worshiped the living God, revealed in Christ, through the power of the Holy Spirit.

Their ecclesia gathered for worship wherever they could—in homes, public buildings, or outdoor settings. And they gathered whenever they could, but mostly at night, since that's when nearly everyone—even the slaves among them—could assemble. They often gathered on Sunday, the day Jesus rose and the day their uprising began, but none of them would argue about which day was best, since every day was a good day to worship God and walk in God's way.

Today: Think of yourself as one cell or one participant in the embodiment of Christ today.

DAY TWO: *The Ecclesia Teaching and Learning*

For the early disciples, worship gatherings included four main functions. They began with the teaching of the original disciples, who were increasingly being called *apostles*. Just as an apprentice carpenter is called a master carpenter once he has learned the trade, well-trained disciples who were sent out to teach others were called *apostles*. The apostles told others the stories of Jesus, events they saw themselves as eyewitnesses or events other credible eyewitnesses passed on to them. They read the law and the prophets, and explained how their sacred texts prepared the way for Jesus and his good news. The apostles and their assistants also wrote letters that were shared from one ecclesia to the next. These letters were read aloud, since many of the early disciples were illiterate and couldn't read on their own. Whether in person or by letter, through the teaching of the apostles the early ecclesia celebrated the words of Jesus, the stories about Jesus, the parables he told, the character he embodied, so they could walk the road he walked.

Today: Contact your pastor, priest, or another spiritual leader and thank them for teaching you about Jesus and his way of life.

DAY THREE: *The Ecclesia Eating and Drinking*

The worship of the early followers of Christ also included a ritual of breaking and eating bread and pouring and drinking wine, as Jesus had taught them to do. Usually, this was part of a full meal they called the "love feast" or "the Lord's table." It was so unlike anything any of them had ever experienced. Everywhere in their society, they experienced constant divisions between rich and poor, slave and free, male and female, Jew and Greek, city-born and country-born, and so on. (Sound familiar?) But at the Lord's table, just as it was when Jesus shared a table with sinners and outcasts, they all were one, all loved, all welcome as equals. They even greeted one another with "a holy kiss." Nobody in Roman culture would ever see a high-born person greeting a slave as an equal—except at the "love feasts" of the ecclesia, where those social divisions were left behind, and where they learned new ways of honoring one another as equal members of one family.

At their love feasts, they repeated the words Jesus said about the bread being his body given for them and the wine being his blood shed for them and for their sins. Those words "for you" and "for your sins" were full of meaning for them. Just as we take medicine "for" an illness, they understood that remembering Jesus's death was curing them of their old habits and ways. For example, when they would ponder how Jesus forgave those who crucified him, they were cured of their desire for revenge. When they saw how Jesus trusted God and didn't fear human threats, they were cured of their fear. When they remembered how Jesus never stopped loving, even to the point of death, they were cured of their hatred, anger, or apathy. When they imagined his outstretched arms embracing the whole world, they felt hearts opening in love for the whole world, too, curing them of their prejudice and favoritism, their grudges and selfishness. No wonder they wanted to celebrate this simple holy meal as often as they could!

Today: Prepare to experience the ritual of bread and wine in a more meaningful way next time you have the opportunity to do so.

DAY FOUR: *The Ecclesia in Fellowship*

Along with the apostles' teaching and the holy meal, early worship gatherings included fellowship or sharing. The people shared their experiences, their sense of what God wanted to tell them, their insights from the Scriptures. They also shared their fears, tears, failures, and joys. There was a financial aspect to their sharing as well. At each gathering they took up an offering to distribute to those who were most in need among them and around them—especially the widows and the orphans. None of them were rich, but through their sharing, none of them were in need, either.

When they gathered, they expected the Holy Spirit to give each individual different gifts to be used for the common good. One person may be gifted to teach or lead. Another may be moved to write and sing a song. One may be given an inspired word of comfort or encouragement or warning for the ecclesia. Someone else may be given a special message of knowledge, insight, or teaching. Someone might speak in an unknown language, and someone else might pray with great faith for a healing or miracle to occur. The same Spirit who gave the gifts taught them to be guided by love in all they would say and do, for love matters most for them. It was even greater than faith and hope!

Today: If you have a faith community where you experience fellowship, thank God for it. If you don't, why not find one today? And if you can't find one, maybe you should consider forming one.

DAY SIX: *The Ecclesia at Prayer*

Along with gathering for teaching, the holy meal, and fellowship, early followers of Christ gathered for prayer. Some of their prayers were requests; they learned it was far better to share their worries with God than to be filled with anxiety about things that were out of their control anyway. They constantly prayed for boldness and wisdom so that they could spread the good news of God's love to everyone everywhere. They brought the needs and sorrows of others to God, too, joining their compassion with God's great compassion. They prayed for everyone in authority—that they would turn from injustice, violence, and corruption to ways of justice, peace, and fairness. They prayed especially for those who considered themselves enemies. The more they cursed and mistreated the ecclesia, the more the ecclesia prayed for God's blessing on them, just as Jesus taught.

Some of their prayers were confessions. They freely confessed their sins to God, because Jesus taught that God's grace freed us from hiding their wrongs or making excuses for them. They didn't want to pretend to be better than we really were, so prayers of confession helped them be honest with God, themselves, and one another.

All of their prayers led them to thanksgiving and praise. They felt such joy to have God's Spirit rising up in their lives that they couldn't be silent. They sang their deep joy and longing, sometimes through the ancient psalms and also through spiritual songs that would spring up spontaneously in their hearts. The more they praised God, the less they were intimidated by the powers of this world. And so they praised and worshiped God boldly, joyfully, reverently, and freely, and they weren't quiet or shy about it.

We shouldn't have the impression that everything was perfect with the early ecclesia. They had lots of problems and a lot to learn. But their problems seemed small in comparison to the joy they felt. This is why, even when they were tired from long days of work, even when they were threatened with persecution, even when life was full of hardships and they felt discouraged or afraid, still they gathered as the ecclesia, the people of the uprising. In the face of Christ, they had come to see the glory of God, the love of God, the wisdom of God, the goodness of God, the power of God, the kindness of God...the fullness of God. In light of that vision of God in Christ, how could they not worship? And what else can we do but join them?

Today: Pray for yourself, for others, for those in authority, for enemies or opponents, and don't forget to add thanksgiving and praise.

THE UPRISING OF PARTNERSHIP

Scripture Readings

Psalm 146
Matthew 10:16–20; 11:28–30; 28:16–20
Acts 16:11–40

Key Verses—Psalm 146:5–7

Happy are those whose help is the God of Jacob,
  whose hope is in the Lord their God,
who made heaven and earth,
  the sea, and all that is in them;
who keeps faith forever;
  who executes justice for the oppressed;
  who gives food to the hungry.

DAY ONE: *Peace at a High Price*

In the decades after Jesus's death, Paul, Timothy, Luke, Silas, Priscilla, Aquila, and many others traveled across the Roman empire, proclaiming the message of justice and joy, reconciliation and peace they had received from Jesus and the original disciples. They developed ecclesia in all the empire's major cities. One such city was Philippi, Greece, about half-way between Jerusalem and Rome. It was a Roman colony, meaning it was like a little outpost of Rome. The people of Philippi were loyal Romans—or at least some of them were.

The slaves there, just like everywhere in the empire, were not so happy with the Pax Romana (the Peace of Rome). They did dispropor-tionately large amounts of work and enjoyed disproportionately small amounts of *pax*. The same could be said for women in the empire. The average Roman woman had to bear a lot of children simply to provide enough sons to go to war to keep the empire secure. Like slaves, most women paid a high price for the *pax*.

It's not surprising, then, that when Paul, Silas, Luke, and others first visited Philippi with the message of Jesus, they were welcomed by a group of women, including a wealthy businesswoman named Lydia who offered Paul and his entourage a place to stay in her large home.

Today: Consider why slaves and women would be the first to welcome a new message of good news, and ponder: Who are their counterparts today, and why?

DAY TWO: *A Challenge to an Oppressive System*

If slaves and women were the worst-off people in the Roman empire, young female slaves were the worst-off of the worst-off.

It was a slave girl who demanded Paul's attention in Philippi. She made a lot of money for her owners by going into a trance and telling fortunes. Whenever Paul and his friends walked by her on the way to the riverside, she would start shouting: "These men are slaves of the Highest God of All. They proclaim to you the way of liberation!"

You can imagine how slave owners would feel upon hearing a slave shouting about liberation. And you can imagine how believers in the pantheon of Greek and Roman gods would feel if she spoke about "the Highest God of All." Their economy and their religion—their whole Roman way of life—were being challenged!

The slave girl's shouting went on for a couple of days until, finally, Paul got annoyed. He may have been frustrated that the girl was drawing attention to them in such an inflammatory way. He may have been embarrassed that a lowly fortune-teller was speaking up about him. But there may have been another reason for his frustration.

In his writings, Paul repeatedly said that all people have equal dignity in Christ, male or female, slave or free, Jew, Greek, Roman, or foreigner. So he may have been frustrated that this outspoken girl with so much energy, intelligence, and courage was reduced to slavery. Anyway, for whatever reason, he finally reached a breaking point. He turned to her and commanded the spirit of fortune-telling to come out of her in the name of Jesus Christ. And from that moment, no more trances. No more fortune-telling. And no more money for the men who exploited her!

Today: A newcomer to a city often notices things that long-time residents have gotten used to and don't even notice. Try to look at your surroundings today as if you were a visitor. What injustices have you gotten used to?

DAY THREE: *You Can't Shut Us Up!*

The situation deteriorated rapidly after the slave girl lost her "knack" for fortune-telling. The furious slave owners grabbed Paul and another disciple named Silas and dragged them into the central plaza of the city where all the markets were. They told the city officials that Paul and Silas were Jewish revolutionaries, advocating a lifestyle that good Romans could never accept. The words *Jew* and *lifestyle* were code words that the city officials picked up. Jews, after all, derived their basic identity from the story of God liberating them from slavery in Egypt. Of all people in the empire, Jews were considered most resistant to Roman domination. The slave owners quickly whipped the people of the market into a patriotic, anti-Semitic frenzy. Soon, by order of the city officials, Paul and Silas were stripped naked, severely beaten, and dragged off to prison, where they were put in chains in the innermost cell.

Late that night, Paul and Silas sang praises to God. It was as if they were saying, "You can lock us up, but you can't shut us up!" Their songs of praise demonstrated that they feared neither the whole Roman system of slavery, domination, and intimidation nor the petty gods that upheld it. The other prisoners, as you could imagine, were quite impressed by their courage, if not their singing voices. Suddenly, around midnight, there was an earthquake. Now earthquakes weren't terribly rare in Philippi, but this kind of earthquake was completely unprecedented. It didn't cause the jail to crash in a heap of rubble. It produced no casualties. It simply shook the jail gates and chains so they came unfastened! It was an earthquake of liberation, not destruction. Imagine that!

When the jailer rushed in to check on his prisoners, he was terrified. He knew that if they escaped, he would be put into prison himself and perhaps tortured, too. So he pulled out his sword and decided that suicide was better than being thrown into the miserable prison system that he managed. Paul shouted out to him, "Don't do it, man! We're all here!"

At this point, the poor jailer was even more shocked. Here his prisoners were concerned about his welfare! They were choosing to stay in prison voluntarily to keep him from suffering for their escape. He brought them outside the prison and fell down on his knees in front of them, trembling with emotion. "Gentlemen, what must I do to experience the liberation you have?" he asked. There was that word *liberation* again—the same word the slave girl had used.

Today: Consider the power of the word *liberation* in relation to the word *salvation*, which is often used as a substitute in English. What does *liberation* say to you that *salvation* doesn't?

DAY FOUR: *Withdrawing Consent*

"Have confidence in the Lord Jesus, and you will be liberated, and so will your whole household," Paul said to the jailer. The jailer must have understood those words *Lord Jesus* to be in contrast to the emperor's title, *Lord Caesar.* He realized that Paul was telling him to stop being intimidated by Caesar's system of threats, whips, swords, chains, locks, and prisons. The jailer heard Paul's words as an invitation to live under a different lord or supreme leader, in a different system, a different empire, a different kingdom—the one Jesus leads, one characterized by true freedom, true grace, and true peace.

If the jailer were liberated from the Roman system of domination and oppression, he would stop dominating and oppressing his family and slaves, which is probably what Paul meant by saying that the jailer's "whole household" would also be set free. The power of the system would be broken if the man at the top withdrew his consent and traded the system's rules for another way of life.

The jailer took Paul and Silas to his own house, washed their wounds, and gave them a good meal. He had already been transformed—from a jailer to a gracious host. When Paul and Silas told the man, his family, and his slaves more about Jesus and the uprising, they all were baptized.

Today: Pray, "Help me have confidence in the Lord Jesus, so I can be liberated—and be a source of liberation for others."

DAY FIVE: *Foiling a Cover-up*

Early the next morning, the day after beating Paul and Silas, the city officials realized that they had violated legal protocols by playing into the wealthy businessmen's demands. They sent police to the jail with orders to get Paul and Silas out of town as soon as possible. But Paul saw what was going on and refused to leave. "They made a mockery of justice by publicly humiliating, beating, and imprisoning two Roman citizens without a trial, and now they want us to participate in a cover-up? No way! If they want us to leave, they need to come in person, apologize, and personally escort us from the city." When the police returned with news that the two prisoners were actually Roman citizens, the city officials were as scared as the jailer had been after the earthquake. Like him, all they could think of was how much trouble they would be in with the higher-ups. They complied with Paul's demands and politely requested that Paul and Silas leave the city immediately.

Paul wasn't in any rush. He decided to stop and spend some time at Lydia's house, where the rest of the disciples were waiting. Paul and Silas shared the story of their arrest, beating, imprisonment, and liberation. Everyone was brimming with excitement, overflowing with joy. They felt that they were partners in an earthquake of liberation. They felt that they belonged to a partnership of liberation—working together so that injustice at every level of society would be confronted, and people at every level of society would be set free.

Today: Imagine what it would be like to be part of a "partnership of liberation" in your town, city, or country.

WEEK THIRTY-EIGHT

THE UPRISING OF STEWARDSHIP

Scripture Readings

Deuteronomy 15:1–11
I Timothy 6:3–19
2 Corinthians 8:1–15

Key Verses—2 Corinthians 8:12–14

For if the eagerness is there, the gift is acceptable according to what one has—not according to what one does not have. I do not mean that there should be relief for others and pressure on you, but it is a question of a fair balance between your present abundance and their need, so that their abundance may be for your need, in order that there may be a fair balance.

DAY ONE: *True Wealth*

By the early AD 50s, there were ecclesia thriving in major cities across the Roman empire. Paul and his friends started a small business making tents so they could cover their own expenses as they traveled from city to city. That way they wouldn't be a financial burden on the little ecclesia they were helping establish.

Paul was very careful about money. You might even say he was suspicious of it. To him, loving money was at the root of all kinds of evil. Real wealth didn't come from possessing gold, but rather from possessing contentment, contentment rooted in gratitude to God. Paul saw contentment as a gift money can't buy, free and available to anyone who seeks it.

Today: Cultivate contentment by cultivating gratitude, and pray, "God, help me appreciate all the gifts that are already mine for free."

DAY TWO: *Luxuries and Necessities*

Paul had a lot to say about money. The drive to accumulate money ultimately brings the heartache of a wasted life, he said: Our real ambition should be to build a big account of good works: acts of generosity and kindness on behalf of those considered the last, the least, and the lost. Paul loved to quote Jesus's words that it is better to give than to receive.

When the spiritual uprising later known as the Christian faith first began in Jerusalem, people held all things in common and shared freely with those in need. As you might expect, that created some problems. Some old tensions sprang up between Jews and Greeks, and some people experienced privilege while others experienced prejudice. A few began playing hypocritical games, pretending to be more generous than they really were. But in spite of the problems, holding all things in common was a beautiful thing, and even in places where "all things in common" wasn't the norm, early participants in the uprising were taught a sense of fairness: It wasn't God's will for some to have luxuries while others lacked necessities. God desired a fair balance.

Today: Compare your luxuries to the necessities lacked by others, and calculate the percentage of your income that you currently give away.

DAY THREE: *What's Mine Is God's*

You could say that the way of life taught by Jesus and the apostles was an uprising against the economies of this world. In God's alternate economy, if we have a lot, we don't hoard it; we share it. If we have been given much in terms of money and power, we don't feel a sense of privilege and superiority but rather a sense of greater responsibility for our neighbors who are vulnerable and in need.

Socially, we measure our well-being and holiness not by our own prosperity and comfort, but by the condition of our weakest and neediest neighbors.

Just as in the Roman empire in the era of the earliest ecclesia, people today exhaust themselves to get rich, and in so doing they cause much harm. Some exploit the land. You might say they are thieves who take more from the bank of creation than they put back, and in that way they steal from unborn generations. Others exploit people of this generation. They are thieves who make big profits through the sweat of their poorly paid neighbors, reducing them if not to slavery then to something almost the same. They are often very subtle in the ways they do this, using banks, investments, and loans to enrich themselves as they impoverish others. It's a dirty economy, and those who profit by it gain the world and lose their souls.

"What's yours is mine," some people say, "and I want to steal it!" "What's mine is mine," some people say. "And I want to keep it!" "What's mine is God's," we are learning to say, "and I want to use it for the common good." We call that attitude stewardship.

Today: Repeat this saying in a prayerful spirit: "What's mine is God's, and I want to use it for the common good."

DAY FOUR: *All Areas of Our Lives*

If we are part of the spiritual uprising of Christ, we participate in God's economy of justice and generosity. We are not driven by the lust for ownership, always seeking more, more, more, more. We are instead guided by the wisdom of stewardship... always working for the common good, seeking to use what we have been given in ways that please God.

Stewardship applies to all areas of our lives: how we use time, potential, possessions, privilege, and power. We seek to make the most of our time, not wasting time—but also remembering that rest and celebration are great uses of time. We seek to develop our potential; we remember that our native abilities are gifts from God, and what we make of them is our gift back to God. We seek to use our possessions for others; if we have homes, we practice hospitality; if we have transportation, we seek to help others in need; if we have extra clothing or equipment or food... we find greater joy in giving than in hoarding. Some of us were given privileges based on our social class, race, or place of birth, and we decide to use our privileges as "haves" to serve the "have-nots," so opportunities are fairly shared. In the same way, whatever power we have we use to empower others.

Whatever we do, we try to give it our very best, because we work for Christ and not just for money and for ourselves. We want no part of dishonest or harmful employment, so if necessary we change jobs, or we work for reform so we can stay in our current jobs or professions with a clear conscience. As we are being transformed personally, we seek to transform our economic systems from corrupt to ethical, from destructive to regenerative, from cruel and dehumanizing to kind and humane.

Anything less would be to put the love of money above the love of God, neighbor, and the holy ground of Earth. This is the way of Christ's uprising.

Today: In prayer, surrender your time, potential, possessions, privilege, and power to God, to be used for the common good.

DAY FIVE: *Love in Action*

Practically speaking, stewardship means living below our means. We do so by dividing our income into three parts. First, we determine a percentage that we will use to provide for our needs and the needs of our families. That's just basic decency. Second, we determine a percentage to save, since wisdom requires foresight for both anticipated future needs and unexpected emergencies. Even ants know to save some of their summer's work to get them through the winter. Third, we set aside the largest portion we can for God's work of compassion, justice, restoration, and peace. Many people discover the blessing of investing a tenth of their income in God's work, and some even go beyond that, increasing their "standard of giving," not just their "standard of living," whenever their income increases.

Some of this third portion goes to today's counterparts of Paul, Silas, Timothy, and others, who lead and serve the ecclesia springing up around the world. Some of it goes to members of the ecclesia who are in need—the sick, the widows, the orphans, the elderly, and those who have lost their homes, their land, and their work. Some of it goes to meet the needs of others near or far—as an expression of God's love and ours. That's what stewardship is, really: love in action.

Today: Commit to giving away a percentage of your income that you feel is good and right, considering your blessings and the needs of others.

DAY SIX: *Foolishness, Selfishness, Godliness*

Paul frequently reminded the early ecclesia that nothing had true value without love, including money... *especially* money.

That explains why money is so deceptive. It deceives people about what has true value. When you overvalue money, you undervalue everything else: your family, your friends, your neighbors, this beautiful Earth, even your own health.

You cannot serve two masters, Jesus taught. If you love God, you will hate money, because it always gets in the way of loving God. If you love money, you will hate God, because God always gets in the way of loving money.

It is *foolishness* to live above your means. It is *selfishness* to spend all your money on yourself. It is *godliness* to give—to produce a surplus that is used for the commonwealth of God, which is an uprising not of greed but of joyful generosity and creative stewardship.

Today: Pray, "God, help me earn all I can, save all I can, and give all I can, and help me experience the great joy of giving."

WEEK THIRTY-NINE

WHATEVER THE HARDSHIP, KEEP RISING UP!

Scripture Readings

> Isaiah 40:27–31
> Acts 9:1–25
> 2 Corinthians 6:1–10; 11:22–33

Key Verses—Isaiah 40:31

> *But those who wait for the Lord shall renew their strength,*
> *they shall mount up with wings like eagles,*
> *they shall run and not be weary,*
> *they shall walk and not faint.*

DAY ONE: *The Gift Nobody Wants, but Everyone Needs*

Year after year, decade after decade, the early ecclesia grew. New leaders were developed, new ecclesia were planted, new people joined the movement, and the uprising gained strength. They experienced discipleship, fellowship, worship, partnership, stewardship, and one thing more: hardship, the gift that nobody wants, but everyone gets, and needs.

There were persecutions from outsiders, betrayals by insiders, and stupid arguments that wasted time and drained energy. There were divisions, moral scandals, and financial improprieties. There were power struggles and all kinds of crazy teachings that confused and distracted and drained precious energy. Like any human endeavor, sometimes the early disciples forgot what their whole uprising was supposed to be about.

But as they offended each other and forgave each other, as they experienced rifts and then reconciliations, as they stumbled and fell and got up again, they developed new strengths, strengths that could be developed in no other way: humility, resilience, and wisdom. God doesn't give us shortcuts around hardships, they learned, but rather God strengthens us through them.

Today: Name your current hardships and consider the strengths that you could develop as you face them wisely. (Also consider the weaknesses you will develop if you don't face them wisely.)

DAY TWO: *Bragging Like a Fool... about What?*

Paul spoke and wrote often about the role of hardships in our spiritual lives, and he knew what he was talking about from personal experience. For example, for the last years of his life, Paul was under house arrest in Rome. At some point, it seemed that everyone in the outside world had either lost track of him or forgotten about him.

Timothy found Paul and brought word back to the ecclesia that Paul was feeling lonely and cold in the winter chill and a little bored, too. So a group of disciples came with Timothy to Rome to comfort him. They brought him a warm coat and things to read, among other things.

You can imagine Paul telling his guests stories about his many adventures, and especially about his struggles and failures. "If I'm going to brag like a fool," he once wrote, "it will be about my weaknesses, limitations, sufferings, and scars."

Paul had many scars—from whippings he received on five occasions, and beatings with rods that he received on three occasions. He knew that even Jesus could only lead the way to God's new commonwealth through suffering, so he understood his own hardships as in some way sharing Christ's ongoing suffering. "Through many hardships you enter the commonwealth of God," he said.

In one of his letters, Paul wrote that when we suffer, we receive God's comfort, so we can pass that comfort on to others who suffer. Our hardships, he understood, increase our compassion.

Today: Pray, "God, help me see my hardships as a way to grow, and help me gain compassion for others through my experiences of suffering."

DAY THREE: *A Road of Hardship*

Paul loved to tell the story of how he first experienced the risen Christ over a three-day period and how from the start he knew that his path would involve suffering and hardship. The uprising had only been underway for about three years, and Saul—the name by which Paul was known back then—was its most passionate enemy. He hated the Way, as it was called back then. He became obsessed with stamping it out. He traveled around the region arresting and imprisoning women as well as men in the name of God and the Scriptures. On at least one occasion, he even took part in a religion-inspired murder.

Once, when he was on his way to Damascus to continue his bloody and hateful work, he was struck to the ground by a blinding light. He heard a voice saying, "Saul, Saul, why do you persecute me?" He asked who was speaking to him, and the voice said, "I am Jesus, the one you are persecuting. Now get up and go into the city and you will be shown what to do next." This shattering experience of spiritual insight left him unable to see physically, so he had to be led into Damascus by the hand. For three days he sat in darkness, unable to see. Obviously, he had a lot to think about.

A complete stranger named Ananias came to visit him. Ananias was a disciple, a follower of Jesus and the Way—exactly the kind of person Paul had come to Damascus to arrest, torture, and kill. Ananias could have killed his blind and defenseless enemy. Instead he spoke words of kindness to him. "Brother Saul," he said, "the Lord Jesus who appeared to you sent me to you so your sight could be restored and so you could be filled with the Holy Spirit." Ananias laid his hands on him and prayed for his vision to be restored.

When Paul opened his eyes, the first face he saw was that of Ananias. Ananias warned him that the road ahead would be full of hardship, and that was the case—for Paul, and for all of us on the Way.

Today: Think about the story of your spiritual life, and the role hardship has played in it. Be thankful for people like Ananias, who have played a role in your spiritual autobiography.

DAY FIVE: *Bitter or Better*

Paul had his share of the normal hardships of life: sickness, setbacks, delays, conflict, struggle. Once, for example, he survived a shipwreck only to get bitten by a venomous snake. Then there was the time he preached for so long that a young man got drowsy, dropped off to sleep, and fell out a second-story window. (Thankfully, that tragic story turned out okay in the end. In fact, after healing the victim of his long sermon, Paul went back and preached for several more hours.)

As Paul got older, he was constantly plagued by eye troubles and other aches and pains. Being under house arrest meant poor food, cold, restricted movement, and uncertainty about what the future might hold, which was an especially great risk with an unstable dictator as emperor. On a personal level, Paul felt deep regret about a break with two of his former friends, Barnabas and John Mark, and he carried a constant concern for the ecclesia spread out across the empire, the way a mother carries her children in her heart even after they're grown.

In the face of all this hardship, Paul admitted to getting depressed at times. But he said that it was only through hardship, through discouragement, through exhaustion, that he learned to draw on the power of God's Spirit within him. It was only when he came to the end of his own strength, and even then refused to give up, that he discovered the depths of God's strength available to him. "When we are weak," he said, "then we are strong."

Hardships can make us bitter...or better. They can lead to breakdown...or to breakthrough. If we don't give up at that breaking point when we feel we've reached the end of our own resources, we find a new aliveness, the life of the risen Christ rising within us. Paul described it like this: "I have been crucified with Christ. So it is no longer my prideful self who lives. Now it is Christ, alive in me."

Hardships not only teach us to live in dependence upon God, but they also teach us interdependence with others. Through hardship, we move from *me* to *we*. Paul's own story illustrated this fact: He discovered Christ not only in his vision, but also in Ananias. After Ananias, he met

Christ in the ecclesia in Damascus, in the ecclesia in Antioch, and in so many individuals, too—in women like Lydia, Prisca, and Julia, in men like Timothy and Titus...and yes, even Barnabas and John Mark, too.

Paul wasn't the least bit shy about speaking of his tenuous future. "The only thing ahead for me is imprisonment and persecution," he said. "But I don't count my life of any value to myself. My only ambition is to finish my course and fulfill the ministry the Lord Jesus has given me: to tell everyone everywhere about the good news of God's grace."

Today: Pray, "God, help me through my hardships to become better, not bitter. Help me to remain faithful and focused right to the end of my life."

DAY SIX: *Death Is Not the End*

At the same time the uprising was spreading across the Roman empire, unrest was building. The Zealots were planning an armed revolt in Jerusalem, to which the Roman military would respond with crushing force, reducing Jerusalem to ashes and rubble. In Rome itself, Emperor Nero was utterly powerful and utterly insane. He took sick pleasure in executing people on a whim, and Paul knew that any day, he could be his next entertainment. But Paul refused to complain. In fact, he couldn't stand complaining. Whatever happened, he would just keep rejoicing and singing and being grateful for each day, each breath, each heartbeat. "For me to live is Christ," he wrote. "But to die will be gain." Paul followed Jesus's example of enduring hardship and seeing joy beyond it, and in so doing, he has set an example for us today.

Paul didn't fear death, and when even death loses its sting, the hardships of life seem smaller and less threatening, too. To Paul, they couldn't compare with the glory that would someday be revealed.

Today: Think of unrest and danger in our world today, and then imagine that beyond this life, there is "an eternal weight of glory" waiting to be revealed. Let that greater glory put today's hardships and dangers in perspective.

IV

ALIVE IN THE SPIRIT
OF GOD

In the previous three sections of this book of daily reflections, we have placed ourselves in the story of creation, the adventure of Jesus, and God's peaceful uprising against the forces of fear, oppression, hostility, and violence. Jesus promised that the Holy Spirit would take the work he began and extend it across space and time, creating a global spiritual community to keep welcoming and embodying what he called the reign or kingdom or commonwealth of God.

In this final section, we ask this key question: How can we participate with the Spirit in this ongoing spiritual movement? That word *spiritual* means a lot of things, but for us, it will mean any experience of or response to the moving of the Spirit of God in our lives and in our world.

WEEK FORTY

THE SPIRIT IS MOVING!

Scripture Readings

John 3:1–21
Acts 2:1–41
Romans 6:1–14

Key Verses—John 3:7–8

"Do not be astonished that I said to you, 'You must be born from above.' The wind blows where it chooses, and you hear the sound of it, but you do not know where it comes from or where it goes. So it is with everyone who is born of the Spirit."

DAY ONE: *Right Here, in Here, Within*

Following Jesus today has much in common with the original disciples' experience. We are welcomed as disciples by God's grace, not by earning or status. We learn and practice Christ's teaching in the company of fellow learners. We seek to understand and imitate his example, and we commune with him around a table.

But there is an obvious and major difference between our experience and theirs: They could see Jesus and we can't. Surprisingly, according to John's gospel, that gives us an advantage. "It's better that I go away so the Spirit can come," Jesus said. If he were physically present and visible, our focus would be on Christ *over there, right there, out there*...but because of his absence, we discover the Spirit of Christ *right here, in here, within.*

Jesus describes the Spirit as *another* comforter, *another* teacher, *another* guide—just like him, but available to everyone, everywhere, always. The same Spirit who had descended like a dove upon him will descend upon us, he promises. The same Spirit who filled him will fill all who open their hearts.

Today: Pray, "Spirit of Christ, fill my life."

DAY TWO: *Paul's Vision of Life*

Paul never saw Jesus in the flesh, but he did experience the Spirit of Christ. That was enough to transform him from a proud and violent agitator of religious hostility to a tireless activist for peace and reconciliation. Through this experience of the Spirit, he seemed to live inside of Christ and look out through Christ's eyes upon the world. And the opposite was equally true: Through the Spirit, Christ lived inside of Paul and looked through Paul's eyes upon the world. "I in Christ" and "Christ in me"—that captures so much of Paul's vision of life.

For Paul, life in the Spirit means a threefold sharing in the death, burial, and resurrection of Jesus. First, as we turn from old habits and patterns, our "old self" with all its pride, greed, lust, anger, prejudice, and hostility dies with Christ. That former identity with all its hostilities is nailed to the cross and left behind. In this way, life in the Spirit involves a profound experience of *letting go* of what has been so far.

Then, Paul says, we join Jesus in the powerlessness and defeat of burial, symbolized by baptism. We experience that burial as a surrender to silence, stillness, powerlessness, emptiness, and rest, a *letting be.*

Then we join Jesus in the dynamic, surprising uprising of resurrection. The surrender, silence, emptiness, and rest of *letting go* and *letting be* make us receptive to something new. Like a vacuum, that receptivity welcomes infilling and activation…and so we experience a *letting come* of the Spirit of God.

Today: Carry in your heart the three movements of letting go, letting be, and letting come.

DAY THREE: *Spirit on the Move*

The Bible describes the Spirit with beautiful and vivid imagery: Wind. Breath. Fire. Cloud. Water. Wine. A dove. These dynamic word pictures contrast starkly with the heavy, fixed imagery provided by, say, stone idols, imposing temples, or thick theological tomes. Through this vivid imagery, the biblical writers tell us that the Spirit invigorates, animates, purifies, holds mystery, moves and flows, foments joy, and spreads peace.

For example, in the first chapter of Genesis, God's Spirit hovers over the primal waters like *wind*, creating beauty and novelty out of chaos. The Spirit then animates living creatures like *breath*. Then, in Exodus, God's Spirit appears as *fire* in the burning bush, beckoning Moses, and then as a pillar of *cloud and fire* moving across the wilderness, cooling by day and warming by night, and leading the way to freedom. Centuries later, when John the Baptist comes on the scene, he says that just as he immerses and marks people with *water*, his successor will immerse and mark people with the Spirit. When John baptizes Jesus, bystanders see the Spirit descending like a *dove* upon him. At the beginning of his ministry, Jesus dramatizes his mission by turning water, which is kept in stone containers used for religious ceremonies, into a huge quantity of *wine* to infuse joy at a wedding banquet. Later, he promises people that if they trust him, they will experience rivers of living *water* springing up from within.

At the core of Jesus's life and message, then, was this good news: The Spirit of God, the Spirit of aliveness, the Wind-breath-fire-cloud-water-wine-dove Spirit who filled Jesus, is on the move in our world. That gives us a choice: Do we dig in our heels, clench our fists, and live for our own agenda, or do we let go, let be, and let come...and so be taken up into the Spirit's movement?

Today: Imagine digging in your heels and clenching your fists, and then, instead, surrender yourself to be taken up into the movement of the Wind-breath-fire-cloud-water-wine-dove Spirit of God.

DAY FOUR: *Unity and Diversity in Harmony*

On the day of Pentecost, according to Luke, the disciples experienced the Spirit as "a mighty rushing wind" and fire. Suddenly, the Spirit-filled disciples began speaking in languages they had never learned. This strange sign is full of significance. The Spirit of God, it tells us, is multilingual. The Spirit isn't restricted to one elite language or one superior culture, as almost everyone had assumed with their nationalistic notions of God and religion. Instead, the Spirit speaks to everyone everywhere in his or her native tongue.

What happened at Pentecost reverses the ancient story of the Tower of Babel, when ambitious Babylonians grasped at godlike power by unifying everyone under one imperial language and culture. At Babel, God opposed that imperial uniformity and voted for diversity by multiplying languages. Now, in the Pentecost story, we discover a third option: not unity without diversity, and not diversity without unity, but unity and diversity in harmony.

Today: Picture "unity and diversity in harmony" sweeping into the world like "a mighty rushing wind" and fire.

DAY FIVE: *Hearts Incandescent*

In the millennia since Christ walked with us on this Earth, we've often tried to box up the "wind" in manageable doctrines. We've exchanged the fire of the Spirit for the ice of religious pride. We've turned the wine back into water, and then let the water go stagnant and lukewarm. We've traded the gentle dove of peace for the predatory hawk or eagle of empire.

When we have done so, we have ended up with just another religious system, as problematic as any other: too often petty, argumentative, judgmental, cold, hostile, bureaucratic, self-seeking, an enemy of aliveness.

In a world full of big challenges, in a time like ours, we can't settle for a heavy and fixed religion. We can't try to contain the Spirit in a box. We need to experience the mighty rushing wind of Pentecost. We need our hearts to be made incandescent by the Spirit's fire. We need the living water and new wine Jesus promised, so our hearts can become the home of dovelike peace.

Today: Strive to maintain a sense of the Spirit of peace, alive in you.

DAY SIX: *Are We Willing?*

Wind. Breath. Fire. Cloud. Water. Wine. A dove. When we open up space for the Spirit and let the Spirit fill that space within us, we begin to change, and we become agents of change. That's why we frequently pause in our journey to gather together around a table of fellowship and communion. Like the disciples in the upper room at Pentecost, we present ourselves to God. We become receptive for the fullness of the Spirit to fall upon us and well up within us, to blow like wind, glow like fire, flow like a river, fill like a cloud, and descend like a dove in and among us. So let us open our hearts. Let us dare believe that the Spirit that we read about in the Scriptures can move among us today, empowering us in our times so we can become agents in a global spiritual movement of justice, peace, and joy.

So are we ready? Are we willing to die with Christ? Are we willing to *let go*?

And are we willing to be buried with Christ? Are we willing to *let be*?

And are we willing to rise with Christ? Can we inhale, open our emptiness, unlock that inner vacuum, for the Spirit to enter and fill—like wind, breath, fire, cloud, water, wine, and a dove? Are we willing to *let come*?

Let it be so. Let it be now. Amen.

Today: In the presence and power of the Holy Spirit, pray throughout the day, "Let it be so. Let it be now. Amen."

WEEK FORTY-ONE

MOVING WITH
THE SPIRIT

Scripture Readings

> John 15:1–8
> Galatians 3:19–4:7; 5:1, 13–26
> Colossians 2:6–7; 3:1–17

Key Verses—Colossians 3:16–17

Let the word of Christ dwell in you richly; teach and admonish one another in all wisdom; and with gratitude in your hearts sing psalms, hymns, and spiritual songs to God. And whatever you do, in word or deed, do everything in the name of the Lord Jesus, giving thanks to God the Father through him.

DAY ONE: *Changing Our Desires*

The wind can be blowing, but if your sail isn't raised, you won't go far. You can be surrounded by oxygen, but if you don't breathe, it won't do you any good. The sap can be flowing, but if a branch isn't connected to the vine, it will wither. If you don't have kindling and wood in your hearth, a lit match won't burn long. It's the same with the Spirit. We are surrounded with the aliveness of the Spirit. All that remains is for us to learn how to let the Spirit fill, flow, and glow within us.

We start in the heart—the wellspring of our desires. That's where our problems begin, and that's where our healing begins, too. When we desire to be filled with the Spirit, the Spirit begins to transform our desires so that God's desires become our own. Instead of doing the right thing because we *have* to, we do the right thing because we *want* to— because we are learning to truly desire goodness. Once our desires are being changed, a revolution is set in motion.

Today: Imagine raising the sail of your soul to God's Spirit.

DAY TWO: *Walking*

The New Testament gives us a simple image for how desire translates into action: *walking*. When we were newborn, we couldn't even roll over, much less crawl, much less walk and run. Eventually, a desire for movement stirred within us, and we gradually and clumsily translated that desire into action—first rolling over, then crawling, then standing and toddling, and eventually walking. Step by step, with lots of stumbles and falls, we eventually mastered the art of translating our desire into movement. And so now, with hardly a thought, we walk, we run, we jump, we dance.

This image of walking is everywhere in the Scriptures. Walk in the Spirit, we are told. Walk in the light. Walk in love. Walk in newness of life. Walk by faith. Walk in good works. Walk in truth. To be a disciple is to follow a mentor, which means walking in the mentor's footsteps. The image is simple...one step at a time, drawn by desire, leaning forward, doing the next right thing, keeping our focus on our goal, leaving the past behind. If you stumble, regain your balance and keep walking. If you fall, get up again and keep walking. If you're distracted or wander off the path, reorient yourself toward your goal and keep walking.

Today: Whenever you walk today, do so mindfully, recalling and embodying the rich imagery of walking in Scripture.

DAY THREE: *Vivid Images*

Jesus used another vivid image to convey how spiritual aliveness grows in us: a branch abiding in a vine. If the branch were to separate itself from the vine, it would wither and die. But if it simply stays connected, the vine's aliveness flows into the branch and bears fruit through it. Likewise, if we abide or remain in vital connection to Christ, the Spirit will flow with God's aliveness in and through us, making us both beautiful and fruitful.

Paul employed several similar images. Stir up the fire in you, he said to his young protégé, Timothy. Just as fires need to be tended, our inner life needs to be tended, too. In his letter to the Colossians, he used the image of welcoming a guest, making room in our hearts so the Spirit of Christ can "dwell in us richly." In Ephesians, he made an analogy to drinking wine. Just as drinking your fill of alcoholic spirits can change your behavior for the worse, being filled with the Holy Spirit will change your behavior for the better.

Today: Choose one of these images and pause to meditate on it throughout the day.

DAY FOUR: *Walking in the Spirit*

If you want to gain practice walking in the Spirit or abiding in Christ or tending the inner flame, you can start when you wake up tomorrow morning. Before your feet hit the floor, open your heart to the Spirit. Ask God to help you walk in the Spirit, step by step through the day. Ask God to help you abide in the vine so good fruit will naturally develop in your life. Ask God to keep the fire burning within you. Just starting the day this way will make a difference.

As you build that habit of yielding yourself to the Spirit morning by morning, you can build the habit of checking in with the Spirit hour by hour throughout the day. At each mealtime, you can offer a prayer of thanksgiving and you can reconnect with the Spirit. As you travel from place to place, as you wait for someone, whenever you have a free moment, you can offer yourself to God: "Here I am, Lord. Please move in and through me to bless others." Whenever an emergency or challenge arises, you can lean on the Spirit: "Give me wisdom, Spirit of God. Give me strength. Give me patience." When you sense that you've let something other than God's Spirit fill you and direct you—anger, fear, prejudice, lust, greed, anxiety, pride, inferiority, or rivalry, for example— you can stop, acknowledge your misstep, and resurrender to the Spirit. It's like breathing—exhaling an acknowledgment of your misstep and inhaling forgiveness and strength to start walking in the Spirit again.

At the end of the day, you can look back with gratitude, resting in the Spirit until a new day begins and you continue walking the journey of faith.

Today: Begin experimenting with the check-ins described in today's reading.

DAY FIVE: *We Walk*

As we walk in the Spirit, we pass through different kinds of terrain. We walk through beautiful valleys where life is full of joy and we feel like dancing. We walk on long, uphill climbs where we seem to slide back two steps for every three steps of ascent. We walk along slippery trails where it's easy to fall and through swampy patches where we can get bogged down. We walk through dark passages where we can easily lose our way and across flat terrain where nothing seems to change mile after mile. We walk through dangerous territory where bullets fly and it's easy to get wounded, and in peaceful places where we can breathe free. Through it all, we need patience, endurance, and perseverance so that no matter what happens, we'll keep putting one foot ahead of the other.

Today: Notice the kinds of terrain—physical and spiritual—you pass through today.

DAY SIX: *Sharing Our Stories*

If we don't give up, as mile adds to mile, each of us will have some stories to tell…stories of how the Spirit guided, empowered, inspired, restrained, sustained, and trained us in the fine art of aliveness. And that's another great blessing of being part of a community of faith. Along the way, we gather around a table or campfire and share our stories about the journey so far. We share our joys and sorrows. We share mistakes we've made and falls we've taken and lessons we've learned. We share ways in which we've experienced the Spirit moving in us, among us, and through us. Through this sharing, we encourage each other. And then we get back on the road.

Today: Get together (or schedule a get-together) with a trusted "soul friend" with whom you can share some stories from your journey, joys and sorrow, mistakes and falls and lessons…and listen to theirs as well.

DAY SEVEN: *Let's Keep Moving*

Sadly, over time, lots of people who began walking in the Spirit get distracted and lose their way. Instead of continuing to walk in the Spirit, they slow down to look back proudly on how far they've come. They become highly impressed by all they've learned: theological concepts, Bible lore, religious history, and so on. Pretty soon, they come to a standstill and brag among themselves, comparing themselves to others who haven't walked as far or fast or cleverly as they have. They form little encampments, sitting around day after day, quarreling about this or that fine point of walking theory. Pretty soon they're so out of shape they give up walking altogether and specialize in talking about the way others walk.

That's their choice. But for us...let's keep walking. Let's keep on the road. However far we've come, there's far more ahead to explore. The Spirit is on the move, so let us keep moving, too.

Today: Each time you're tempted to criticize someone else's "walking," refocus on your own path and how far you have to go.

WEEK FORTY-TWO

SPIRIT OF LOVE: LOVING GOD

Scripture Readings

Psalm 116
Romans 8:1–17
Ephesians 3:14–21

Key Verses—Psalm 116:1–2

I love the Lord, because he has heard
my voice and my supplications.
Because he inclined his ear to me,
therefore I will call on him as long as I live.

DAY ONE: *A Name of Something Ugly*

Wherever God's Spirit is at work in the world, people are drawn more deeply to love...beginning with loving God.

Of course, we must acknowledge that the word *God* has become a big problem for a lot of people. How can they love a God who is an angry old white man with a beard, oppressing women and minorities, promoting discrimination and war, and blessing the destruction of the planet? How can they love the curator of a religious museum who seems to have a taste for all that is outdated, archaic, dour, and dusty? How can they love the host of an unending religious broadcast where everyone is always artificially smiling and excessively, unrealistically happy, desperate for you to send in your next generous financial contribution? How can they love a testy border guard who won't let new arrivals through heaven's passport control office unless they correctly answer a lot of technical doctrinal questions with a score of 100 percent?

Hot-headed religious extremists, lukewarm religious bureaucrats, and cold-hearted religious critics alike have turned the word *God* into a name for something ugly, small, boring, elitist, wacky, corrupt, or violent—the very opposite of what it should mean. Maybe God is more turned off to the word *God* than anyone else! And maybe the distaste of many for the word *God* as it is commonly used actually reveals a corresponding love that longs for what God truly is.

Today: In light of how the word *God* has been corrupted and reduced, try to think of fresh ways of addressing "the One frequently called God."

DAY TWO: *Moving Toward*

Whatever ember of love for goodness flickers within us, however feeble or small...that's what the Spirit works with, until that spark glows warmer and brighter. From the tiniest beginning, our whole lives—our whole hearts, minds, souls, and strength—can be set aflame with love for God.

Even those of us who have always believed in God's existence and never had any big problems with the word *God*...when it comes to actually loving God, we can feel a little intimidated. We don't know where to begin.

But really, it's not so different from loving another human being.

When we speak of loving another human being, we naturally move toward that person in a special way. We appreciate the qualities of the beloved. We respect and honor the beloved's dignity. We enjoy the beloved's company and feel curious about the beloved's personhood. We want to support the beloved's dreams and desires. And we make ourselves available for the beloved to respect, honor, enjoy, know, and support us, too, because to be "in love" is to be in a mutual relationship.

Today: Practice moving toward God in your heart.

DAY THREE: *Showing Up*

When we learn to love God, we appreciate God's qualities. We honor and respect God's dignity. We enjoy God's presence and are curious to know more and more of God's heart. We support God's dreams coming true. And we want to be appreciated, honored, enjoyed, known, and supported as well—to surrender ourselves to God in mutuality.

It all begins with moving toward God, taking a first step by simply showing up, becoming aware of God's presence and presenting ourselves to God. It's as simple as saying, "God, here I am," or "God, here you are," or even better, "God, here we are, together."

A second step is appreciation. Sometimes we take a spouse, child, parent, or friend for granted. Then some shock or threat occurs—an accident, a disease, or an argument through which they are nearly taken from us. Suddenly, we appreciate afresh this precious person we've been taking for granted. If we don't want to take God for granted, we can express gratitude and appreciation for what it means to have God in our lives. That's why many of us try to begin each day and each meal with a prayer of thankful appreciation—it's a way of being sure we don't take God and God's blessings for granted. If the simple word *here* helps us show up, the simple word *thanks* can help us with appreciation.

We all know that we do the opposite of loving God sometimes. We remain aloof or preoccupied, we complain instead of appreciate, and we ignore or disrespect rather than honor God. That's where a fourth step comes in: learning to say we're sorry and to express to God our regrets. When we say and mean a simple sentence like "I'm sorry" or "Lord, have mercy," we move toward God again, receiving forgiveness and renewing our loving connection.

Today: Use some simple phrase ("Here we are, together," or "Thanks," or "Lord, have mercy") to help you "show up" with God.

DAY FOUR: *Supporting Dreams*

If love means supporting the beloved's dreams and plans, we love God by expressing our support for what God desires. We express this support whenever we pray, "May your kingdom come. May your will be done on Earth as it is in heaven." We do so whenever we come to God in empathetic concern for others, joining our compassion with God's compassion for those in need, sorrow, or pain. By refusing to allow numbness or hardness of heart to gain a foothold in our lives, we keep our hearts aligned with God's heart, and in this way, express love for God. Sometimes, holding up the name or face of a person in God's presence, simply breathing the words "please help him" or "please bless her" can be a way of loving God by loving those God loves.

If love is about mutuality, love also means opening ourselves for God to support our dreams and desires. In that way, every time we cry out, "Help me, Lord!" we are expressing love for God. Why that is the case becomes obvious when we consider the opposite. Imagine shutting out a friend, parent, or spouse from our need, sorrow, or pain. Imagine never asking for help. That would be a sign of indifference and distrust, not love. Opening ourselves to God when we're in need says that we trust God and want God to accompany us, support us, and befriend us in every way.

We trust those we love most with our deepest fears, doubts, emptiness, and disillusionment. We love God when we share those vulnerable aspects of our lives with God. Just as a little child in the middle of a temper tantrum can shout "I hate you, Mommy!" only because he knows his outburst will not end their relationship, we can express to God our deep doubts, anger, or frustrations only because we possess an even deeper trust in God's love. At times, then, our hearts cry out, "When, Lord? How long, Lord?" or "Why?" or even "No!" But the fact that we share this pain with God rather than withhold it turns out to be an expression of love.

Today: Open your heart to the Spirit by saying, "I support your dreams," and be aware that your dreams are supported, too.

DAY FIVE: *To Love and Be Loved*

Imagine an elderly couple who have loved each other through a long lifetime or an adult child sitting at the bedside of a dying parent. Often, their love is expressed most powerfully by presence and touch, not by words. Simply being together, holding hands, smiling, sitting close in mutual enjoyment—these are profound expressions of love, beyond words. Something like this develops over time in our relationship with God.

Like one tuning fork that resonates effortlessly with another, we release our whole being to resonate with the love, grace, and joy of God. We feel a habitual attentiveness to God that spontaneously smiles or reaches out in an affectionate touch—without obligation, without trying, without even thinking. No words are necessary as we simply and deeply enjoy being together here and now. We are not alone. We are loved. We love.

Remembering our true identity in the family of creation, being rooted and grounded in love, we experience the multidimensional love of Christ that surpasses all knowledge, and we are filled with the very fullness of God. In that fullness, we simply breathe, be, and let be. This is life in the Spirit, being in love, with God—true aliveness indeed.

Today: Find a place where you can sit silently in God's presence...simply breathe, be, and let be.

WEEK FORTY-THREE

SPIRIT OF LOVE:
LOVING NEIGHBOR

Scripture Readings

Acts 10:1–48
I Corinthians 13:1–13

Key Verses—I Corinthians 13:12–13

*For now we see in a mirror, dimly, but then we will see face to face. Now I
know only in part; then I will know fully, even as I have been fully known.
And now faith, hope, and love abide, these three; and the greatest of these is love.*

DAY ONE: *Who Is Our Neighbor?*

Where the Spirit is moving, love for God always, always, always overflows in love for neighbor. And according to Jesus, our neighbor isn't just the person who is like us, the person who likes us, or the person we like. Our neighbor is anyone and everyone, like us or different from us, friend or stranger—even enemy. As Peter learned in his encounter with Cornelius, the Spirit wants to break down walls of prejudice and hostility so that we stop judging *us* as clean and *them* as unclean, opening the way for strangers and enemies to become neighbors, friends, family.

Today: Wherever you go, when you see people, identify them to yourself as, "My neighbor. My relation."

DAY TWO: *A New Way*

It's time to find a better way to live together on a crowded planet. It's time to graduate from thinking in terms of "our kind versus their kind" to thinking in terms of "humankind." It's time to turn from the ways of our ancestors and stop trying to kill off, subjugate, or fend off everyone we judge different and dangerous. It's time for a new approach, to make a new road, to pioneer a new way of living as neighbors in one human community, as brothers and sisters in one family of creation.

Today: Say to yourself, "It's time," and recall the message of today's reading.

DAY THREE: *Unity Energized by Diversity*

The apostle Paul repeatedly describes how in Christ we see humanity as one body and our differences as gifts, not threats, to one another. In Christ, Paul came to realize that people aren't different because they're trying to be difficult or evil; they're different because the Spirit has given them differing gifts. Just as a foot needs an eye to tell it where to step, and just as a nose needs a hand to grasp the food it smells, and just as feet, eyes, noses, and hands all need kidneys and bones and skin…we humans need other humans who are different from ourselves. The Spirit of God, we learn, is a team spirit, and in the holy team Spirit, we experience a unity that is energized by diversity.

Today: As you notice people, ask yourself, "What unique gifts have they been given to share with others?"

DAY FOUR: *A New Fuel*

All our social groups don't need to wear the same paint and feathers, speak the same language, cook with the same spices, and celebrate the same religious holidays. But all our social groups—nations, religions, cultures, parties—need to convert from what we might call dirty energy to clean energy to fuel our tribal life. True, the dirty energy of fear, prejudice, supremacy, inferiority, resentment, isolation, and hostility is cheap, abundant, and familiar. That's why our societies run on it, even though it's destroying us. More than ever before in our history, we need a new kind of personal and social fuel. Not fear, but love. Not prejudice, but openness. Not supremacy, but service. Not inferiority, but equality. Not resentment, but reconciliation. Not isolation, but connection. Not the spirit of hostility, but the holy Spirit of hospitality.

Today: Monitor what is fueling you throughout the day: clean fuel or dirty fuel?

DAY FIVE: *Majoring in Love*

There is a "most excellent way," Paul said. It is the way of love. Old markers of gender, religion, culture, and class must recede: "There is neither Jew nor Gentile, slave nor free, male nor female, for you are all one in Christ Jesus." Old in/out social indicators, he says, count for nothing: "the only thing that counts is faith working through love." Where the Spirit is, love is. Where the Spirit teaches, people learn love. Faith communities at their best are Spirit-schools of love, engaging everyone, from little children to great grandparents, in lifelong learning. In the school of the Spirit, everyone majors in love.

Today: Whenever you see yourself in a mirror today, say: "I am a student in the school of love."

DAY SIX: *One Another*

If love remains a generality, it's just a word. That's why the New Testament is serious about translating love into practical, specific, concrete, down-to-earth action. Because each of us has something to give and much to receive, the term *one another* keeps popping up on page after page of the New Testament. These "one-anothers" tell us what the prime directive—*love one another*—looks like in action:

1. "Love one another as I have loved you." (John 13:34; John 15:12, 17; Rom. 13:8; I Thess. 4:9; Heb. 13:1; I Pet. 1:22, I Pet. 3:8, I Pet. 4:8; I John 3:11, 23; I John 4:7, 11; 2 John 1:5)

2. "Wash one another's feet…serve one another in love." (John 13:14, Gal. 5:13)

3. "Be at peace with each other." (Mark 9:50, I Thess. 5:13, I Pet. 3:8)

4. "Be devoted to one another with mutual affection." (Rom. 12:10)

5. "Honor one another above yourselves." (Rom. 12:10)

6. "Live in harmony with one another." (Rom. 12:16)

7. "Stop passing judgment on one another." (Rom. 14:13)

8. "Accept one another as Christ accepted you." (Rom. 15:7)

9. "Greet one another with a holy kiss." (Rom. 16:16, I Cor. 16:20, 2 Cor. 13:12, I Pet. 5:14)

10. "Agree with one another so that there may be no divisions among you and that you may be perfectly united in mind and thought." (I Cor. 1:10)

11. "When you come together to eat, wait for each other." (I Cor. 11:33)

12. "But God has combined the members of the body and has given greater honor to the parts that lacked it, so that there should be no division in the body, but that its parts should have equal concern for each other." (I Cor. 12:24–25)

13. "Let us not become conceited, provoking and envying each other." (Gal. 5:26)
14. "Carry each other's burdens, and in this way you will fulfill the law of Christ." (Gal. 6:2)
15. "Be completely humble and gentle; be patient, bearing with one another in love." (Eph. 4:2, Col. 3:13)
16. "Be kind and compassionate to one another, forgiving each other, just as in Christ God forgave you." (Eph. 4:32, Col. 3:13, I Thess. 5:15)
17. "Submit to one another out of reverence for Christ." (Eph. 5:21)
18. "Do not lie to each other." (Col. 3:9)
19. "Let the word of Christ dwell in you richly as you teach and admonish one another with all wisdom, and as you sing psalms, hymns, and spiritual songs with gratitude in your hearts to God." (Eph. 5:19, Col. 3:16)
20. "Therefore encourage one another and build each other up." (I Thess. 5:11, Heb. 3:13)
21. "And let us consider how we may spur one another on toward love and good deeds. Let us not give up meeting together...but let us encourage one another." (Heb. 10:24–25)
22. "Brothers and sisters, do not slander one another." (James 4:11)
23. "Don't grumble against each other." (James 5:9)
24. "Therefore confess your sins to each other and pray for each other so that you may be healed." (James 5:16)
25. "Offer hospitality to one another without grumbling." (I Pet. 4:9)
26. "Clothe yourselves with humility toward one another." (I Pet. 5:5)

For all of us who want to be part of the movement of God's Spirit in our world, there is no more important and essential pursuit than love.

That's why we walk this road. That's why we seek to improve our fluency and grace in "one-anothering"—especially with people who seem very different from us. For in the story of creation, in the adventure and uprising of Jesus, and in the movement of the Spirit, to love is to live.

Today: Look for opportunities to practice these "one anothers."

WEEK FORTY-FOUR

SPIRIT OF LOVE: LOVING SELF

Scripture Readings

Proverbs 4:1–27
Romans 12:3–21
James 1:2–8; 3:13–18

Key Verses—Proverbs 4:5–7

Get wisdom; get insight: do not forget, nor turn away
from the words of my mouth.
Do not forsake her, and she will keep you;
love her, and she will guard you.
The beginning of wisdom is this: Get wisdom,
and whatever else you get, get insight.

DAY ONE: *Pro-Pleasure*

If love for God is always linked with love for others, and if we are to love others *as we love ourselves*, what does it mean to love ourselves? Could the Spirit of God teach us a holy and healthy kind of self-love?

Of course, advertisers and politicians often tempt us to become more *selfish* or *self-centered*—our doing so is often in their *self-interest*. But the Spirit teaches us a profoundly different way of loving ourselves— a way of maturity that involves self-examination, self-control, self-development, and self-giving. These practices of mature self-care enable us to love God and others more fully and joyfully.

Now, our struggles with self are often struggles with pleasure, for the self is, among other things, a pleasure-seeking entity.

Pleasure, of course, was originally the Creator's idea. By giving us taste, smell, sound, sight, and touch, God was making possible an amazing array of pleasures: from eating to sex, from music to sport, from painting to gardening, from dance to travel. Human pleasure is a good and beautiful creation, mirroring, it would seem, a great capacity for enjoyment that exists in God. We are told that God takes pleasure in creation and in us, something all parents, teachers, and artists understand in relation to their children, students, and works of art. So again and again in the Bible, we are reminded that our Creator has given us all things to enjoy richly, and that in God's presence is fullness of joy. The Creator is definitely pro-pleasure.

Today: Notice what experiences give you pleasure.

DAY TWO: *Learning to Say No*

If God is so pro-pleasure, why do we find so many warnings and rules about pleasure in the Bible? Those rules make sense when you realize how easily all life's great pleasures—food, drink, sex, owning, winning, resting, playing, working—can become addictive and destructive. When we indulge in pleasures without self-examination or self-control, great pleasure can quickly lead to great pain—for the addicts themselves and for those whose lives are touched by their addiction.

So rules about pleasures have an important place. The desire center within us that demands "what I want, when I want it, as much as I want" can all too easily become an addictive dictator. We all need to learn to say, "No, that's not right," or "No, this isn't the right time," or "No, that's enough for now." Without wise rules and that basic level of self-control to follow them, we'll all be stuck in childish, selfish, self-destructive, and even suicidal immaturity.

Today: Notice times when you say "no" (or should have said "no") to potentially problematic pleasures.

Living by rules—"law" in the Bible—is important, but it's only a beginning. At best, it's like primary school.

Primary school has its place, but if we're never allowed to graduate to secondary school, it feels like a prison. So when we're ready, the Spirit always leads us to graduate from rule-oriented primary school to secondary school with its new emphasis: wisdom. From basic questions like *Is this right or wrong, legal or illegal?* we graduate to questions of wisdom: *Will this help or hinder me in reaching my highest goals? Where will this lead short-, medium-, and long-term? What unintended consequences might it entail? Who might be hurt by this? Are there better alternatives? Is now the best time? Should I seek wise counsel before moving forward?*

Today: Ask yourself the questions of wisdom.

DAY FOUR: *What Wisdom Does*

Wisdom helps us see how a hasty purchase of a desired indulgence can lead to the long-term pressure of debt. Wisdom reminds us that a one-night sexual liaison can lead to lasting tragic consequences for both parties, plus their spouses, children, parents, and many others—literally for generations to come. Wisdom knows that a single ill-advised business shortcut to increase profits can ruin a reputation earned over decades—as can one careless sentence spoken in anger or dishonesty. Wisdom remembers that habitual overindulgence in alcohol, drugs, tobacco, or even food can greatly shorten your life. And wisdom warns that even one night of drunkenness or one outburst of anger can end your life and the lives of others. Wisdom guides us to see beyond life's immediate pleasures to potential consequences that are less obvious and less pleasant.

Wisdom also helps us see how excessively denying ourselves pleasure can itself become unwise. For example, if a mom and dad are so exhausted from the work of parenting that they forget to keep their romance alive, they can drift apart even though they're sleeping under the same roof. Wisdom guides them to nurture their romance and sexuality so they'll be less vulnerable to infidelity—and so their family will stay in a sustainable, healthy, life-giving balance. The same goes for someone who loves his work and gets great pleasure from it. If he works too much, his life will fall out of balance…and soon he will hate his work. A wise person learns that he must find pleasures outside of work so that his work will remain pleasurable rather than addictive. A wise person in this way practices self-care, sometimes stepping on the brakes and sometimes stepping on the accelerator of pleasure.

Today: Pray, "Spirit of Wisdom, help me grow in wisdom!"

We all need wisdom to know our limits and keep our balance, to know when to say yes and when to say "That's enough" or "That's unwise" or "This isn't the right time." We need wisdom to know when to ask for help—from a friend or professional—when we are in over our heads. We need wisdom to monitor the difference between legitimate desires and dangerous temptations. We even need wisdom to keep different kinds of pleasure in a healthy and sustainable balance. As a wise teacher said, "Watch over your heart with all diligence, for from it flow the springs of life" (Proverbs 4:23, NASB).

After all, nobody is more likely to ruin your life than you. By pursuing wisdom, you get out of your own way. You learn to be a friend to yourself instead of your own worst enemy. You learn self-examination, self-control, self-development, and self-care—so you can better practice true self-giving toward God and others. Rules are good, wisdom is better, and love is best of all.

Could this be a central purpose of the universe—to provide an environment in which self-control, wisdom, and love can emerge and evolve? Could this be a central purpose in our lives—to mature in self-control, wisdom, and love? And could this be a central purpose of religion and spirituality—to multiply contagious examples of maturity, to create communities where the more mature can mentor others, to build a global Spirit movement toward individual and collective maturity?

Today: Aspire to be a "contagious example of maturity."

DAY SIX: *The Spirit's Love*

So. You have this self. What you do with it matters a lot. You can be self-absorbed, self-contained, self-centered, selfish, self-consumed—and your closed-in self will stagnate, spoil, and deteriorate over time. Or you can engage in Spirit-guided self-examination, self-control, self-development, and self-giving—and your self will open and mature into a person of great beauty and Christlike maturity.

God, it turns out, isn't a divine killjoy. God wants you to love you the way God loves you, so you can join God in the one self-giving love that upholds you and all creation. If you trust your self to that love, you will become the best self you can be, thriving in aliveness, full of deep joy, part of the beautiful whole. That's the kind of self-care and love of self that is good, right, wise, and necessary. And that's one more reason we walk this road together: to journey ever deeper into the beautiful mystery of the Spirit's love. There we find God. There we find our neighbor. And there we find ourselves.

Today: Draw near to God as the "one self-giving love that upholds me and all creation."

SPIRIT OF UNITY AND DIVERSITY

Scripture Readings

Proverbs 8:1–36
John 17:1–23
Ephesians 4:1–16

Key Verses—John 17:22–23

The glory that you have given me I have given them, so that they may be one, as we are one, I in them and you in me, that they may become completely one, so that the world may know that you have sent me and have loved them even as you have loved me.

DAY ONE: *Trinity*

In the centuries after Jesus walked this Earth, theologians and mystics who reflected on Jesus's life and teaching were faced with a paradox. They agreed there was only one God as their tradition had taught. But the oneness of the Creator wasn't as flat or static as they had assumed. In Christ and through the Spirit, they came to see that God's unity was so deep and dynamic that it included diversity. This diversity didn't compromise God's unity but made it more beautiful and wonderful. Over time, they tried to describe this mysterious paradox. After much dialogue and debate, a radically new understanding and teaching about God emerged. They had to create a new term to convey it: *Trinity*.

First, through Jesus and his good news they had come to know and relate to God in a parental way. Like a parent, God was the source of all creation, the giver of all life and existence. God's parental love held all creation in a family relationship. This parental givingness, this reproductive creativity and fertility, this primal motherly and fatherly generosity, they called *God the Father*. There were reasons they only rarely used *motherhood* to describe God back then. Were they here today, they would probably include both *motherhood* and *fatherhood* and speak of God's parental love.

Second, in Jesus they came to see a childness in God, a givenness of the child-life corresponding to the givingness of the parent-life. If God the Father gave of God's self, the self-gift was simultaneously God and an offspring, or self-gift, of God. If God the Creator was self-expressive, the self-expression, or Word, was simultaneously God and the Word, or expression, of God. This primal givenness, self-outpouring, or expressivity they called *God the Son* or *God the Word*.

Through Jesus and his good news, they had also experienced a third reality: the loving, harmonious Spirit that flowed in and between and out from the first and the second. This loving and unifying presence, this primal harmony, this deep, joyful, contagious communion they called *God the Spirit*.

Today: Open your mind and heart to wider, deeper understandings of God.

DAY TWO: *The Mystery of One-Another*

Trinitarian talk sounds highly speculative, but it was a sincere attempt to put into words the radical way Christian thinkers in the first several centuries were rethinking and freshly experiencing God in the aftermath of their experience of Jesus. By God's parental love, through Christ's beautiful life, death, and uprising, and through the Holy Spirit, they felt that they had been caught up into this divine communion themselves. God could never again be for them a distant, isolated One to whom they were "the other." Now they knew God as a dynamic and hospitable one-another in whom they lived, moved, and had their being. The Trinity described how they experienced God "from the inside."

Because they had been trained in Greek philosophy as well as in the Bible, of course they used philosophical language in their deliberations. Sometimes they overestimated the capacity of their philosophical terms to capture God's unfathomable depths. When they erred in this way, they grew proud and used the new teaching of the Trinity as a weapon. But at their best, they remained humble and awestruck by the realization that God was a mystery so big and deep and beautiful that human words could never fully contain it. Like fingers, words could point up and out and in to God, but they could never grasp God like a flipped coin caught in a clenched fist. When they spoke from this humility and awe, the teaching of the Trinity brought healing—reminding us that the word *doctrine* and the word *doctor* share a common root.

Today: Cultivate humility and awe in the presence of mysteries too big and deep to be captured in words.

DAY THREE: *A Kind and Caring Parent*

The healing teaching of Trinity began unleashing a revolution that is still unfolding today in at least five distinct but related ways.

First, the teaching of the Trinity leads us beyond *violent* understandings of God. The many Greek and Roman gods of ancient tradition were, truth be told, a gang of overgrown adolescents who had more power than moral maturity. They were competitive and egotistical projections of human nature, glorious and gracious one minute, vindictive and cruel the next. But now, imagine the shift when we understand our source and destiny not as a rivalrous gang but as a loving, nonviolent community.

This insight was revolutionary, because even the Supreme Being of monotheism was often seen as the violent patron of one nation, religion, and culture. Such a Supreme Being typically ruled by instilling fear, making threats, and crushing the noncompliant. But again, imagine the change when our vision of God shifts from a violent dictator to a kind and caring parent who loves all and wants the best for all. Imagine how in the Son, or Word, we see God as one who identifies, serves, and suffers with creation as Christ did, who would rather be tortured and killed than torture or kill. Then, imagine how the image of a violent commander sending us into the world to wage war is eclipsed by the image of a gentle, healing, reconciling, purifying, empowering Spirit who descends upon us like a dove. A healing teaching indeed!

Today: See yourself being sent into the world to wage peace and healing.

DAY FOUR: *To a Dancing God*

The healing teaching of Trinity leads us beyond *fixed* or *frozen* understandings of God. After all, if God in Christ surprised us once, showing us we had a lot left to learn, shouldn't we expect more surprises? If Jesus told us the Spirit would guide us into more truth when we were ready to bear it, shouldn't we expect to learn more whenever we can bear more? And so the old image fades of God as a removed and unmoved mover, static, fixed, and frozen. In its place, we see God as a whirling, intimate, glorious dance of eternal, creative, joyful movement. What a revolution!

Today: Pray, "God, keep me open to new surprises!"

DAY FIVE: *Us and Them United*

Through the Trinity we transcend *us–them, in–out thinking*. Imprisoned in our old familiar dualistic thinking, we were always dividing the world into *mine* and *yours, one* and *other, same* and *different, better* and *worse*. In the Trinity, we move beyond that dualism so that *mine* and *yours* are reconciled into *ours*. *One* and *other* are transformed into *one another*. *Same* and *different* are harmonized without being homogenized or colonized. *Us* and *them* are united without loss of identity and without dividing walls of hostility. To put it in philosophical terms, dualism doesn't regress to monism. Dualism is transcended and included in something wider and deeper.

Today: Look for dualism—us versus them, in versus out, good guys versus bad guys—and look for a vantage point where the two opposites can be transcended and included.

DAY SIX: *Equality, Empathy, Generosity*

The healing teaching of Trinity also helps us transcend *top-down* or *hierarchical* understandings of God. If God's Father-ness elevates and includes Son-ness in full equality, do you see what that means? If God's Son-ness doesn't grasp at equality, but rather mirrors the Father's self-giving and self-emptying love, do you see what that means? If the Spirit is not subordinated as inferior but is honored and welcomed as equal, do you see what that means? God is characterized by equality, empathy, and generosity rather than subordination, patriarchy, and hierarchy.

Today: Hold equality, empathy, and generosity in your mind and heart.

DAY SEVEN: *Holiness Perfects Imperfection*

Our ancestors assumed that God's holiness would be polluted by any contact with imperfection, so in their minds, God was *exclusive* and unwilling to associate with any imperfection. But Jesus, in his habit of eating with "sinners," gave us a new vision of God. God's holiness is drawn to unholiness the way a doctor is drawn to disease. Rather than catching disease, God's holiness "infects" the sick with a chronic case of regenerating health. Rather than being polluted by association with imperfection, God's holiness perfects imperfection. In this way, the healing teaching of Trinity undermines *exclusivist* understandings of God, presenting us with a God who doesn't reject imperfection but embraces it, and in so doing, perfects it and makes it holy.

Sadly, too often our forbears wielded a warped and jagged understanding of the Trinity as a weapon. In so doing, they reinforced violent, static, dualist, hierarchical, and exclusive understandings of God. But it's still not too late. If we open our hearts, we can feel the Spirit guiding us now to let the healing teaching of the Trinity continue its joyful revolution. Perhaps we are now ready to bear it…and to dare to practice it. Because if God is not violent, static, dualist, hierarchical, or exclusive, neither should we be.

To join the movement of the Spirit is to let our Trinitarian tradition continue to live, learn, and grow…so the hostile one-versus-otherness of Earth can become more like the hospitable one-anotherness of heaven. From beginning to end, the Spirit leads us into vibrant diversity and joyful unity in beautiful harmony.

Today: See God's presence as a chronic case of regenerating health.

WEEK FORTY-SIX

SPIRIT OF SERVICE

Scripture Readings

Matthew 23:1–12
John 13:1–15
Philippians 2:1–11

Key Verses—Philippians 2:3–5

Do nothing from selfish ambition or conceit, but in humility regard others as better than yourselves. Let each of you look not to your own interests, but to the interests of others. Let the same mind be in you that was in Christ Jesus . . .

DAY ONE: *Leading Downward*

The Spirit leads us downward.

That may come as a surprise to people who are raised in a culture that is obsessed with upward mobility. We climb social ladders. We rise to a higher standard of living. We reach for a higher position. We want to be on top. Some use drugs so that whatever their actual circumstances, they will at least feel high. Even our religious communities often have an "up, up, and away" mentality: flying away to heaven, leaving this old Earth below and behind.

But the Spirit leads us downward. To the bottom, to the place of humility, to the position and posture of service...that's where the Spirit, like water, flows.

Jesus modeled this for us. Before Jesus, and even after him, most people assumed that God was at a great distance above us. To approach God meant to leave this world. But Jesus modeled a profoundly different vision. God comes down. God meets us where we are, in our neighborhood, on our level, where we need God most. God descends to the pit of need, suffering, and abandonment. God is not distant from us, aloof, across a chasm, far above looking down. No, God is with us. Here. Now. In reach.

While we race to get to the head of the table, Jesus shocks everyone and takes the role of a servant, washing their feet. While we push and squeeze into the inner circle, Jesus shocks everyone and walks out to the margins to hang out with the outcasts and outsiders. While we struggle to make ourselves rich—often at the expense of others—Jesus shocks everyone. He pours out everything he is and has. While we fight to seize power over others, Jesus empowers others by standing with them in solidarity, by listening to them with respect, by seeking to make them successful, even at great cost to himself.

Today: Look around for signs of people climbing to the top, and each time you see such a sign, ponder where the Spirit might lead you downward.

DAY TWO: *Those in Need*

If you listen to the Spirit, here is what will happen to you. You'll be at a party and you'll notice on one side of the room all the beautiful people laughing and having fun together. In a far corner, you'll notice a person who is alone, feeling awkward, not knowing anyone. The Spirit will draw you to the person in need. You may become the bridge that connects the outsider to the insiders—and in that connection, both will be better off.

Here's what will happen if you listen to the Spirit. You will see a person or a group being vilified or scapegoated. Everyone is blaming them, shaming them, gossiping about them, feeling superior to them, venting their anxieties on them. If you join in, you'll feel part of the group. If you are silent, they'll assume you're with them. But the Spirit will draw you to differ courageously and graciously. "I'm sorry," you'll say, "but I see things very differently. I know this person. He is my friend. She is a good person. They are human beings just like us." You will risk your reputation in defending the person or people being scapegoated. And in that risk, both you and they will know that God's Spirit is alive and at work in your midst.

Today: Look for people who are alone, feeling awkward, not knowing anyone, or who are being vilified or scapegoated, and let the Spirit draw you to be in solidarity with them.

DAY THREE: *Practicing Humility*

Here's what will happen to you if you listen to the Spirit. You will realize that someone is angry at you or resentful toward you. You will hear that someone has spread false information about you or worked behind your back to do you harm. Everything in you will want you to write them off or get them back. But the Spirit will draw you toward them in humility. "I have a problem and need your help," you will say. "I feel there may be some tension or distance between us. I want to close the gap and be sure things between us are good." Your opponent may be too angry or insecure to respond well, but whatever happens, know this: The Spirit is at work in you.

Here's what will happen if you listen to the Spirit. You will make a mistake and you will be tempted to cover it up, minimize it, make an excuse for it, hide it from view. But the Spirit will draw you to admit it, first to yourself and to God, and then to those who deserve to know. You will say, "Here's what I did…I was wrong. Will you forgive me?" In that acknowledgment, God will be real. In your humility, God will be present. For the Spirit moves downward.

Today: At moments when you are tempted to write people off or get them back, or at moments when you are tempted to make excuses and cover up your own faults, weaknesses, or failures, let the Spirit lead you downward.

DAY FOUR: *A Simple Act of Service*

If you listen to the Spirit, here's what will happen to you. It will be late. You will be tired. There will be dishes to do or clothes to pick up or trash to empty. *Someone else should have done this,* you will think with anger. You will rehearse in your mind the speech you will give them. And then you will think, *But I guess they're just as tired and overworked as I am. So maybe I can help.* You won't do this as a manipulative ploy but as a simple act of service. Or maybe, if their negligence is habitual, you won't step in, but you will find a way to gently, kindly, wisely speak to them and help them better fulfill their responsibilities. Either way, as you serve, you will know that God is real, for God is alive in you.

Today: Let the Spirit energize you to do an act of service or kindness that someone else forgot or was too tired to do.

DAY FIVE: *Standing in Another's Shoes*

Here's what will happen to you if you listen to the Spirit. You will be in a public place. You will see a person who, by their dress or language or mannerisms, is clearly from another religion, another culture, another social class. That person will be uncomfortable or in need. And you will feel the Spirit inspiring a question within you. *If I were in their shoes—in an unfamiliar or uncomfortable environment, what would I want someone to do for me?* And you will move toward them. You will overcome differences in language or culture. Your kind eyes and warm smile and gentle presence will speak a universal language of neighborliness. In that moment, they will feel that God is real, for God's Spirit is alive in you.

Today: Look for opportunities to move toward the other.

DAY SIX: *You Fall into God*

There is a prison near you. A hospital. A park or a bridge or an alley where homeless people sleep. A playground or shopping center where teenagers hang out and get into trouble. Or there's a country in great need or a social problem that few people notice. If you listen to the Spirit, you will be drawn toward an opportunity to serve. At first, the thought will frighten or repel you. But when you let the Spirit guide you, it will be a source of great joy—one of the richest blessings of your life.

One more thing: There will be times in your life when you will need to be served—not to be the one serving. But even then, you will have the opportunity to appreciate, bless, and thank those who serve you, and in so doing, you and they will experience mutual service, one of life's greatest joys.

The Spirit of God leads downward. Downward in humility. Downward in service. Downward in solidarity. Downward in risk and grace. You used to strive to be cool, but the Spirit makes you warm. You used to strive to climb over others, but the Spirit leads you to wash their feet. You used to strive to fit in among the inner circle, but the Spirit dares you to be different on behalf of the outcasts and outsiders. You don't find God at the top of the ladder. No, you find God through descent. There is a trapdoor at the bottom, and when you fall through it, you fall into God.

It happened to Jesus. It will happen to you, too, if you follow the Spirit's lead.

Today: Pray, "God, help me find the trapdoor at the bottom, so I can fall into you."

WEEK FORTY-SEVEN

THE SPIRIT CONSPIRACY

Scripture Readings

> Ephesians 5:15–6:9
> Philemon 1:8–19
> Hebrews 13:1–8
> James 5:1–6

Key Verses—Hebrews 13:1–2

> *Let mutual love continue. Do not neglect to show hospitality to strangers, for by doing that some have entertained angels without knowing it.*

DAY ONE: *Your Family*

There are circles of people that the Spirit of God wants to touch and bless, and you are the person through whom the Spirit wants to work. Your mission, should you choose to accept it, is to conspire with the Spirit to bring blessing to others.

Let's start with your family. Nobody is better positioned to wound and harm your spouse than you, and nobody better to enhance your spouse's thriving than you. The same goes for your parents, your children, your siblings. The Spirit wants to conspire with you in making their lives rich, full, free, good, and fruitful.

When Jesus wanted to confront religious hypocrisy in his day, he pointed out the way hypocrites served their religion at the expense of their families. Paul picked up this theme in his letters to the early churches, calling such behavior worse than unbelief. So Paul urged husbands and wives to submit to each other and show each other true love and respect. Although his writings may strike us as chauvinistic by today's standards, they were progressive by the standards of his time, because they promoted mutual responsibility, not merely top-down privilege. Similarly, he told children to obey and honor their parents, and parents to nurture their children and raise them without frustrating them—presumably by excessively high or unclear demands. And Paul repeatedly showed special consideration for widows—which today might mean an elderly aunt, uncle, or grandparent, or any family member who is alone and vulnerable.

Today: Make a list of your closest relatives, and choose at least one to be the recipient of some act of unexpected kindness today.

DAY TWO: *The Circle of Work*

Paul taught that the Spirit works through us not only in the circle of our families, but also in the circle of work. In his day, slavery was a social norm. Where he had the opportunity—as he did with a church leader named Philemon—he urged slave owners to release their slaves and accept them as equals. Where that couldn't be done, he urged slave owners to transcend the normal master-slave relationship and dare to treat their slaves with kindness—to mirror the kindness of God.

Similarly, he urged slaves to transcend social norms by doing their work with pride and dignity. Before, they might have given the least required by a human master. But now in the Spirit, they would work for and with God. They would do whatever was required and even more, giving their best.

James took Paul's concern for a Spirit-led work ethic to the level of business management and economic policy. In strong language, he warned rich employers not to underpay their workers. What employers might call "keeping labor costs low," James called wage theft, and he reminded employers that God hears the cries of every underpaid laborer.

Our economic behavior will change greatly when we stop asking typical questions like "How little will the market or the law allow me to pay this person?" Instead, the Spirit leads people to conspire around new questions like "What would God consider fair and generous pay to this person? How can we expand the bottom line from economic profit to something deeper and broader—economic, social, and ecological benefit? How could our business and economic systems and policies become less harmful and more beneficial to aliveness on planet Earth—for us and for future generations? Could we measure success not by how much we consume and how fast we consume it, but by how well we live, care, and serve?" Just imagine how the business world would change if more and more of us went to work conspiring goodness in the Spirit.

Today: Seek to bring the spiritual awareness in today's reading to your work life.

DAY THREE: *Neighbor a Stranger*

In the next circle out beyond family and work relationships, the Spirit activates our concern for people in our neighborhoods, including strangers we meet on the street. Whatever their race, class, religion, political party, or sexual identity, they, too, are our neighbors, and the Spirit will constantly awaken us to opportunities to serve and care. Biblical writers constantly emphasize the importance of hospitality—especially to strangers. "As you have done for the least of these, you have done for me," Jesus said. So the Spirit is looking for conspirators who are interested in plotting goodness in their communities. "What would our community look like if God's dreams for it were coming true?" we ask. The answer gives us a vision to work toward.

From the circles of family, work, and neighborhood, the Spirit moves us to another sphere of concern: vulnerable people who would normally be forgotten. According to James, our religion is nothing but hot air if we don't translate our faith into action in regard to the vulnerable and easily forgotten around us. The Spirit invites us to conspire for the well-being of orphans, widows, undocumented aliens, refugees, prisoners, people with special needs, the sick, the poor, the homeless, the uneducated, the unskilled, the unemployed, and the underpaid.

Today: Keep your eyes open for someone who needs some extra encouragement. Through a surprisingly generous tip, a surprisingly kind conversation, a surprisingly gracious gift, give them evidence that a gracious God is present.

DAY FOUR: *Civic and Community Life*

Beyond the circles of family, friends, work, and neighborhood, the Spirit works through us in the still larger circle of our civic and community life. We're also given the example (through Peter and Paul especially) of standing up to political leaders when necessary, speaking truth to power, and refusing to be conformed to harmful norms of society. In our economic lives, we're told in the New Testament to pray for and show due respect for our political leaders. We're told to avoid debt—except the perpetual debt of love that we owe to every human being. In today's world, that means everyone on the planet, because as never before our world is bound together in one global ecology, one global economy, and one global military-industrial complex. To be in tune with the Spirit is to transcend all smaller boundaries and to conspire in terms of the planetary whole.

We can't forget that this larger circle includes our critics, opponents, and enemies—the people who annoy us and those we annoy, the people who don't understand us and those we don't understand, the people who try our patience and those whose patience we try. Rather than write them off as unimportant and unwanted, we need to rediscover them as some of the most important people we know. If we ignore them, our growth in the Spirit will be stunted. If we let the Spirit guide us in what we say to their faces and behind their backs, we will become more Christlike.

Today: Pray, "God, help my circle of concern grow to the circumference of yours."

DAY FIVE: *Control the Tongue*

One of the most important ways the Spirit moves us to care for people in all these circles is by training us to control the tongue. Words can wound, sometimes deeply: careless words, critical words, condemning words, harsh words, insulting words, dehumanizing words, words of gossip or deception. If your life were a ship, your words would be its rudder, James implies (3:1–12). So if you want to be a mature agent in the movement of the Spirit in our world, conspire with the Spirit in your choice of every single word.

You'll never regret forgoing an unkind word. And you'll never regret uttering a kind and encouraging word. An overworked person doing customer service, a housekeeper in a hotel, a landscaper or janitor, a harried mother on a plane with a cranky child, the cashier at a busy fast food joint, your child's third-grade teacher, the nurse in the emergency room—how much could they be encouraged today by a kind word from you, not to mention by a card, a gift, a large tip, a written note? If you're a part of the Spirit's conspiracy, you can be God's secret agent of blessing to anyone in any of these circles.

Today: Pay special attention to your words, foregoing unkind and needless words, indulging in kind and encouraging ones.

DAY SIX: *God's Secret Agent*

There's one other circle in which the Spirit seeks to work through you: the circle of your community of faith. It's the learning circle that forms whenever we encourage each other to let the Spirit keep flowing and moving in one another's lives. Keep showing up and doing so with a good attitude. It's especially important to be a channel of blessing to those who lead in your community of faith...being sure they don't have to worry about money, for example, and being sure they feel truly appreciated. Their work is so important and surprisingly hard. Your encouragement could make the difference in whether they give up or keep giving their best.

The largest circle of all extends beyond humans and includes all living things and the physical structures on which we all depend: air, rain, soil, wind, climate. You can't claim to love your neighbors and pollute the environment on which they depend. You can't claim to love the Creator and abuse the climate of this beautiful, beloved planet. The Spirit that moves among us is the same Spirit that moves in and through all creation. If we are attuned to the Spirit, we will see all creatures as our companions...even as our relatives in the family of God, for in the Spirit we are all related.

Your mission, should you choose to accept it, is to be a secret agent in God's Spirit conspiracy that is spreading quietly across the world, joining with other secret agents to plot goodness and foment kindness wherever you may be.

Today: Think of yourself as an agent in God's Spirit conspiracy, bringing blessing to our world in word and deed.

WEEK FORTY-EIGHT

SPIRIT OF POWER

Scripture Readings

> Acts 4:1–31
> 1 Thessalonians 5:1–11
> 2 Timothy 1:1–14
> Ephesians 6:10–20

Key Verses—Ephesians 6:10–12

> *Finally, be strong in the Lord and in the strength of his power. Put on the whole*
> *armor of God, so that you may be able to stand against the wiles of the devil.*
> *For our struggle is not against enemies of blood and flesh, but against the rul-*
> *ers, against the authorities, against the cosmic powers of this present darkness,*
> *against the spiritual forces of evil in the heavenly places.*

DAY ONE: *Count the Cost*

Sooner or later, everyone should be arrested and imprisoned for a good cause. Or if not arrested and imprisoned, put in a position of suffering and sacrifice. Or if not that, at least be criticized or inconvenienced a little. Because if we're coconspirators with the Spirit of God to bring blessing to our world, sooner or later it's going to cost us something and get us in trouble.

Jesus told his followers to "count the cost." He promised that those who walk his road would experience pushback, even persecution. And he often described that pushback as demonic or Satanic in nature. Some people today believe Satan and demons to be literal, objective realities. Others believe they are outmoded superstitions. Still others interpret Satan and demons as powerful and insightful images by which our ancestors sought to describe shadowy realities that are still at work today. In today's terminology, we might call them social, political, structural, ideological, and psychological forces. These forces take control of individuals, groups, and even whole civilizations, driving them toward destruction.

Today: Try to discern the social, political, structural, ideological, and psychological forces that have control of people, groups, and civilizations.

DAY TWO: *A Will of Its Own*

Consider this: You can have a crowd of normal, happy people dancing in a popular nightclub. Suddenly someone shouts, "Fire!" and people panic. Within seconds, everyone stampedes toward the exits. Soon, some people are being trampled—even killed—in the chaos, which means that others are doing the trampling and killing. None of the happy dancers in that club would have been seen as heartless killers before the scare. But we might say "the spirit of panic" possessed them and drove them to violence. That spirit had a will of its own, as it were, turning peaceful, decent individuals into a ruthless, dangerous mob that became every bit as dangerous as the threat it feared.

Now imagine a similar spirit of racism, revenge, religious supremacy, nationalism, political partisanship, greed, or fear getting a foothold in a community. You can imagine previously decent people being possessed, controlled, and driven by these forces, mind-sets, or ideologies. Soon, individuals aren't thinking or feeling for themselves anymore. They gradually allow the spirit of the group to possess them. If nobody can break out of this frenzy, it's easy to imagine tragic outcomes: vandalism, riots, beatings, lynchings, gang rapes, house demolitions, plundered land, exploited or enslaved workers, terrorism, dictatorship, genocide. Bullets can fly, bombs explode, and death tolls soar—among people who seemed so decent, normal, and peace loving just minutes or months before.

Today: As you check the news headlines, look for the spirits that are getting a foothold in our world today.

DAY THREE: *Lying to Ourselves*

You don't need to believe in literal demons and devils to agree with Jesus and the apostles: There are real and mysterious forces in our world that must be confronted. But how? If we respond to violence with violence, anger with anger, hate with hate, or fear with fear, we'll soon be driven by the same unhealthy and unholy forces that we detest and are trying to resist. To make matters worse, we'll be the last to know what's driving us, because we'll feel so pure and justified in our opposition. "We must be good and holy," we will say to ourselves, "because what we're fighting against is so evil!"

We can see in this light why ancient people described Satan as a deceiver, an accuser, and a liar. When we allow ourselves to come under the spell of an ideology or a similar force, we feel utterly convinced that evil is over there among *them*, and only moral rightness is here among us. In this accusatory state of mind, focused so exclusively on the faults of our counterparts, we become utterly blind to our own deteriorating innocence and disintegrating morality. Even when we begin to inflict harm on those we accuse, we are unable to see our actions as harmful. Self-deceived in this way, we lie to ourselves and live in denial about what we have become.

Today: Pray, "Spirit of truth, wake me up when I am slipping into self-deception. Keep my vision clear and my conscience activated."

DAY FOUR: *Unhealthy Spirits*

Paul had much to say about "spiritual warfare" against "the principalities and powers" that rule the world. He kept reminding the disciples that they weren't struggling against flesh-and-blood people. They were struggling against invisible systems and structures of evil that possess and control flesh-and-blood people. The real enemies, back then and now, are invisible realities like racism, greed, fear, ambition, nationalism, religious supremacy, and the like—forces that capture decent people and pull their strings as if they were puppets to make them do terrible things.

In that light, being filled with and guided by the Holy Spirit takes on profound meaning—and practical importance. Where unholy, unhealthy spirits or value systems judge and accuse, the Holy Spirit inspires compassion and understanding. Where unholy, unhealthy spirits or movements drive people toward harming others, the Holy Spirit leads us to boldly and compassionately stand up for those being harmed. Where unholy, unhealthy spirits or ideologies spread propaganda and misinformation, the Holy Spirit boldly speaks the simple truth. Where unholy, unhealthy spirits or mind-sets spread theft, death, and destruction, God's Holy Spirit spreads true aliveness.

Today: Use your breath to meditate on today's reading. Breathe out the unholy; breathe in the Holy.

DAY FIVE: *Overcome Evil with Good*

How do we resist being "possessed" by the unholy, unhealthy systems that are so prevalent and powerful in today's world? Sometimes it's as simple—and difficult—as responding to harsh words with a kind, disarming spirit. When a website vilifies a group, for example, you might add a gentle, vulnerable comment: "You're talking about people I count among my closest friends." When a religious group, overly confident in its own purity or rightness, condemns others, you might humbly and unargumentatively quote a relevant Scripture: "Whoever thinks he stands should take care, lest he fall," or "Knowledge puffs up, but love builds up." When powerful forces organize to do harm, you may need to form or join some sort of collective, nonviolent action—a march, a boycott or buy-cott, a protest, even nonviolent civil disobedience. Whether in small, quiet ways or big, dramatic ones, if we join the Spirit in the ongoing mission of Jesus, we won't be overcome by evil; we will overcome evil with good.

Today: Notice people who are organizing to overcome evil with good, and see this as the Spirit's work.

DAY SIX: *Power, Love, and a Sound Mind*

Don't expect overcoming evil with good to be popular, easy, convenient, or safe, as Paul's words to his young protégé, Timothy, make clear: "God has not given us a spirit of cowardice but of power, love, and a sound mind." When people are threatening you, hating you, and calling you a heretic, an infidel, or worse, a bold and courageous spirit of empowerment, love, and a sound mind is exactly what you need.

Paul, of course, spoke from personal experience. He had once been a confident, accusatory, violent persecutor of those he considered evil—utterly sure of himself, utterly convinced of his moral rightness in all he did. When he encountered Jesus and was filled with the Holy Spirit, he soon became the one being persecuted. The Spirit gave him nonviolent boldness to face repeated arrests, beatings, imprisonments, and ultimately, according to tradition, beheading by Nero in Rome. Clearly, for Paul, being a leader in the Spirit's movement wasn't a boring desk job!

No wonder one of the most oft-repeated themes in the New Testament is to *suffer graciously*, echoing Jesus's words about turning the other cheek. In I Peter 2:21 and 23, for example, we read, "Christ left you an example so that you might follow in his footsteps...When he was insulted, he did not reply with insults. When he suffered, he did not threaten revenge. Instead, he entrusted himself to the one who judges justly." To do that takes courage and power. It takes love. And it takes a sound—or nonreactive—mind.

When a crisis hits, unprepared people may be paralyzed with fear, but we'll set an example of confidence and peace. Unprepared people may not know where to turn, but we'll have this circle of peace in which to welcome them. Unprepared people may turn on one another and pull apart, but we'll turn toward one another and pull together. Unprepared people may withdraw into survival mode, but we'll have strength enough to survive, and more to share. Through the Spirit, we will have unintimidated power, unfailing love, and a sound, nonreactive mind. When necessary, we will suffer graciously. For we will know that for us, whatever happens, even the end of the world...isn't really the end of the world.

Today: Imagine some crises that might hit—global crises, personal crises, even persecution for doing what is right—and ask the Spirit to prepare you with power, love, and a sound mind.

WEEK FORTY-NINE

SPIRIT OF HOLINESS

Scripture Readings

> Psalm 98
> John 14:15–18, 25–27; 15:26–27; 16:33
> I Corinthians 3:9–15; 15:20–28

Key Verses—Psalm 98:7–9

> *Let the sea roar, and all that fills it;*
> > *the world and those who live in it.*
> *Let the floods clap their hands;*
> > *let the hills sing together for joy*
> *at the presence of the Lord, for he is coming*
> > *to judge the earth.*
> *He will judge the world with righteousness,*
> > *and the peoples with equity.*

DAY ONE: *Justice Beyond the Grave*

Jesus promised his followers three things. First, their lives would not be easy. Second, they would never be alone. Third, in the end, all will be well.

But all is not well now, and that raises the question of how: How does God get us from here to there? How does God put things right?

The word in the Bible for putting things right is *judgment*. Unfortunately, many today, drawing from the concept of a judge in today's court system, understand *judgment* to mean nothing more than condemnation and punishment. In contrast, in biblical times, good judges did more than condemn or punish. They worked to set things right, to restore balance, harmony, and well-being. Their justice was restorative, not just punitive. The final goal of judgment was to curtail or convert all that was evil so that good would be free to run wild.

It's obvious to everyone that this kind of justice doesn't always happen in a satisfying way in this life. So people of faith have trusted that God can continue to set things right on the other side of the threshold of death. Through the idea of final judgment, we have dared to hope that somehow, beyond what we see in history, restorative justice can have the last word.

Today: When you see things that are wrong, speak to yourself: Someday, this will be set right.

DAY TWO: *God's Ultimate Justice*

Final judgment, or final restoration, means that God's universe arcs toward universal repentance, universal reconciliation, universal purification, universal "putting wrong things right." That means more than saying that everything that can be punished will be punished: It means that everything that can be restored will be restored. It means the disease will be treated and healed, not just diagnosed. It means everything will, in God's ultimate justice, not only be evaluated: It will be given new value.

So when we say, with the writer of Hebrews (Hebrews 9:27), that "it is appointed for mortals to die once, and after that the judgment," we are not saying, "and after this, the condemnation." We are saying, "after this, the setting right." With John, we dare to believe that to "see God as God is," to be in God's unspeakable light, will purge us of all darkness:

> *How great is the love the Father has lavished on us, that we should be called children of God! And that is what we are!...Dear friends, now we are children of God, and what we will be has not yet been made known. But we know that when he appears, we shall be like him, for we shall see him as he is. All who have this hope in them purify themselves, just as God is pure. (1 John 3:1–3)*

Since "what we will be has not yet been made known," it is hard to say anything more, except this: in the end, God will be all in all, and all will be well.

Today: Hold this simple phrase in your heart: *All will be well.*

DAY THREE: *The Purifying Fire*

Does "all will be well" mean there will be no cost, no loss, no regret, no mourning? This is where the so often misused image of fire comes in. Many a hellfire-and-brimstone preacher has depicted fire as an instrument of torture, but it is far better understood as an instrument of purification. Paul describes it this way: God's purifying fire can't consume "gold, silver, and precious stones," because in so doing, God would be destroying something good, which would render God evil. The cleansing or refining fire of God must destroy only the "wood, hay, and stubble" of hypocrisy, evil, and sin.

If some of us have constructed our lives like a shoddy builder, using worthless building materials, there won't be much of our life's story left. We will experience the purification of judgment as loss, regret, remorse. We thought we were pretty smart, powerful, superior, or successful, but the purifying fire will surprise us with the bitter truth. In contrast, others of us who thought ourselves nothing special will be surprised in a positive way. Thousands of deeds of kindness that we had long forgotten will have been remembered by God, and we will feel the celebration of God: "Welcome into my joy!"

Today: Pray, "God, may I live my life like a wise builder, with the 'gold, silver, and precious stones' of goodness, beauty, and truth."

DAY FOUR: *The Hope of Restorative Judgment*

When you understand God's judgment after death as restorative rather than merely punitive, you live differently before death. This understanding makes you eager to use your wealth to make others rich, not to hoard it. It inspires you to use your power to empower others, not to advance yourself. It liberates you to give and give so that you will finish this life having given more than you received. It encourages you to try to be secretive about your good deeds because you would rather defer the return on your investment to the future. In fact, this hope makes you willing to give up this life, if necessary, for things that matter more than survival.

And this hope also changes the way you see trials and difficulties in this life. If you see trials and difficulties not as a punishment for your wrongs but as a refining fire to strengthen and purify you, trials become your friends, not your enemies.

So, in this light, delay is like a fire that burns away impatience. Annoyances are like flames that burn away selfishness. The demands of duty are like degrees of heat that burn away laziness. The unkind words and deeds of others are like a furnace in which your character is tempered, until you learn to bless, not curse, in response. It's not even worth comparing our short-term trials, Paul said, to the long-term glory that comes from enduring them. Whatever we face—ease or struggle, life or death—Paul's encouragement is the same: "Therefore, my beloved, be steadfast, immovable, always excelling in the work of the Lord, because you know that in the Lord your labor is not in vain."

Today: As you experience the fires of trial and difficulty, try to name what is being burned away.

DAY FIVE: *No Fear*

If we believe in judgment—in God's great "setting things right"—we won't live in fear. We'll keep standing strong with a steadfast, immovable determination, and we'll keep excelling in God's good work in our world. If we believe the universe moves toward purification, justice, and peace, we'll keep seeking to be pure, just, and peaceable now. If we believe God is pure light and goodness, we'll keep moving toward the light each day in this life. Then, someday, when our time comes to close our eyes in death, we will trust ourselves to the loving Light in which we will awaken, purified, beloved, forever.

Today: Imagine the whole universe moving toward purification, justice, and peace.

DAY SIX: *The Spirit Is Working*

At this moment, the Spirit is working, leading us along in that great arc toward restoration and healing. Like a mother in childbirth, groaning with pain and anticipation, the Spirit groans within us. She will not rest until all is made whole, and all is made holy, and all is made well.

This is true of you as an individual, just as it is true for all other persons, no exceptions. It is also true for history as a whole. The Spirit is working, like wind hovering over the water, evoking hope from despair, beauty from ashes, and resurrection from death.

Life will not be easy. We will never be alone. In the end all will be well. That is all we know and all we need to know. Amen.

Today: Find some time to simply be quiet, holding these words: "Life will not be easy. We will never be alone."

WEEK FIFTY

SPIRIT OF LIFE

Scripture Readings

Psalm 90
Luke 20:27–38
Philippians 1:20–30

Key Verses—Philippians 1:20–21

It is my eager expectation and hope that I will not be put to shame in any way, but that by my speaking with all boldness, Christ will be exalted now as always in my body, whether by life or by death. For to me, living is Christ and dying is gain.

DAY ONE: *A Doorway to Heaven*

We all will die someday. Mortality rates remain at 100 percent, and nobody among us is getting any younger. Among the Spirit's many essential movements in our lives is this: to prepare us for the end of our lives, without fear.

So many of us are afraid to even think about death, much less speak of it. That fear can enslave us and can rob us of so much aliveness. The Spirit moves within us to help us face death with hope, not fear; with quiet confidence, not anxiety. "The law of the Spirit of life in Christ Jesus," Paul said (Romans 8:2), "has set you free from the law of sin and of death."

Here's a way to think about death. We often speak of God as the one who was, who is, and who is to come. The God who *was* holds all our past. The God who *is* surrounds us now. And the God who *is to come* will be there for us beyond this life as we know it. With that realization in mind, death could never mean leaving God, because there is nowhere we can escape from God's presence, as the psalmist said (139:7). Instead, death simply means leaving ~~the presence of God in~~ this little neighborhood of history called the present. Through death, we join God in the vast, forever-expanding future, into which both past and present are forever taken up.

Some religious scholars tried to trap Jesus once by bringing up a conflict between moral sense and belief in the afterlife. If there is life after death, they asked, does that mean that a woman who was widowed seven times in this life will have seven husbands in the next? You can almost see them smirking, thinking themselves very clever for stumping the rabbi. In response, Jesus said that to God, all who ever lived are alive (Luke 20:38). In that light, death is merely a doorway, a passage from one way of living in God's presence in the present to another way of living in God's presence— in the open space of unseized possibility we call the future.

Today: Think of death as a doorway.

DAY TWO: *Liberated from the Fear of Death*

We've all heard the cliché about someone being "so heavenly minded he's no earthly good," and maybe we've met people on whom the cliché fits like an old bedroom slipper. But there is also a way of being so earthly minded that you're no earthly good. And there's a way of being heavenly minded so that you are more earthly good than you ever could have been any other way. To be liberated from the fear of death—think of how that would change your values, perspectives, and actions. To believe that no good thing is lost, but that all goodness will be taken up and consummated in God—think of how that frees you to do good without reservation. To participate in a network of relationships that isn't limited by death in the slightest degree—think of how that would make every person matter and how it would free you to live with boundless, loving aliveness.

Today: Consider how being heavenly minded can make you be of more earthly good.

DAY THREE: *What Might We Expect?*

So what might we expect to happen when we die? Nobody knows for sure, but in light of Jesus's death and resurrection, we can expect to experience death as a passage, like birth, the end of one life stage and the beginning of another. We don't know how that passing will come...like a slow slipping away in disease, like a sudden jolt or shock in an accident. However it happens, we can expect to discover that we're not falling out of life, but deeper into it.

On the other side, we can expect to experience as never before the unimaginable light or energy of God's presence. We will enter into a goodness so good, a richness so rich, a holiness so holy, a mercy and love so strong and true that all of our evil, pride, lust, greed, resentment, and fear will be instantly melted out of us. We will at that moment more fully understand how much we have been forgiven, and so we will more than ever be filled with love...love for God who forgives, and with God, love for everyone and everything that has like us been forgiven.

Today: Pray, "God, help me understand even now how much I have been forgiven, and help me, the more I'm forgiven, to be filled with more forgiving love for others."

DAY FOUR: *A Sense of Reunion*

We can expect to feel, on the other side of dying, a sense of reunion—yes, with loved ones who have died, but also with our great-great-great-great grandparents and our thirty-second cousins a thousand times removed whose names we've never known but to whom we are in fact related. That sense of relatedness that we now feel with closest of kin will some-how be expanded to every person who has ever lived. And that sense of relatedness won't stop with human beings, but will expand infinitely outward to all of God's creation. We can expect to feel the fullest, most exquisite sense of oneness and interrelatedness and harmony—a sense of belonging and connection that we approached only vaguely or clumsily in our most ecstatic moments in this life.

We can expect to feel differently about our sufferings. We will see not the short-term pain that so preoccupied us on the past side of death but instead the enduring virtue, courage, and compassion that have been forged in us through each fall of the hammer on the anvil of pain. We will bless our sufferings and feel about them as we feel about our plea-sures now. What has been suffered or lost will feel weightless compared to the substance that has been gained.

We can expect to feel a limitless sense of "Ah yes, now I see." What we longed for, reached for, touched but couldn't grasp, and knew in part will then be so clear. All of our unfulfilled longing on this side of death will, we can expect, enrich and fulfill the having on that side of death. We can expect to feel as if we're waking up from being half asleep, wak-ing into an explosion of pure, utter gratitude as we suddenly and fully realize all we've had and taken for granted all along.

Of course, we don't have to wait until the other side of death to feel these things. They are available to some degree to us right now, if we have eyes to see and ears to hear.

Today: Imagine waking into an explosion of pure, utter gratitude.

DAY FIVE: *The Dual Pull*

You may imagine that dying will be like diving or falling or stepping into a big wave at the beach. You will feel yourself lifted off your feet and taken up into a swirl and curl and spin more powerful than you can now imagine. But there will be no fear, because the motion and flow will be the dance of Father, Son, and Holy Spirit. The rising tide will be life and joy. The undertow will be love, and you will be drawn deeper and deeper in.

We normally don't look forward to the process of dying, and most of us would be happy if the dying process were as short and painless as possible. But if we allow the Spirit to prepare us for dying by contemplating it in these ways, we can begin to understand the dual pull that Paul wrote about: "For me to live is Christ but to die is gain." On the one hand, we feel a pull to stay here in this life, enjoying the light and love and goodness of God with so many people who are dear to us, with so much good work left to be done. On the other hand, we feel an equal and opposite pull toward the light and love and goodness of God experienced more directly beyond this life.

Today: Practice holding life lightly by being freed from the fear of death.

DAY SIX: *Our Last Act of Love*

Many of us remember the experience as children of "waiting your turn." Maybe it was waiting your turn to ride a pony at the county fair, or waiting your turn to play a game, or waiting your turn to ride a sled down a hill in winter snow. Imagine the feeling of having had your turn on this Earth and having enjoyed it thoroughly. Now you are ready to step aside to let someone else have their turn. In that way, even dying can be an act of love and generosity: vacating space to make room for others, especially generations as yet unborn, just as others vacated their space so you could have your turn in this life. Perhaps the act of letting others have their turn will be one of our most mature and generous actions, a fitting end to our adventure in this life. At that moment, it will be our turn to graduate into a new adventure, beyond all imagining.

As we walk this road, we not only remember the past, we also anticipate the future, which is described as a great banquet around God's table of joy. When you pass from this life, do not be afraid. You will not pass into death. You will pass through death into a greater aliveness still— the banquet of God. Trust God, and live.

Today: Say, "I will someday pass through death into a greater aliveness still."

WEEK FIFTY-ONE

SPIRIT OF HOPE

Scripture Readings

> Psalm 126
> Revelation 1:9–19; 19:11–16; 21:1–8; 22:16–21

Key Verses—Revelation 21:3–5a

And I heard a loud voice from the throne saying, "See, the home of God is among mortals. He will dwell with them; they will be his peoples, and God himself will be with them; he will wipe every tear from their eyes. Death will be no more; mourning and crying and pain will be no more, for the first things have passed away." And the one who was seated on the throne said, "See, I am making all things new."

DAY ONE: *An Open Future*

The last book in the Bible is the Book of Revelation, also known as the Apocalypse (or unveiling). Some people ignore it, wondering why such an odd composition was even included in the biblical library. Other people seem obsessed by it. They are certain that it is a coded "history of the future," telling us how the world will someday end.

That way of reading Revelation is based on a lot of assumptions that deserve to be questioned. For example, did God create a closed and predetermined universe or a free and participatory one? Is the future a movie that has already been shot, so to speak, and we are just watching it play? Or is the future open, inviting us not simply to resign ourselves and adapt, but to be protagonists who invent, improvise, and help create the outcome as God's coworkers and fellow actors?

Today: See yourself as God's coworker and fellow actor.

DAY TWO: *Rediscovering Revelation*

Having left behind the "history of the future" way of reading Revelation, more and more of us are rediscovering it in a fresh way. The first step in this fresh approach is to put the text back in its historical context. Our best scholars agree it was composed during the bloody reign of either Nero in the AD 60s or Domitian in the AD 90s. Life was always hard in the Roman empire for poor people, and most of the followers of Jesus were poor. But life was extremely precarious when the man at the helm of the empire was vicious, paranoid, and insane, as both Nero and Domitian were. Life got even tougher when the madman on the throne demanded to be worshiped as a god, something followers of Jesus would never do.

In this light, Revelation was the very opposite of a codebook that mapped out the end of the world in the distant future. It addressed the crisis at hand. Even if the emperor is mad, Revelation claimed, it's not the end of the world. Even if wars rage, it's not the end of the world. Even if peace-loving disciples face martyrdom, it's not the end of the world. Even if the world as we know it comes to an end, that ending is also a new beginning. Whatever happens, God will be faithful and the way of Christ—a way of love, nonviolence, compassion, and sustained fervency—will triumph.

Today: When you find yourself anxious about something, say, "Even the end of the world isn't the end of the world."

DAY THREE: *Literature of the Oppressed*

Along with understanding the historical context of the Book of Revelation, we would be wise to understand its literary context, which is *literature of the oppressed*. Literature of the oppressed arises among people living under dictatorships who have no freedom of speech. If they dare to criticize the dictator, they'll be "disappeared" and never seen again. Before being executed, they may be brutally tortured so their oppressors can extract names of others they should go arrest, torture, and elicit still more names from. No wonder people learn to be silent in a dictatorship.

But being silent in the presence of injustice feels like a way of cooperating with it.

As literature of the oppressed, the Book of Revelation provided early disciples with a clever way of giving voice to the truth—when freedom of speech was dangerous in one way, and remaining silent was dangerous in another. Instead of saying, "The emperor is a fraud and his violent regime cannot stand," which would get them arrested, Revelation tells a strange story about a monster who comes out of the sea and is defeated. Instead of saying, "The religious establishment is corrupt," it tells a story about a prostitute. Instead of naming today's Roman empire as being doomed, they talk about a past empire—Babylon—that collapsed in failure.

Today: Consider how fearful silence can be self-destructive.

DAY FOUR: *Take the Historic and Literary Context Seriously*

If we keep reading Revelation as the history of a predetermined future, the consequences can be disastrous. For example, we may read the vision of Jesus coming on a white horse (Rev. 19:11 *ff.*) and think that's about a Jesus completely different from the one we met in the gospels. This Jesus won't be a peace-and-love guy anymore but a violence-and-revenge guy. What might happen if we leave the peace-and-love Jesus in the past and follow a violence-and-revenge Jesus into the future?

We may read about people being thrown into a lake of fire at the end of Revelation (20:7 *ff.*), and if we take it literally, we may see God as some kind of a sadistic torturer. If God tortures for eternity, might it be okay for us to do the same in our next war or political upheaval? Or if we interpret literally the passage in Revelation (21:1) that makes it sound like the Earth will be destroyed, might we think, *Hey, why worry about overconsumption, environmental destruction, or climate change? God is going to destroy the world soon anyway, so we might as well pitch in!* There is a high cost to reading Revelation outside its historical and literary context.

Today: Ponder the dangers of trying to interpret the Bible outside of its historical and literary context.

DAY FIVE: *More Powerful Than Swords*

People who read Revelation without understanding its literary and historical context tend to miss some telling details. For example, when Jesus rides in on the white horse, his robes are bloodstained and he carries a sword. Many have interpreted this scene as a repudiation of Jesus's non-violence in the gospels. But they miss the fact that he carries his sword in his mouth, not his hand. Instead of predicting the return of a killer Messiah in the future, Revelation recalls the day in the past when Jesus rode into Jerusalem on a donkey. His humble words of peace, love, and justice will, Revelation promises, prove more powerful than the bloody swords of violent emperors. In addition, we notice his robe is bloodstained before the battle begins, suggesting that the blood on his robe is not the blood of his enemies, but is his own, shed in self-giving love. In that light, Revelation reinforces rather than overturns the picture we have of Jesus in Matthew, Mark, Luke, and John.

Today: Let go of violent depictions of Jesus you may have heard from people who misinterpret Revelation.

DAY SIX: *The Spirit Says Come!*

What was true for Revelation's original audience is true for us today. Whatever madman is in power, whatever chaos is breaking out, whatever danger threatens, the river of life is flowing now. The Tree of Life is bearing fruit now. True aliveness is available now. That's why Revelation ends with the sound of a single word echoing through the universe. That word is not *wait!* Nor is it *not yet!* or *someday!* It is a word of invitation, welcome, reception, hospitality, and possibility. It is a word not of ending, but of new beginning. That one word is *come!* The Spirit says it to us. We echo it back. Together with the Spirit, we say it to everyone who is willing. *Come!*

Today: Hear the Spirit saying, "Come!"

GOD IN THE END

Scripture Readings

Luke 15:11–32
Romans 8:31–39
I Corinthians 15:50–58

Key Verses—Romans 8:38–39

For I am convinced that neither death, nor life, nor angels, nor rulers, nor things present, nor things to come, nor powers, nor height, nor depth, nor anything else in all creation, will be able to separate us from the love of God in Christ Jesus our Lord.

DAY ONE: *A Big Celebration*

Astronomers tell us that in a little less than eight billion years, our sun will turn into a red dwarf and Earth will be incinerated. Before that time, they offer a number of other scenarios that could wipe out human civilization on our planet: a massive comet or asteroid, a black hole, or a hypernova elsewhere in our galaxy, not to mention likely fruits of human stupidity in the form of nuclear or biological warfare, climate catastrophe, and environmental collapse.

Somewhere between science and science fiction is the possibility of escaping Earth and populating other planets elsewhere in the universe if we ruin this one. But even if we manage a "Plan B," scientists tell us that the entire universe is winding down. It will eventually end either in a Big Freeze or a Big Crunch, after which there will be nobody left to remember that any of this ever existed. If this prediction is the whole truth, our unremembered lives and their illusory meaning will be reduced to nothing, gone forever—utterly, absolutely, infinitely gone.

In the biblical library, in contrast, neither a Big Freeze nor a Big Crunch gets the last annihilating word. Instead, we are given an ultimate vision of a Big Celebration or a Big Consummation. From Genesis to Revelation we find the story of an infant universe into which is born an infant humanity that grows, comes of age, makes mistakes, learns lessons, and finally reaches maturity. Like most coming-of-age stories, this one ends with a wedding, as humanity welcomes God into its heart.

Today: Ponder three possible futures for the universe: Big Freeze, Big Crunch, or Big Celebration.

DAY TWO: *The Parental Love of God*

What could a story of Big Celebration mean as the finish line of creation as we know it? What could it mean to us right now? Jesus gave us a clue in one of his best known but least understood parables. In it, human history can be seen as the story of a family, a father and two sons. The family experiences conflict. The rebellious younger son runs away and for a while forgets his true identity. The dutiful older son stays home but also forgets his true identity. The younger son reaches a crisis and comes home. He is welcomed by the father, which then creates a crisis for the older son. Of course, the story isn't only about the identity crises of the sons. It also reveals the true identity of the father, whose heart goes out to both brothers, who graciously loves them even when they don't know it, and even when they don't love each other. The story ends with a celebration—a welcome-home party, a reunion party.

Like many of our best stories, it doesn't have to be factual to tell the truth, and its ending is left unresolved. Will the older brother remain outside, nursing his petty resentments? Or will he come inside to join the Big Celebration and rediscover his true identity in the family? We find ourselves cheering for him: "Come inside, man! Come on! Don't hold back! Come in!" That word *come*, interestingly, is the same word we find echoing at the end of the last book in the biblical library.

If we enter this story and let it do its work on us, we can look out from within it and see ourselves and all creation held in the parental love of God. We can empathize with God, who wants all to come, all to enjoy the feast, all to discover or rediscover their true identity in God's family, in God's love.

This short parable is one of the best mirrors of humanity ever composed. In it, both the rebellious and the religious can see themselves. But more important, it is one of the best windows into God ever composed, because it shows a gracious and spacious heart that welcomes all to the table.

Today: Open your heart to God as the gracious and spacious heart that welcomes all to the table.

DAY THREE: *Try to Imagine*

The Big Freeze or Big Crunch predictions of the astronomers may be accurate on some limited level, but they don't have the right instruments to detect the widest, deepest dimensions of reality. It takes stories like the ones we have been exploring to help us imagine those deeper and bigger dimensions.

Imagine a moment before the Big Bang banged. Imagine a creativity, brilliance, fertility, delight, energy, power, glory, wisdom, wonder, greatness, and goodness sufficient to express itself in what we know as the universe. Try to imagine it, even though you know you cannot: a creative imagination and energy so great that it would produce light, gravity, time, and space...galaxies, stars, planets, and oceans...mountains, valleys, deserts, and forests...cobia, bison, dragonflies, and meadowlarks...gorillas, dolphins, golden retrievers, and us.

And then dare to imagine that this is the great, big, beautiful, mysterious goodness, wholeness, and aliveness that surrounds us and upholds us even now.

Finally, try to imagine that this is also the great, big, beautiful, mysterious goodness, wholeness, and aliveness into which all of us and all creation will be taken up—in a marriage, in a homecoming, in a reunion, in a celebration.

Today: Hold the image of creation being drawn toward a marriage, a homecoming, a reunion, a celebration.

DAY FOUR: *Flowing Toward Reconciliation*

We inherited various words to name the ultimate mystery. In English, *God*. In Spanish, *Dios*. In French, *Dieu*. In Russian, *Bog*. In Mandarin, *Thianzhu*. *Mungu* in Swahili. *Allah* in Arabic. *Edoda* in Cherokee. *Elohim* and *Adonai*, and many others, in Hebrew. *Wakan Tanka* in Sioux, and so on. So many books have been written to describe and define this mystery. Sadly, so many arguments and inquisitions have been launched and wars waged over it, too. But here in Jesus's parable, as in the closing chapters of Revelation, we get a window into its true heart, its intention, its flow. The whole story flows toward reconciliation, not in human creeds or constitutions, but in love, the love of the One who gave us being and life. We can boast of knowing the "right" name and still have the wrong understanding. But if we have eyes to see and ears to hear, the great, big, beautiful, wonderful, holy, mysterious, reconciling heart of God waits to be discovered and experienced.

Today: Pray, "I open my eyes, ears, and heart to the beautiful mystery of You."

DAY FIVE: *That Is Why We Walk This Road*

Big Bang to Big Death? Or Big Bang to Big Celebration? If the biblical story is true, it is the latter. In the end as Paul envisioned it, death is swallowed up in a great big victory, as if death were a tiny drop in comparison to God's huge ocean of aliveness. A contemporary writer put the same insight like this: "All the death that ever was, set next to life, would scarcely fill a cup."

Human speculation—whether religious or scientific—does the best it can, like a little boat that ventures out on the surface of a deep, deep ocean, under the dome of a fathomless sky. Our eyes cannot see beyond the rim. Our ears cannot hear the music beneath the silence. Our hearts cannot imagine the meaning above us, below us, around us, within us. But the Spirit blows like wind. And so this mystery humbles us even as it dignifies us. This mystery impresses us with our smallness even as it inspires us with our ultimate value. This mystery dislodges us from lesser attachments so we sail on in hope. This mystery dares us to believe that the big love of God is big enough to swallow all death and overflow with aliveness for us all.

"Do not fear," the Spirit whispers. "All shall be well." That is why we walk this road, from the known into the unknown, deeper into mystery, deeper into light, deeper into love, deeper into joy.

Today: Imagine yourself walking deeper into mystery, light, love, and joy.

ABOUT THE AUTHOR

Brian D. McLaren is an author, speaker, activist, and public theologian. He leads the Convergence Leadership Project (convergenceleadership .org) and is a popular conference speaker and a frequent guest lecturer for denominational and ecumenical leadership gatherings in the United States and internationally. He is an Auburn Senior Fellow and is active in multi-faith work. Brian's writing spans more than a dozen books, including *Why Did Jesus, Moses, the Buddha, and Mohammed Cross the Road* and *Everything Must Change*. He is an active and popular blogger, a musician, and an avid outdoor enthusiast. Brian is married to Grace, and they have four adult children and five grandchildren. Learn more at his website, www.brianmclaren.net.

This book is dedicated to
unsung heroes of local churches,
saints who serve selflessly and ceaselessly
behind the scenes
week after week
without ribbons or rewards or recognition—
for sweeping up after church meals,
for counting every Alabaster Offering penny,
for stacking chairs and scrubbing floors,
for fixing and tending and cleaning.
You give much
simply because you have been given much.
Thank you.

When Jesus was commissioning His disciples, He didn't say, "Go and build a church building and huddle there until folks show up." Rather, He said, "Go and make disciples." Every body of believers can do this. It depends not on your building, the size of your congregation, your location or your style. It does depend on your willingness to make some changes. In the pages of this book you will not read from the pen of theorists. You will hear from leaders of churches that took Christ's commission seriously, made some "shifts," and began to see God bless their efforts. The USA/Regional Office of the Church of the Nazarene sends this book and video resource with the prayer that God will bring vibrant renewal to every church.

Bob Broadbooks
Regional Director
USA/Canada Region Church of the Nazarene

CONTENTS

SHIFT (VERB)

1. to adjust in order to move forward
2. to change from one thing to another; to move ahead

6

FOREWORD

Many churches stuck on a plateau or spiraling into decline can discover the joy of reaching the peak of revitalization. In many ways, the North American church has forgotten the joy of climbing the mountain peaks of ministry. It has become overweight with modern techniques and methodologies and lost sight of its true mission and purpose to simply make more and better followers of Jesus Christ.

Why not plant new churches? It's a fair question. I've often said, "It's easier to birth a baby than raise one from the dead." Neither is easy, but one is far more common. While I have spent much of my life planting new churches and mentoring church planters, I realize the kingdom of God needs both church planting and church revitalization.

In my book *Comeback Churches* I cowrote with Mike Dodson, we sought to identify principles that could guide pastors and churches down the path of revitalization. Many of the conclusions drawn in our book resonate with what you will find in the pages ahead.

Like any resurrection, a spiritually dead church requires the power of God to live again. Often pastors have failed in ministry because they have cut their churches off from the power of God through prayer, either by failing to lead in prayer or by neglecting prayer as a priority.

Respondents to a survey for *Comeback Churches* were asked to identify the top three factors leading to their churches being revitalized. Their responses clearly revealed prayer as the number one factor inhibiting their churches from shifting from sickness to health.

The book you are about to read is designed to facilitate the kind of shift God wants for your church, the shift from sickness to health, spiritual death to spiritual life, spiritual apathy to spiritual energy. Pastoring a church in need of revitalization can be personally taxing. Pastors seldom burn out at healthy churches. And the situation seems hopeless when all of the factors inhibiting the shift God desires for your church seem out of your control. But the reality of your situation, of my situation, is we serve a God who delights to work in relationship with us toward a common mission. Only when we turn Godward in prayer and focus on His mission are we able to make the shifts our churches so desperately need.

We can discover the joy of reaching the peak of revitalization because of God's omnipotence. The same God who heals the sick, restores sight to the blind, and raises His Son to new life is inviting you on His mission. Your response to His invitation holds the key to unlock the glorious gospel revitalization awaiting all those who seek God.

You hold in your hand the product of years of study and research by people under the conviction of the Holy Spirit that nothing will overcome Christ's Church (Matthew 16:18). Though my Nazarene brothers and I are separated by denominational affiliation, we are unified by God's mission (28:19-20). It's both personally challenging and encouraging to see the five key strategies highlighted by Bill Wiesman, particularly the "vibrant church renewal" initiative. May you find what you seek, and may God breathe new life into missional communities in North America, to the ends of the earth.

—*Ed Stetzer*
President of LifeWay Research

PREFACE

The Church of the Nazarene has a rich heritage of making Christlike disciples in the nations. From our earliest days we have multiplied churches and disciples across the United States and Canada and out to the "uttermost parts" (Psalm 2:8, KJV) of the world. Today we have over twenty-seven thousand churches in almost one hundred sixty countries around the world. Growth has been rapid and dynamic in recent years in world areas, but here in the USA/Canada Region our growth has slowed and plateaued. In 2009 and 2010 USA/Canada Regional Director Bob Broadbooks sought input from hundreds of pastors, superintendents, laypeople, and denominational leaders in leading the region to identify five key strategies for the future:

1. **Intentional Leadership Development**—Recognize, develop, train, and release passionate leaders with a Wesleyan-Arminian focus.

2. **Vibrant Church Renewal**—Help each local church discover new missional life.

3. **Clear and Coherent Theological Identity**—Facilitate communication and collaboration between the Global Ministry Center, educational regions, educational institutions, ministers and laity through print, electronic media, civil conversation, and clear preaching.

4. **Passionate Missional Outreach**—Release and encourage our people to embrace with open arms and hearts both the needy and the new people groups among us.

9

5. **Multifaceted New Church Development**—Foster an environment and enthusiasm for starting new churches through districts and local churches.

This book is the result of an ongoing initiative to develop Strategy Number 2, Vibrant Church Renewal. Recognizing that we could not study all "vibrant churches," we did our best to locate churches that positively fit the following characteristics.

1. Turnaround churches, previously plateaued or declining but have since turned around
2. Breakout churches, which have suddenly taken off

We further identified four major factors:

1. Internal institutional factors, such as programs, ministries, emphasis, staff, and so on—this is the area that local leaders have the most control over.
2. Internal contextual factors, such as aging congregation, poor location, deferred maintenance, historical precedents—less control by local leaders.
3. External institutional factors, such as the positive or negative impact of being part of a connectional system or denomination, with almost no control by local leaders.
4. External contextual factors—for example, the town is dying or changing—with no control by local leaders.

To narrow the scope of our study, we chose to look at only the first two factors, internal institutional factors and internal contextual factors. These are those over which local leaders have the most control. We narrowed the scope of our study even further by looking at only the seventy percent of our Nazarene churches that had fewer than one hundred in average attendance prior to shifting to a higher level of health and effectiveness.

When these are analyzed statistically, we see that groups of churches go through a life cycle similar to that of other organizations: birth, growth, maturity, plateau, decline, dropout, and death. Because of the dynamic presence of the Holy Spirit, though, there is hope for many of our aging churches. Anecdotally we know that all churches do not go through this life cycle. Some continue to refocus and reinvent and redevelop and make Christlike disciples in ongoing cycles of health and vibrancy. Why does God seem to bless in some places and not in others? Are there commonalities in churches that are experiencing renewal? We wanted to find out.

So with the help of the Nazarene Research Department, the over five thousand USA/Canada churches were put through more and more stringent filters until only a handful were left. Nine pastors met, presented papers, answered survey questions, and allowed their ministries to be subjected to in-depth analysis to discover helpful commonalities. These pastors and churches generally fit the following criteria:

1. The church has existed since at least 1990.
2. The pastor has served at least five years.
3. At the beginning of the pastorate, the church had fewer than one hundred members and fewer than one hundred in average worship attendance.
4. Since the beginning of the pastorate, average annual membership growth has at least doubled the average population growth during the decade.
5. Since the beginning of the pastorate, average annual worship attendance growth has at least doubled the average population growth during the decade.
6. Since the beginning of the pastorate, new Nazarenes have been received each year.
7. Since the beginning of the pastorate, the average total of annual new Nazarenes has at least equaled one-third of that of the beginning membership.

The nine churches that form this study are listed here:

District	Church	Pastor
East Ohio	Massillon	John Stallings
Mid-Atlantic	Owings Mills, Maryland, Latin American First	Walter Argueta
Northwestern Illinois	Princeton, Illinois, New Hope	Laura Root
Virginia	Winchester, Virginia, The Core	*James Asberry
Virginia	Waynesboro Community Fellowship	*James (Jeff) Griffith
Tennessee	Clarksville Grace	*Tony Miller
Canada Central	London, Ontario, First	Junior Sorzano
New Mexico	Farmington Crossroads Community	David West
Tennessee	Waverly	Daron Brown

*Pastor has since relocated to another church.

Finally, we must celebrate and recognize Pastor Daron Brown of the Waverly, Tennessee, Church of the Nazarene, one of the churches that formed a part of this study. When asked, Daron willingly stepped into the role of facilitator and leader of the study. He is the author of this book. Thank you, Daron, for your contribution for our Lord and His kingdom.

—*Bill Wiesman*
Evangelism Ministries Director

ACKNOWLEDGMENTS

This book is far from a solo effort. It is the result of many hearts, minds, and lives. I offer great thanks to the following.

Bob Broadbooks: your vision for churches to experience vibrant renewal has inspired this effort. Thank you.

Bill Wiesman: thank you for composing the "Next Steps" strategies and holding my hand in the process.

Our vibrant pastors: Tony Miller, Junior Sorzano, Laura Root, Walter Argueta, Fernando Ibanez, David West, John Stallings, James Asberry, and Jeff Griffith. Thank you. Being with you makes me a better pastor.

Shelma Warner, Joy Wilson, and Wesley McKain: your hard work has made everything else happen. Thank you.

Lyle Pointer, Michael Curry, Terry Williams, Eric Bryant, Bryon McLaughlin, Greg Sheffer, Rich Housel, and Dale Jones: you elevated the quality of this work by lending your voices.

Our vibrant churches: your faithfulness is the story.

The people of Waverly, Tennessee, Church of the Nazarene: you are a vibrant church. You gave me time and space to write this book. Your prayers made it possible. Thank you.

My *Shift* prayer team. I needed your prayers.

Katie: thank you for reaching for my hand.

Kendall, Parker, and McCauley: your hugs and kisses are everything.

My Lord Jesus: thank you for apprehending me.

The problem is not that we're small.
The problem is that we've forgotten
what God does with small.
—Dan Boone
President, Trevecca Nazarene University, Nashville

14

INTRODUCTION

I was eighteen years old when I first saw the film *Rudy*. The story of Daniel E. "Rudy" Ruettiger took hold of me. I ached as the small-framed, big-hearted college kid willed himself to play football for the Fighting Irish. My own heart fell into the rhythm of the chant "Rudy, Rudy, Rudy . . ." and every last nerve ending soared with sheer elation as number forty-five finally charged onto the field.

The story of *Rudy* is nothing new. Many of us while growing up fed on stories like *The Little Engine That Could* and *Cinderella*. We root for the college basketball teams who bust their way through brackets every spring. We are drawn to stories where barriers are shattered, norms are upended, and expectations are exceeded. We like stories in which small becomes success, where unlikely equals reality.

As followers of Christ, we believe God does something with small.

Small Israel.

Small David.

Small stones.

Small baby.

Small Twelve.

Small loaves and fish.

Small bread and wine.

The landscape of North America is filled with small established churches that struggle to move forward. With God's help, some of those established churches are experiencing renewed life and growth. Once our nine vibrant churches were identified (see the criteria in the Foreword), their pastors gathered for three summits and completed multiple surveys. Visits were made to their campuses. We collaborated to discern commonalities in our settings. The results are nine vibrant church characteristics, nine common traits between our churches. Those characteristics are shared in the nine chapters of this book.

The first section is titled "First Things" simply because the first two commonalities are preliminary to the other seven. Vibrant pastors and laypeople regard these two as most vital. Once the first two are in place, the groundwork is laid for the next seven, which are described in a series of shifts. It became clear throughout our conversations that each of our churches experienced specific shifts, series of movements from one thing to another. In order for these churches to shift forward, a series of minor movements was necessary. The described shifts involved changes in both attitude and action. The second section describes *pastor shifts,* and the third shares *people shifts.* Each shift chronicles Spirit-led movement that took place in order for old patterns of plateau and decline to give way to vibrant growth.

Shift is not a novel concept. Some of our best biblical and theological expressions are *turn, convert, repent, transform, sanctify, be born again, renew, restore, regenerate,* and *change.* Each of them communicates the same thing: *Don't stay put. Hear the voice of God calling you away from where you are. Allow Him to bring you in a different direction.* This message is not only for our individual lives but also for our churches.

Throughout the book, our nine pastors are referred to as "vibrant pastors," and their churches are designated as "vibrant churches." This is not to suggest, of course, that vibrant churches do not exist outside of this group. These designations are simply for purposes of communicating the shared stories of the churches who are part of our study. And you will find that *vibrant* is an appropriate adjective for the churches described in the pages ahead. You will also find continuous comparisons between the churches prior to vibrant renewal and after vibrant renewal. The before-and-after comparisons and the methods by which they went about transition are designed to highlight each shift.

The purpose of this book is not to offer a recipe for church growth. Instead, it is a report. We simply seek to find common ways that the Holy Spirit is working in some vibrant churches today. By describing what He is doing in these churches, you may gather helpful insight into what God desires in your own context.

The pastors and people from our vibrant churches clearly give God credit for what has happened in their settings. In no way do we desire to give the impression that we are the heroes of our stories. While our discernment and obedience are vital, our roles are secondary. Our activity is in response to the Holy Spirit, who is the primary agent in the stories of these local churches.

17

Furthermore, this book is not about simply shifting from small to big. Instead, it's about moving from where you are to where He wants you. Shifting often involves addressing barriers that prevent churches from being faithful and fruitful. And while the churches sought and profiled in this book began with fewer than one hundred in average worship attendance, the content is applicable to churches of all sizes.

This book is written to be a practical resource for laypersons, local church leaders, church boards, pastors, and staffs. Stories from the nine churches are included. The end of each chapter leads into a brief section called "Next Steps," in which Bill Wiesman provides strategies, questions to stimulate group interaction, and suggested books for further reading. Instead of giving you long lists of resources in each area, we chose to share only a few solid resources that tie into the theme of each chapter. All the resources listed have been selected by vibrant pastors because they have been useful in their churches' vibrant renewal.

I am not a writer or an expert. I am a theologian only in the broadest sense of the word. What I am is a *pastor*. I have a heart for local churches to be faithful and fruitful. As I pass along the stories of these nine churches, my hope and my prayer is that you will be better equipped to serve the Lord in your local setting.

SECTION 1
FIRST THINGS

When we vibrant church pastors gathered to discern common characteristics in our churches, we came to realize that not all characteristics are equal. All of them are crucial to each church's vibrant renewal, but two of them are of supreme importance. The first two characteristics are *first things*. They are first simply because they matter most and provide the necessary groundwork for the others.

The *first things* set the stage for the remaining seven characteristics. Without these two, the next seven are not possible. And not only do the *first things* set the stage for the subsequent seven, but they also provide an undercurrent for the rest of the characteristics. They flow into and through the remaining characteristics, feeding and giving life to them.

Our *first things* are (1) *powered by prayer* and (2) *a holy core*. Vibrant pastors determined that their churches had to establish these two before they could move toward vibrant renewal. Therefore, these pastors and churches focused their time, energy, and efforts toward strengthening these two areas. While our *first things* are listed as number one and number two, this is not to suggest that they are sequential or that one is more important than the other. In fact, both rely on each other. They are simultaneous, interdependent, and woven throughout the seven subsequent shifts.

These *first things* are inherently spiritual. They necessitate heart change, transformed lives, and the genuine desire to live in right relationship with Christ. But because they are spiritual in nature, it would be a mistake to assume that they are void of action. The *first things* call for specific actions related to prayer and holiness lived out among the church's core leadership.

When these two are firmly in place, possibilities for vibrant renewal become more than possibilities.

one

SHIFT | POWERED BY PRAYER

When Pastor John Stallings answered the call to restart
the Massillon, Ohio, Church of the Nazarene,
his first initiative was to gather a group of fifty intercessors
who committed to pray daily for the church. Some were
nearby, while others lived far away. John communicated
with them regularly to let them know how to pray
for the church throughout the critical process.
John points to this initiative as the first and
most important reason the Massillon church
has survived and thrived.

All nine of the pastors highlighted in this book point to prayer as the most significant factor in their churches' renewal. All nine of these churches are *powered by prayer*. To say that prayer *powers* ministry is not to suggest that the work of the church is generated by human effort. On the contrary, the very reason why prayer powers ministry is because we humbly seek the Powerful One. Rightly put, it is the Spirit of God who *empowers* when His people reach out to Him. While all churches pray, there are a few commonalities in how these nine churches went about the work of prayer.

PRAY FIRST

Prayer is primary. Massillon, Ohio, Church of the Nazarene is a prime example. Prayer is the first order of business. Prayer is not another activity tacked onto an already busy church schedule. Prayer is not peripheral. Instead, it is preeminent. Each of the pastors of this and the other eight churches knew that before sleeves were rolled up, knees had to get dirty.

At the Owings Mills, Maryland, Latin American First Church of the Nazarene, Pastor Walter Argueta describes prayer as the foundation of the church. From the beginning of his ministry, Pastor Argueta created a schedule for prayer and fasting. Every person in the church is asked to give two days a week to pray and fast. As the church has expanded, Pastor Argueta says it has been crucial for this prayer ministry to expand as well.

Pastor Tony Miller of Clarksville, Tennessee, Grace Church of the Nazarene describes "one of the most significant prayer and spiritual breakthrough moments as a result of three solid months of prayer cottages on Tuesdays and Thursdays . . . until one specific weekend called 'Lay Witness Mission.'"

The entire congregation was assigned a prayer cottage according to the area within which they lived. About fifteen homes were open for prayer between the hours of six and eight in the evening, and each group was given a new list of prayer requests. Primarily, it was a time to pray for revival. At the end of three months we gathered together as a congregation on Friday, all day Saturday, and all day Sunday to hear testimony and teaching about God's transforming power. Over one hundred fifty people came to the altar that one Sunday! We gained one hundred new people in the next month and never declined. Pastor Miller shares another powerful prayer story:

We needed $5,000 for a new sign before opening day of our new building. I called the board and asked anyone else who would come together to meet in the parking lot of our new church building one week before our first Sunday. We marched around the church seven times praying and shouting praise and then gathered in one circle holding hands in prayer. After a good while, one man lifted his head and said, "The Lord just told me to give five hundred dollars for our new sign." We had not even mentioned the need at this point. Soon another followed and then another until all $5,000 was promised, and we opened the church one week later with the new sign.

Pastor Miller is quick to point out that the sign is not the point of the story. The point is that prayer was their first order of business in a time of need.

For each of our vibrant churches, seasons of prayer are planned prior to significant events, revivals, major decisions, and steps of faith. Prayer is powerful because prayer is *primary.*

PRAY MUCH

23

Second, prayer is pervasive throughout each church. Multiple, organized, ongoing prayer initiatives are prevalent in each setting. Pastor David West at the Crossroads Community Church of the Nazarene in Farmington, New Mexico, makes sure every lay leader has a prayer partner. Prayer partners make weekly contact for accountability and intercession.

Similarly, Pastor James Asberry of The Core Church of the Nazarene in Winchester, Virginia, has "pastor and leadership prayer partners," who "pray specifically for a certain pastoral family or one of our leadership team and their family."

At the Waverly, Tennessee, Church of the Nazarene, each newly elected church board has its first meeting around the altar. Board meetings often feel more like prayer meetings. Another vital prayer effort from Waverly is the church's prayer and care group. This is a Wednesday night option that meets simply to pray for people and to write cards to them, letting them know that the group has prayed for them. Each week cards reach those who are ill or grieving, veterans, schoolteachers, pastors far and wide, and many others who need prayer.

Pastor Tony Miller established a prayer closet at his church. People signed up to gather in the prayer closet during morning worship services and prayed specifically for the pastor while he preached, that people would respond to the messages. Pastor Miller noted immediate positive change as a result.

Each of the nine pastors and churches has established multiple, ongoing prayer efforts such as prayer teams, prayer groups, prayer chains, community prayer walks, forty-day seasons of prayer and fasting, and twenty-four-hour prayer vigils. And each church's regular slate of ministries and events (such as small groups, business meetings, and outreach events) is bathed in prayer from beginning to end.

Pastor Walter Argueta expressed this point well. When asked to list the prayer ministries of his church, he simply began listing every single ministry of his church. Every ministry is saturated with prayer. Like blood circulating throughout our bodies, delivering oxygen to billions of cells, prayer circulates through these churches, saturating each ministry, fueling every effort. Prayer is pervasive.

PRAY FORWARD

Third, the content of each church's prayers is significant. When asked, "Specifically, what does your church pray for?" pastors not only responded with expressions like *needs* and *intercession* but also listed *the community, our building, the future of our church, our vision, God's plans for us, our mission, the unchurched,* and *the pastor.* In other words, prayer is both reactive and proactive. While prayer in response to needs, illnesses, and issues is necessary and vital, these churches also pray forward. They make their church's mission and future a prayer priority.

The Crossroads church designates each season of Lent for prayer and fasting for the church's future. Pastor West says these forty-day prayer periods have triggered numerous outreach and ministry opportunities, including the purchase of land, the establishment of a Christian school, the spawning of a day care center, and the purchase of a new facility.

The Waverly, Tennessee, church is in the process of a capital fund-raising campaign called Faith for the Future. Alongside the fund-raising campaign is a prayer campaign called Prayer for the Future, which consists of several prayer efforts intended to fuel the vision. One example, phone alarms are set at 1:27 PM daily to remind people to pray for the future. The time was chosen because Psalm 127:1 is the driving verse for the focus: "Unless the LORD builds the house, the builders labor in vain."

In order to pray for the community, Pastor Junior Sorzano and the people of London, Ontario, First Church of the Nazarene place prayer cards inside bags of food distributed to those in need. People respond by writing their prayer needs and returning the cards to the church. Not only does this ministry offer prayers for those in need, but it also gives the church a

25

second contact with those who return the cards. In addition, the church periodically engages in Sunday evening prayer walks throughout the community.

PROMOTING PRAYER

Pastors were asked, "How do you help people *want* to pray?" Vibrant pastors agree that the best way to motivate people to pray is to celebrate previous answers to prayer, which is done through testimonies, social media, newsletters, prayer chains, and in worship services. Pastor Sorzano and the people of his congregation set aside time in each weekly worship service to celebrate answers to previous prayers. Pastors also noted that prayer breeds prayer. Praying churches naturally attract and raise up prayer warriors. Praying churches become magnets for praying people.

The pastor plays a central role when it comes to prayer. Churches that are powered by prayer have *pastors* who are powered by prayer. Our nine pastors have a deep hunger for God. They want to meet with Him regularly and repeatedly. Pastor Miller states, "Before pastors can lead a church in prayer, they have to come to terms with whether they're convicted of prayer themselves."

Pastor Sorzano made a point in the early days of his ministry to go straight to the altar every time he entered the doors of the church building. Pastor David West missed the worship service on his first Sunday at Crossroads Community Church. Instead of meeting with the church family, he ventured into the community for a prayer walk. On his walk he gathered twelve stones to bring back to the church as a reminder.

These pastors continually seek an encounter with a living God. They live in the thick of the presence of God. They are not praying mechanically or out of a sense of obligation.

26

Instead, they have a deep desire to be in constant communion with Christ.

Several common threads run through our nine churches when it comes to prayer. One key adjective that continually surfaced throughout our conversations was *intentional*. These churches are intentional about teaching and practicing prayer. They are deliberate about when and how and how often people pray. Their pastors are praying. Their initiatives are creative. Their passion is abundant. They clearly understand that prayer is their power source. They pray first. They pray much. And they pray forward.

In Acts 12 the Early Church was facing great opposition and trial. Stephen had been killed. Persecution was spreading. Judean believers faced financial hardship. King Herod was arresting believers. James, the brother of John, was put to death by sword. And Peter was imprisoned. In the midst of this growing persecution and hardship, verse 5 stands out as a welcome ray of hope: "but the church was earnestly praying to God for him." When the church earnestly prays, chains fall and prison doors swing wide open. When the church earnestly prays, renewal is realized and obstacles are overcome. When the church earnestly prays, communities are changed and the mission is materialized. Whatever is happening in your context, let it be said of you, "The church is earnestly praying to God."

27

NEXT STEPS

Chapter 1: Powered by Prayer

1. Chapter 1 key thoughts
   a. Our *first things* are (1) powered by prayer and (2) a holy core.
   b. "*First things* call for specific actions related to prayer . . . lived out among the church's core leadership."

       c. Pray first, pray much, pray forward, promote prayer, intentionally pray.

  2. Discussion starters

     a. Read Acts 4:23-24, 29-35. When the Early Church faced their first crisis, what was their first response? How can your church be mobilized to respond the same way?

     b. Does your community consider your church a house of prayer? Do people who do not attend your church seek out your members and request that the church pray for them?

     c. How does your church behaviorally demonstrate that prayer is not just "another activity" among many others?

     d. A number of illustrations were given in this chapter concerning prayer. Which of these has your church practiced before? Which might be incorporated into the prayer life of your church?

       (1) Use of a prayer closet during worship services. Where? Who?

       (2) Scheduling of specific times of prayer and fasting. When?

       (3) Seasons of prayer prior to significant events. Which events?

       (4) A prayer partner for every leader. Who?

       (5) Praying forward for the church's mission and future. How? When?

       (6) Prayer walks through the community. Where? When?

       (7) Celebrating answers to prayer in every service. How?

       (8) Prayer retreat for the pastor and leadership. When?

  3. Suggestions for further reading

       Jim Cymbala, *When God's People Pray* (Grand Rapids: Zondervan Publishing House, 2007).

28

Jonathan L. Graf and Lani C. Hinkle, eds., *My House Shall Be a House of Prayer* (Colorado Springs: NavPress, 2001).

John Wesley, *How to Pray: The Best of John Wesley on Prayer* (Uhrichsville, Ohio: Barbour, 2007).

two

SHIFT A HOLY CORE

There is an "aha" God experience
before there is an "aha" growth experience.
—Pastor Tony Miller

Every church has a core, a nucleus, a hub of people who hold authority. These are people to whom others look when decisions must be made. They may or may not be elected to official leadership positions within the church. But they are leaders. They may or may not have keys to the church building. But they possess keys to the church itself.

As the core goes, so the church goes. When this inner circle is divided, so is the rest of the church. When the core lacks spiritual maturity, the church follows suit. When the core is idle or self-focused, the rest of the people fall in line. Conversely, when a core becomes healthy, good health seeps into the rest of the body. When a core is filled with missional impulses, those impulses surge through the church body. When a core group is unified, their unity permeates the people. Like a rudder on a vessel, the core group of a church sets the course for the church as a whole.

Before any church can experience renewed life and growth, changes need to happen within the core. In a word, the core must be *holy*. The command to "be holy, because I am holy" (Leviticus 11:44; 1 Peter 1:16) is a thread that runs throughout the whole of Scripture. God's people are called to surrender their hearts, their wills, and their lives to the lordship of Christ. Made possible by only God's grace, the goal of the Christian in this life is to be cleansed from sin, renewed in the image of God, and empowered to love fully. The call to holiness is the call to Christlikeness.

This call to holiness is both individual and corporate in nature. Not only are just *you* or just *I* called to be holy—*we* are called to be holy. When the core group of a church is holy, not only does each individual leader embody Christlikeness, but the whole group is marked by a sanctified spirit. A holy core displays spiritual maturity. A holy core is together, even in the midst of disagreement. Our nine pastors agree that a holy core is one of the *first things* a church needs in place before it can begin to experience authentic vibrant renewal.

In John 17 we hear Jesus' intimate and powerful prayer to the Father. He poured out His heart in this last prayer before being arrested. Jesus beautifully weaved together the themes of unity, holiness, and mission. Like three strands of the same cord, these inseparable threads are components of a faithful people. Jesus prayed fervently for us to become unified, holy, and missional. The core group of every church sets the tone for the rest of the church. The core helps determine if Jesus' prayer will be answered affirmatively in their setting.

Vibrant pastors entered their churches at varying stages of health. One of the nine was technically a restart. While the others were not restarts per se, each of the pastors knew that significant work lay ahead. When asked to describe their

31

churches prior to renewal, our pastors used the following ex-pressions: *unhealthy, focused on minors and ignored majors, survival mode, afraid of change, lacking in vision, focused on past and petty things, not unified, spiritually sick,* and *leadership based on worldly success.*

These pastors realized something early on. If necessary changes were going to take place within the whole church, they had to begin with the core leaders. We asked these pastors to share specifically what they did to help their leaders grow in spiritual maturity.

PERSONAL HOLINESS

The core of a church obviously includes the pastor. The pastor's spiritual maturity has a direct effect on the spiritual maturity of the remaining core and the whole church. A great responsibility rests with the pastor to set the spiritual tone and level of expectation for the core group. Robert Murray M'Cheyne, Scottish pastor and writer from the mid-1800s, said, "The greatest need of my congregation is my own personal holiness."[1] While the implementation of strategies and tools is helpful, it becomes woefully insufficient if the pastor is not modeling a life submitted to the lordship of Christ.

Pastors, your church's greatest need is your own personal holiness. Their greatest need is not your faithful preaching, your administrative capabilities, or your relational skills. More than anything, your church needs a pastor who is living in total submission to the lordship of Jesus. There is a direct connection between your personal holiness and your church's corporate holiness. Your constant message to the core group of your church should be these words of the apostle Paul to the Corinthian believers: "Follow my example, as I follow the example of Christ" (1 Corinthians 11:1).

32

More important, *your* greatest need is *your own* personal holiness. Aside from your responsibility to your church, your holiness is a matter of personal obedience. You need to be holy, not just to lead your church somewhere but because your holiness is an end in itself. Are you living in fullness of relationship with God? Have you abandoned self-will? Are you completely surrendered to Christ?

Unless you are living in complete submission to Jesus, filled with His Holy Spirit, then ministry practices become mere tactics, tricks of the trade, hollow methods that might give the appearance of authentic renewal. I don't mean to give the impression that pastors struggle because they are not holy. I know plenty of holy pastors who struggle in their personal lives and their churches. Instead, what I'm saying is this: Your church will not experience authentic vibrant renewal without a holy core. And a core will not be a holy core without a holy *pastor.*

IT'S NOT ABOUT US

Pastor John Stallings is quick to point out that the single thing that impacted his core group the most was "loving others." Conventional wisdom might say, "Focus on the core to strengthen the core." Pastor Stallings did the opposite. He turned the core group's attention outside itself in order to be strengthened. As church leaders embraced those in need, not only were they obedient by loving and serving others, but God used that mind-set and those encounters to increase the spiritual maturity of the group.

The prayerful tone of the church board meetings at the Waverly, Tennessee, church was mentioned in the first chapter. It applies here as well. The first board meeting of every year around the altar sets a spiritual tone for the rest of the year. Unity is reinforced. Common vision is upheld. And every

33

meeting thereafter is saturated with vision and prayer. Our final agenda item for every board meeting is the discussion of new people to our church family. *Who has begun coming? What is God doing in their lives? How can we better connect them to the body?* When we conclude each board meeting with this agenda item, we leave remembering why we do everything else. While establishing committees and addressing finances are necessary work for a board, we are reminded that our most important work is people.

Lay leaders in the Waverly church adopted a common phrase a long time ago: *It's not about me.* Holy leaders know that it's not about them. It's not about their agenda or their opinions. Instead, it's about God's purposes. It's about people who don't yet know him. Holy leaders are willing to sacrifice their sentiments for the greater good of the body. More than once in board meetings in Waverly a leader has said something like "I don't know about this. I'm not sure this is the best direction—but I trust our pastor. And I trust the rest of you. So I'm with you." When leadership teams are filled with people who possess such a Spirit-filled, selfless mind-set, we become powerful tools in the hands of a mighty God.

34

LEADERSHIP ACCOUNTABILITY

Some of our pastors noted that they raised the level of accountability and expectation for those who serve in positions of leadership. Pastors Jim Asberry, David West, and Junior Sorzano require lay leaders to go through intensive discipleship training courses. Crossroads Community Church has a mandatory seventeen-week course for leaders. The Core offers a thirty-six-week discipleship program. And London, Ontario, First Church has a Leadership Training Institute that draws curriculum directly from the Church of the Nazarene's Continuing Lay Training program.[2] In each of these cases the core group is willing to require themselves and other leaders to submit to the process.

Pastor Sorzano has established regular prayer emphases and leadership retreats in which he continually examines and emphasizes the mission and purpose of the church. Through these retreats he reinforces the core group's agenda harmony. Several other pastors emphasize the value of ongoing training for board members and lay leaders. These training sessions, however they happen to be executed, offer spiritually rich, targeted training for leaders. Throughout these training sessions, leaders are developed, and the core group harmonizes around common values and vision.

At the Waverly church, much of this work is done on Sunday nights and Wednesday nights. People who typically attend those services are the core group. Instead of cluttering the calendar with additional training sessions, those services are designated for leadership development. They are not always labeled as such. Whether the people realize it or not, each Bible study, each devotional, and each topic of discussion on Sunday nights and Wednesday nights serves the purpose of growing and maturing leaders.

35

In addition to meeting stated requirements for service on the local church board, several of our pastors ask the nominating committee to consider only those who are actively serving in some form of ministry in or through the church. The leadership bar is then raised to include only those who are invested enough in the church to give themselves to the ministry of the church. From a pastor's perspective, it is important to have only those who are regularly committed to the ministry of the church to be in position to make crucial leadership decisions for the church.

A few of our pastors honestly admitted that in order for their church's core to be strengthened and sanctified, sometimes that meant certain leaders needed to step away from their official positions of leadership. In some cases the leader did not adhere to stated requirements for leadership. In other cases they were clearly morally unfit, while sometimes they simply weren't in line with the larger vision of the church. While such action is never ideal, there were times in which these waters needed to be delicately and prayerfully navigated in order for the church's core group to become healthier, more missional, and unified.

HOLINESS IS OUR CORE

A holy core group is crucial, because holiness is our core. It is the centerpiece of what it means to be followers of Jesus, the heart of what we believe and hold dear. Holiness is life lived in radical obedience to Jesus through the power of the Holy Spirit. When leadership groups of local churches, including pastors, boards, and lay leaders, give themselves and their efforts over to the power of a holy God, then whole churches begin the process of authentic renewal. When agendas are laid aside and opinions are measured against God's vision, the core group becomes a mighty tool for God's purposes. The entire church need not be in one accord for the church to move forward, but the core group (including pastor, staff, and lay leadership) must be in harmony with God and one another. Each of these churches teaches us that a holy core is an essential *first thing* for any local church to move forward. There is power in a holy core.

NEXT STEPS

Chapter 2: A Holy Core

1. Chapter 2 key thoughts

   a. Our *first things* are (1) powered by prayer and (2) a holy core.

   b. "*First things* call for specific actions related to being a holy core . . . lived out among the church's core leadership."

   c. As the core goes, so the church goes. The church's greatest need is the pastor's personal holiness, a pastor who is living in total submission to the lordship of Jesus. It's not about us—our most important work is people. Leaders must be accountable. A holy core group is crucial because holiness is our core; it is the centerpiece of what it means to be followers of Jesus. There is power in a holy core.

2. Discussion starters

   a. Read John 17. Do your core leaders have unity, holiness, and missional focus for the lost? Is this behaviorally displayed? How?

   b. Do your core leaders reflect the image of Christ toward one another and toward others? How?

   c. Have your core leaders reflected spiritual maturity even in the midst of disagreement? When?

   d. What additional corporate spiritual practices could your leaders engage in to intentionally develop as a holy core? When?

   e. What ongoing training is provided for the leaders of your church to develop common values and vision? What might be added? When?

37

f. Does anything need to be removed from my life in order to reflect the holiness of God? What? How will I deal with this?

g. Am I loving God completely and my neighbor as myself? Is this behaviorally demonstrated? How?

3. Suggestions for further reading

Nina G. Gunter and Gay Leonard, *Holy Leadership in a Hectic World* (Kansas City: Beacon Hill Press of Kansas City, 2009).

Bill Wiesman, ed., *A Holy Purpose: 5 Strategies for Making Christlike Disciples* (Kansas City: Beacon Hill Press of Kansas City, 2011).

SECTION 2
PASTOR SHIFTS

I wish I could bring you to the table. When our nine vibrant pastors met for three summits, our meeting times were marked with rich, Spirit-filled dialogue. They shared inspiring stories and told what God taught them. Their faith is contagious. Their passion is abundant. And their humility is remarkable. My greatest joy in all my endeavors on the Vibrant Church Task Force is to be among these eight men and one lady. Being with them energizes me.

There is much that could be said and should be said about these pastors. All of them name mentors who have significantly impacted their lives and ministries. Their longevity in their churches has earned them credibility to lead the churches through the changes laid out in this book. Most important, each of these pastors' hearts beats for God's heart. These nine pastors exemplify the *first things*. They are powered by prayer, and they live holy lives. I have been charged with the nearly impossible task of expressing their hearts on these printed pages.

While much could be said about these pastors, they put their fingers on two specific areas, which we will call *pastor shifts*. All the characteristics of vibrant churches obviously relate to the pastor. He or she has a significant responsibility to lead churches in each of the nine areas and beyond. But two of our shifts directly involve the pastor's role and activity. Vibrant pastors determined that these two *pastor shifts* were essential for each of their churches' renewed life and growth.

The pastor shifts are (1) *doer* to *equipper* and (2) *desk* to *field*. Vibrant pastors had to change their mind-sets and their actions related to these two shifts. First of all, these shifts are biblically based. Our scriptures are clear. These shifts articulate God's design for Kingdom leaders. Second, these shifts free pastors from outdated, ineffective ministry models. Many pastors' hands are tied because of errant expectations or assumptions related to pastoral ministry.

While these are not "people shifts," the laypersons of vibrant churches were not without responsibility. In order for each pastor to effectively make these paradigm changes, the support and blessing of lay leadership were required. Vibrant pastors could have had every desire and intention to make these changes. But if their lay leaders had not been willing to allow their pastors to function differently, these shifts would not have become reality.

40

When pastors begin to imagine and operate differently, both pastors and laypersons are released to experience the joy of fulfilling their Kingdom calling. And the potential for vibrant church renewal becomes palpable.

three

SHIFT DOER TO EQUIPPER

I recognized that we had to change the mind-set and philosophy of the church board and its leaders. We sought to reeducate the leadership on the "role of the pastor," to release the pastor to do the ministry of equipping others. We began a series on discipleship, seminars on finding and using your spiritual gifts, established a Leadership Training Institute, and had fifteen individuals enrolled in the first series of courses. In raising up a generation of competent and Spirit-filled leaders, I was freed up to concentrate on specific areas of ministry without other areas in the church being neglected. Today we have a leadership team of about twenty-eight individuals who meet bimonthly for equipping, training, prayer, and accountability.

—Pastor Junior Sorzano

41

One might assume that the word *pastor* appears in the Bible dozens of times. In fact, the word is recorded only once in Scripture: "Christ himself gave . . . *pastors* . . . to equip his people for works of service, so that the body of Christ may be built up" (Ephesians 4:11-12, emphasis added). This passage is crucial for developing a healthy, biblical understanding of the role of a pastor. The verb that is used in conjunction with *pastor* is *equip*. Going back to the original language, we find that one definition of *equip* is "to make ready for use."

Needless to say, pastors of all ages, church sizes, personality types, and denominations easily become consumed by multiple demands. Whether pastors are driven by models they learned, the expectations of the people, their perfectionism, or the assumption that the work won't get done unless the pastor does it himself or herself, too many pastors are doing too many things.

One significant commonality among our vibrant pastors is the intentional shift from *doer* to *equipper*. All nine went about the challenging work of shifting this paradigm. Prior to this shift, vibrant pastors report performing the following regular duties: janitorial services, maintenance, making coffee, secretarial work, taking out the garbage, creating and folding bulletins, locking and unlocking doors, landscaping, direct oversight of various ministry projects, and more. These are noble and necessary tasks. And there may be instances in which pastors need to lead by example when it comes to humble service. But the pastor's schedule can easily be filled with *doing* to the extent that it prevents the pastor from *equipping*.

Some of our pastors recognized the need for this shift from the beginning. From the start they laid the groundwork for less doing and more equipping. Other pastors fully embraced the paradigm of doing, only to find themselves stretched because of ministry demands. Their realization of the need to shift was a reaction to their overwhelming workload. Regardless of whether they came to the shift reactively or proactively, each of our pastors had to shift from *doer* to *equipper*.

One of the first tasks in equipping is locating leaders. Finding the right person for the right ministry task is a univer-

42

sal challenge for pastors. Locating leaders takes Spirit-led discernment. Each of our pastors went about the rigorous work of identifying people for service. Locating leaders is not an exact science. All pastors can share numerous stories of successes and failures in this area. Multiple tools were used, such as ministry surveys, spiritual gifts testing, personality-type testing, ministry fairs, and ministry coaches. At the most basic level, it takes knowing people, trusting the Spirit, and simply asking them to serve. In many cases it's as simple as "You do not have because you do not ask" (James 4:2).

When asked about this particular shift, several of our pastors used the same word: *release*. They talked about *releasing* ministry to the people. The assumption might be that a strong leader is one who keeps, controls, and contains ministry. Vibrant pastors take a different approach. In a spirit of true humility, they freely give ministry to others. Not only do they delegate smaller duties, but they willingly share larger tasks as well.

For example, three of our nine vibrant churches have a regular pulpit rotation. One might assume that a task as significant and central as preaching would be kept solely within the pastor's realm of duties. Instead, these particular pastors regularly step aside in order to release the preaching ministry to others who are called and gifted. Such release requires a small ego and large confidence in God's work through others. These pastors realize that they don't need to have their hands in every area of ministry, even the areas that are traditionally considered central to pastoral work.

Delegation is key. But equipping requires far more than delegating. In addition to locating the right person for the right task, pastors must resource them to sufficiently complete the work. At Crossroads Community Church, Pastor David West's mandatory seventeen-week leadership course serves this very

43

purpose. He also regularly steers ministry leaders toward Nazarene Bible College's online training program. The church budgets money to pay for leaders' tuition costs. Pastor West also implemented what he calls The Jesus Principle. Thinking in terms of concentric circles, he personally invests in three to five individuals that are his inner circle (his Peter, James, and John). He then surrounds himself with an outer circle of eight to twelve who may one day be part of the inner group. The goal is to resource these few in order to reach many. Other vibrant pastors take a similar approach, intentionally bringing a small group of leaders or potential leaders around them in order to equip them to serve others.

Pastor Tony Miller says,

> My main vehicle to carry the primary leadership team (paid and non-paid staff) is monthly ministry meetings, which are something other than board meetings. Second, twice per year I bring in a specialist and have every leader over every ministry as well as all teachers attend a Saturday workshop. I make sure they are the best of the best, and I also try to gently "require" the attendance of all leaders.

Each of our other pastors implemented similar training programs. They took different forms in each setting. Some used Saturday training workshops. Some brought in outside experts. Some used Sunday nights and Wednesday nights for equipping. Each church implemented a structure for equipping. And each pastor held as one of their primary preaching goals "to equip his people for works of service, so that the body of Christ may be built up" (Ephesians 4:12).

Pastor Jim Asberry speaks for all the vibrant church pastors when he says, "We work hard to create an atmosphere of involvement with our congregation." Through preaching, teaching, and one-on-one interaction, the message is constantly sent to the church body that the expectation is for all people to serve. One of the primary ways this is accomplished is through new member orientation or membership classes. Pastor Tony Miller asked the question in each new member orientation: "How are you going to serve?" Similarly, at Waverly Church of the Nazarene each group of people who enter the church orientation course are told, "We don't want you to join. Instead, we want you to join *in*." Some people think of joining the church as a mere affirmation of shared belief and a desire to be officially affiliated with the church. While shared belief and church affiliation are important, more is expected. We want people to join *in* the work of the church. The new member orientation course gives great opportunity to be upfront about vision, values, and expectations of people before they make a commitment. Doing so communicates expectation, creates a climate of involvement, and imparts the church's DNA into newcomers.

While books, training programs, sermons, and other resources are valuable equipping tools, there is no greater tool than simple trial and error. Pastor Miller says, "The best 'gift testing' I have found, after explaining the different gifts, is to follow your desires and 'trial and error.'" Laura Root of New Hope Church of the Nazarene, Princeton, Illinois, says the best way to equip people for service is to take them with her while doing ministry. She says, "It's better caught than taught." People do not learn, *then* serve. They often learn *by* serving. Like on-the-job training, there is no better way to equip people to serve than to give them the opportunity to serve. Doing otherwise would be like reading a manual on swimming before you get wet. You learn to swim by getting into the water and flopping and splashing until you eventually swim.

45

In the same way, people learn how to serve by actually serving. This was Jesus' preferred method of equipping. Instead of putting the disciples into a classroom until He deemed them ready for the mission, the classroom *was* the mission field. They learned as they served. There is no better method of equipping than bringing people with you into ministry, adequately resourcing them, and patiently trusting that the Spirit will impart wisdom and skill in due time.

We recognize that all believers are called to be ministers. God also calls some to vocational ministry; some full-time, others part time. The strong culture of equipping present in our vibrant churches is evidenced by the number of people who have been called to vocational ministry from each church. During each pastor's tenure, multiple people have been called to vocational ministry. The fewest number of people called to ministry within the pastor's tenure in a vibrant church is four. The largest number is sixteen. Each pastor has an eye for laypersons within whom God may be stirring a summons to the vocation of ministry. Each pastor makes a serious effort to come alongside those who are potentially called, develop them, resource them, and encourage them forward. Most of those who are called within vibrant churches have become staff members of their respective churches. Others have been sent into other congregations and contexts in order to fulfill God's call upon their lives.

Upon beginning their tenures, eight of the nine vibrant pastors were the only ministry staff personnel in their churches. The lone exception: one of the nine churches had a children's pastor at the beginning of the pastor's tenure. Because of the strong culture of equipping, vibrant churches currently average five ministry staff persons per church. If additional ministry ventures such as day cares and thrift stores are included

46

in the calculation, vibrant churches average almost eight staff persons per church. Some of these are part-time or non-paid. All of them are designated as staff. And the strong majority of these staff positions are filled from within each church. Vibrant church staff members are home-grown. Because each church has a strong culture of equipping, there is less need to venture outside the church to bring staff personnel on board. Potential ministers are identified, equipped, resourced, and elevated to leadership within each church. And once they are in place, senior pastors of vibrant churches make sure staff members understand that one of their primary roles is to equip others for ministry. Pastor Tony Miller regularly reminded staff members that sixty percent of their work is recruiting and developing others to lead. The shift from *doer* to *equipper* is not limited to the senior pastor but must be the mind-set of staff as well.

The shift from *doer* to *equipper* is clearly a *pastor shift*. But the laity share great responsibility here. This shift is often made difficult by expectations of laypersons that come in direct conflict with equipping. "That's what we pay the pastor for" is a cliché that causes pastors to cringe. In many churches, laypersons hold expectations of the pastor to *do* the ministry of the church. While these expectations may be well-intentioned, they prevent the pastor from fulfilling his or her biblical call to *equip* people. Pastors' calendars can be so cluttered with the demands of *doing*, that there is not enough time or energy for *equipping*. The end result is a lowered ceiling. The work of the church is limited to the giftedness and time of one person. It is crucial for laypersons, specifically those on lay leadership teams, to understand the need for this shift to take place. Permission must be given for pastors' job duties to change. Sometimes that means releasing certain duties that are commonly

47

associated with traditional pastoral care. Not only must permission be given, but lay leaders should encourage and hold their pastors accountable to less *doing* and more *equipping*. Lay leaders should periodically ask, "Pastor, what can we take off your plate?" or emphatically state, "Pastor, you're doing too much!" Such accountability enables the pastor to better fulfill his or her biblical call to equip. A crucial accountability tool for laypersons regarding this *pastor shift* is a written job or ministry description for the pastor. Few pastors can point to a written job description, which often subjects them to the multiple expectations of the many people in the church. No pastor can live up to such a varied set of expectations. A clearly written job or ministry description that is approved by the church's lay leadership team is a weight-lifting blessing for pastors.

The *pastor shift* from *doer* to *equipper* is good not only for the pastor and for ministry effectiveness. It is also good for the people of the church. Simply put, God calls people to ministry. And there is great joy in fulfilling that call. When pastors are doing ministry to the detriment of equipping others, then people are robbed of the joy of doing the ministry to which they are called. If God's people are truly a "royal priesthood" (1 Peter 2:9), then this shift is necessary not only for ministry effectiveness but also to every Christian's development as a Kingdom servant.

The story of Moses and Jethro in Exodus 18 provides welcome solace for any pastor who is strapped with the demands of *doing*. Jethro's prophetic instructions for Moses are just as prophetic for pastors today. Hear Jethro's bold directive:

> What you are doing is not good. You and these people who come to you will only wear yourselves out. The work is too heavy for you; you cannot handle it alone. Listen now to me and I will give you some advice, and may

God be with you. You must be the people's representative before God and bring their disputes to him. Teach them his decrees and instructions, and show them the way they are to live and how they are to behave. But select capable men from all the people—men who fear God, trustworthy men who hate dishonest gain—and appoint them as officials over thousands, hundreds, fifties and tens. Have them serve as judges for the people at all times, but have them bring every difficult case to you; the simple cases they can decide themselves. That will make your load lighter, because they will share it with you. If you do this and God so commands, you will be able to stand the strain, and all these people will go home satisfied (*Exodus 18:17-23*).

When pastors and churches embrace the *pastor shift* from *doer* to *equipper*, the biblical model for ministry is realized. Both pastors and laity are freed to fulfill their respective callings. Leaders are developed. Ministry is maximized. The church is energized. The kingdom of God advances. And this one shift sets the whole church in forward motion toward greater health and vibrant renewal.

NEXT STEPS

Chapter 3: *Doer* to *Equipper*

1. Chapter 3 key thoughts
   a. Vibrant pastors determined that two *pastor shifts* were required for renewed life and growth of their congregations: (1) *doer* to *equipper* and (2) *desk* to *field*.
   b. Lay leaders must be willing to allow their pastor to make this shift.

49

    c. An intentional shift—less doing, more equipping. Locating leaders takes Spirit-led discernment. Releasing and resourcing lay ministry leaders is key. Create an atmosphere of involvement—not "join" but "join *in*."

2. Discussion starters

    a. Read and discuss Ephesians 4:11-12. What does this scripture teach about the primary role of the pastor? On a scale of 1 to 10, with 1 being "not at all" and 10 being "all the time," how well does your church reflect the primary role of pastor as equipper?

    b. Have the laypeople in this church given the pastor permission to delegate and release ministries?

    c. If you are a lay leader, are there areas of ministry that you could do that are now being done by the pastor? Which ones?

    d. If you are a pastor, are there areas of ministry that could be delegated to lay leaders? Which ones?

    e. Tools such as ministry surveys, spiritual gifts testing, ministry fairs, and so on are used to help identify leaders. Are there tools to identify and equip leaders used by this church? Which ones?

    f. Does this church intentionally develop an atmosphere of involvement in service to others? How?

    g. Estimate how many people in the past five years have been called into full-time vocational ministry from your church. How might an atmosphere be developed for the Holy Spirit to work where it is normal for people to be called into vocational ministry?

3. Suggestions for further reading

Dennis Bickers, *The Healthy Pastor: Easing the Pressures of Ministry* (Kansas City: Beacon Hill Press of Kansas City, 2010).

Bill Hybels, *The Volunteer Revolution: Unleashing the Power of Everybody* (Grand Rapids: Zondervan Publishing House, 2004).

Andy Stanley, *Next Generation Leader: Five Essentials for Those Who Will Shape the Future* (Portland, Oreg.: Multnomah Press, 2003).

four

SHIFT DESK TO FIELD

My most memorable story would be about Brenda, manager of a nearby BP convenience store. For five years I invited her to Friend Day. For four years she said she would come but never did. All the while I bought my coffee and gas from her. For five years I stopped by every other day, asking about her family and business. Soon she began to open up and confide in me when no other customers were around. Sometime in the fifth year she asked, "Aren't you going to invite me to Friend Day?" Of course I did. She came, and she was saved. Then she brought her two teenage children, her brother, and her husband! They all gave their hearts to Jesus too. Praise His holy name! That Easter one whole row was filled by this family and their friends. They are faithful today. And it took a relationship of five years.
—Pastor Tony Miller

It took a pastor who ventured away from his desk. It took a pastor who intentionally built a relationship over the long haul with an unchurched person. It took weeks and months and years. It took a shift—from the *desk* to the *field*.

One remarkable commonality between our nine vibrant pastors is that they regularly leave the confines of their studies. Not that there isn't enough work to do behind their desks. There always is. These pastors understand the importance of their personal movement into the mission field. While sermon-planning, study, prayer, and administration are vital ministry endeavors, so is pulling away from church buildings and church people in order to interact with those who don't yet know Christ. Our second *pastor shift* is from *desk* to *field*. This shift is evidenced in a number of creative ways.

PUBLIC SCHOOLS

We at the Waverly Church of the Nazarene have adopted the elementary school across the street. My regular volunteer service at Waverly Elementary School began for a number of reasons: (1) Our church property sits directly across the street from the school campus. (2) Our church officially adopted the school several years ago. (3) One of our church's primary areas of focus is children's ministry. (4) My service at the school gives me more opportunities to interact with people from the community than any other form of community service. (5) Children are often gatekeepers when it comes to reaching whole families with the gospel. And (6)—it's just plain fun.

I greet at the front doors of the school Monday through Thursday. Alongside other volunteers from the community, I open car doors, assist children into the building, help traffic flow quickly and safely, and provide a warm welcome to children, parents, and school employees. I regularly read books to classes. One teacher has me visit every Wednesday to read to her class. In addition, I help chaperone field trips and class parties and make myself available however needed.

53

Pastor Jeff Griffith of Waynesboro, Virginia, Community Fellowship Church also gives his time at a local elementary school. He regularly tutors children who need help with schoolwork, and once a week he is a "lunch buddy," eating lunch in the school cafeteria and building relationships. The majority of his work in the school is spent with children who come from single-parent homes.

It is no secret that public schools are mission fields. Schools are places where children spend the majority of their waking time. Teachers and other school employees are charged with great responsibility to shape and educate our children. These are primary places where children receive their education. They are educated officially by teachers and receive an unofficial education, whether good or bad, from their peers. When pastors are granted access, few places in the community offer as much opportunity to connect with people who need to experience the love of Christ.

School administrators and teachers have expressed their concern that many children lack positive adult male relationships. Many come from single-parent homes. Most of those are cases in which the mother is the single parent. And the majority of elementary schools have mostly female staffs. For these reasons, positive male presence is lacking in the lives of many young people. Pastor Jeff and I recognize the special privilege of being male volunteers in schools. We have a great opportunity to offer service, provide positive male presence, and witness to children, their families, the school staff, and our communities.

COMPASSIONATE LIFESTYLE

Vibrant church pastors realize that preaching and teaching compassionate ministry is not enough. For their sake and for the sake of their churches, these pastors actively engage needy people on a regular basis.

Pastor Junior Sorzano of London, Ontario, talks about his shift from *desk* to *field*: "I decided to lead by example and got involved in our community. I started and led two nursing home ministries by conducting monthly services, and I served with Mission Services of London in their drug and alcohol program. Tuesday is my community outreach day. I visit the local prison and conduct two chapel services, and I have also joined our outreach team in a street hot dog ministry. I also participate in a quarterly on-call chaplain program at one of our hospitals."

Pastor Laura Root also serves as a hospital chaplain. In addition, she leads a twelve-step recovery group. And Pastor Laura has personally taken on the demanding work of foster parenting.

Pastor John Stallings exemplifies this all-important shift. Because his church was a restart, he began with a clean slate. From day one, Pastor John began pouring himself into compassionate ministry in his community. He says, "For me it was never the *desk*. I told them up front that I did not 'do office' well. 'If you need me,' I told them, 'call my cell phone.' I started the restart from the *field*." Consequently, Pastor John is the president of the Massillon Area Homeless Taskforce. He leads the church's Hope House, a center for women who are giving up drugs, prostitution, or abusive relationships. He also leads the Hope Home and Hope Home 2, which offer shelter to the same women. He regularly spends time in jails and hospitals. And he is always on the lookout for people in the community who need trees cut or houses painted. Because Pastor John's life embodies this shift so thoroughly, his long hours spent in the courtroom have gained him credibility with the courts. One judge periodically consults Pastor Stallings when it comes

55

to sentencing and decision-making on the best course of action for rehabilitation.

Much of Jesus' work was meeting real human needs. Whether it was feeding the hungry, embracing the poor, or healing the sick, Jesus' eyes and arms were consistently directed toward "the least of these." These vibrant pastors take seriously the biblical commands to come alongside those who suffer. As they shift from *desk* to *field*, compassion is their way of life.

EVERYDAY INTERACTION

Like Pastor Tony Miller and Brenda, the convenience store manager, vibrant pastors make the most of everyday opportunities to build relationships and witness to those with whom they come in contact. Pastor Tony regularly connects with unchurched people in social settings. Through activities like fishing and golf, he spends time with people who need Christ. Through these encounters, he leads them to the place where they can come to know Jesus.

Pastor Jim Asberry of The Core Church of the Nazarene in Winchester, Virginia, does not have to go out of his way to interact with unchurched people. Instead, he views everyday contacts as Spirit-led opportunities to make connections. His insurance agent, the bank teller, his son's teammates' parents, and the server in his favorite restaurant are all people who need to know Christ. Pastor Jim is intentional about the relationships he already has.

On the other hand, Pastor Jeff Griffith does go out of his way to interact with unchurched people. Today his church has almost seven hundred members and nearly five hundred in Sunday morning worship attendance. Pastor Jeff is bivocational. But it's not because he must be. In fact, he gives away the money he earns from his secular job. Three days a week,

56

hours before he begins his day in the church office, Pastor Jeff gets up at three o'clock in the morning to go to his part-time job at a FedEx shipping center. He moves packages and builds relationships. Over time, Pastor Jeff has become the "chaplain" of his workplace. His reliability and genuine concern for his coworkers gains credibility with them. Being the only pastor many of them know, Pastor Jeff preaches their families' funerals and officiates their wedding ceremonies. Most important, he witnesses to them. His coworkers see the love of Christ as a result of Pastor Jeff's efforts.

GET BEHIND ME, CHURCH!

In each case, vibrant pastors live missionally in their communities. The nature of their community involvement takes different forms, depending on their context and giftedness. And these are more than token efforts. All of them give significant amounts of time, effort, and resources to local missions work. They don't have just missional hearts—they have missional *hands*.

There are two primary reasons why they have adopted this lifestyle. First of all, they engage unchurched people because they are devoted to God's call upon their lives to live missionally. They want people to know Jesus. If you ask any of these pastors, they will tell you that their community involvement is a matter of personal obedience.

The second reason these pastors engage their communities is because they are intentionally modeling missional living for their churches. They realize that the best way for their congregations to engage their communities is for the pastor to lead them there. Vibrant pastors can credibly preach and teach about missional living because they spend their weeks in the trenches.

Imagine being part of the Massillon, Ohio, Church of the Nazarene. When you witness Pastor John spending the majority of his week with the homeless and destitute of the community, it would be hard not to follow him there. If you were part of the Waynesboro Community Fellowship Church of the Nazarene, listening to Pastor Jeff preach and teach about service and mission, knowing that he inconveniences himself by getting up long before sunrise three times a week to go to a second job, you would find that his words would carry more weight with you.

Several of our pastors mentioned the value of inviting others to come alongside them as they serve. Pastor Tony Miller makes a habit of bringing staff members with him on evangelistic calls. Pastor John Stallings regularly involves laypeople in his community service. Such efforts become opportunities for equipping others to embrace missional living. This is where our two pastor shifts intersect. Equipping people to serve and moving into the field are simultaneous shifts that work together to achieve greater faithfulness and Kingdom fruit.

58

Few pastors need to be convinced of the importance of shifting from the desk to the field. We understand the rationale. We are fully aware of God's repeated command to "go" (Genesis 12:1; Mark 16:15; Matthew 28:19), and we want to be "witnesses in [our] Jerusalem" (Acts 1:8). The shift from the desk to the field often requires trimming the workload in other areas. Like the first pastor shift, this one also depends on the support and accountability of laypeople. Pastors need faithful laypeople to assist with responsibilities that pastors routinely perform in order to free their schedules. Pastors need faithful laypeople who understand that they must be released from "office hours" to personally engage the community. This shift necessitates a shift not only in the pastor's activity but also in the people's mind-set.

To find a model for this shift, we need look no further than Jesus himself. First, the incarnation provides a powerful theological framework for moving from the *desk* to the *field*. The second Person of the Trinity "made himself nothing by taking the very nature of a servant, being made in human likeness" (Philippians 2:7). Coming from heaven to earth, Jesus exemplified this shift. Second, Jesus' three years of ministry were constantly spent engaging those in need. Instead of being tied to the Temple, His "office hours" were in the field—among the poor, the sick, and the needy. He said, "It is not the healthy who need a doctor, but the sick. I have not come to call the righteous, but sinners to repentance" (Luke 5:31-32). By speaking these words and living this life, Jesus clearly illustrates the importance of this shift.

The *pastor shift* from the *desk* to the *field* is integral to the health and renewal of the church as a whole. In order for local churches to become agents of healing and mission for their communities, their pastors must first personally, continually embrace those outside the church. When pastors make this shift, the Holy Spirit uses their efforts to begin the forward movement of His people.

59

NEXT STEPS

Chapter 4: *Desk* to *Field*

1. Chapter 4 key thoughts
    a. Vibrant pastors determined that two *pastor shifts* were required for renewed life and growth of their congregations: (1) *doer* to *equipper* and (2) *desk* to *field*.

    b. Personal involvement in the mission field. Interaction with those who don't yet know Jesus. Public schools. Compassionate lifestyle. Everyday interaction. Missional hearts *and* hands.

2. Discussion starters

    a. Read John 4:35-36 and Luke 10:2-3. What does Jesus say about the harvest? Why does Jesus say, "Go"? Why can't we stay in the safety of the church and wait for the harvest to come to us?

    b. Is there a public school that your church could adopt? How? When?

    c. If not a school, then is there another area of ministry your church could start?

    d. Are you modeling a lifestyle of compassion? How?

    e. Are there unchurched people you are intentionally developing a relationship with? Whom?

    f. Are you making the most of the relationships with the unchurched that you already have? How? Are there ways that you might increase the effectiveness of your ministry to the unchurched? How?

    g. Lay leader, are you overly jealous of your pastor's time? Are there ways that you can open doors for your pastor to be better connected in the mission field? How? When?

3. Suggestions for further reading

The Acts of the Apostles (This entire book of the Bible serves as a template for leadership on the mission field.)

Michael Frost and Alan Hirsch, *The Shaping of Things to Come: Innovation and Mission for the 21st Century Church* (Peabody, Mass.: Hendrickson Publishers, 2003).

Alan J. Roxburgh and Fred Romanuk, *The Missional Leader: Equipping Your Church to Reach a Changing World* (San Francisco: Jossey-Bass, 2006).

SECTION 3
PEOPLE SHIFTS

It is not only imperative for pastors to imagine and operate differently. It is also crucial for laypeople to do the same. After all, the identity of a church has less to do with stones and steeples. And it has everything to do with the faithful people who are members of one body (see Romans 12:4). On behalf of me and the other eight vibrant pastors, we recognize the essential role that the good people of our churches have undertaken. For the sake of the Kingdom, they have made changes. These changes were often inconvenient and sometimes painful. Because the people of our churches embodied the *first things* (powered by prayer, a holy core), they willingly endured specific shifts. These shifts did not take place in isolation. They were the direct results of praying, holy people.

People shifts are changes in mind-set, attitude, and action that lay leaders and entire congregations embraced in order to welcome a new day in their local settings. These *people shifts* were vital for our nine churches to experience vibrant renewal.

Our five *people shifts* are (1) *fuzzy* to *focused*, (2) *inside* to *out*, (3) *single-cell* to *multi-cell*, (4) *established worship* to *energized worship*, and (5) *obstacles* to *opportunities*. There is nothing novel about the themes of these shifts. There are plenty of books, seminars, and other resources that have to do with these topics. What sets the following chapters apart from many other resources is the descriptions of how these nine churches made significant shifts in these areas.

Admittedly, there is overlap within these five shifts, and there is great overlap between these five and the first four that were previously described. Our nine characteristics are not separate, isolated efforts. Instead, all nine work together, often at the same time. This series of Spirit-led micro-shifts work in conjunction to bring about a macro-shift for an entire local church. When people embrace this series of movements, each modeled by the practices of the Early Church, congregations follow the Holy Spirit toward vibrant renewal.

five

SHIFT
FUZZY TO FOCUSED

Our church was growing, and at times we seemed to be too busy with many programs and activities. We wanted to ensure our "back door" was not larger than our "front door" and that we were not just experiencing transfer growth but also making disciples who were committed to the mission of the church. We simplified and aligned all our activities toward fulfilling our mission. Our church and people have become Kingdom-focused and are a "sent" church who seek to fulfill the great commission, experience discipleship, and pursue spiritual formation.
—Pastor Junior Sorzano

Like London, Ontario, First Church of the Nazarene, many churches are busy—and they are busy with good things. But *busy* isn't always good. Church calendars are bounded by bake sales, banquets, basketball tournaments, and the like. None of which are wrong in and of themselves. The problem comes when churches offer too many programs, ministries, and activities that do not tie in to a larger, cohesive vision.

I enjoy food. Like you, I have my favorite restaurants. And like you, there are restaurants I avoid. One popular type of restaurant is the kind that offers every food under the sun. Multiple buffet tables offer a broad selection of everything from seafood to Mexican cuisine to piles of pasta. You want it? They have it. It's just a matter of finding the right buffet line. While those types of restaurants are common Sunday afternoon fare, they are not my first choice. In their attempts to offer everything, most of their menu is mediocre at best. To find good Mexican food, I would rather search out a restaurant that specializes in Mexican menu items. For good seafood, I scope out a restaurant that concentrates specifically on great seafood. In many cases, restaurants that attempt to serve *everything* often don't serve *anything* well.

When churches operate in similar fashion, serving up a wide array of disconnected ministries, the quality of ministry is often sacrificed. Thom Rainer and Eric Geiger are more blunt: "Busyness is a great disguise for the lack of life. The complexity is a great cover-up. Churches can sometimes be fancy coffins."[1]

Before our nine vibrant churches experienced renewal, each was busy with multiple, disconnected ministries. Each indiscriminately spent its time and energy on activities that always sounded good and sometimes were good. More than enough wheels were spinning—but the car wasn't going anywhere. They may have had a good-sounding mission statement tucked away in their worship bulletin. Some of the church people may have even been able to verbalize some vague purpose of their church that made sure to include a biblical reference or two. But truth be told, each church was disjointed and aimless.

NARROWING FOCUS

Through prayerful discernment, visionary pastoral leadership, and willingness to make hard changes, each of the nine churches shifted from *fuzzy* to *focused*. Amid the complexity of multiple, fragmented ministries, they first went about the challenge of identifying their single purpose. And once their single purpose was made known, they accepted the even greater challenge of aligning all of the church's ministries with that purpose. By doing so, they willingly examined their very own DNA.

Thankfully, it is not up to us to conjure the mission of the church. The church does not belong to us. And neither does the mission. The mission to recover lost people and to make them into Christlike disciples is first and foremost God's mission. And He commands us to participate in His mission. Jesus gave us our marching orders in the Great Commission:

All authority in heaven and on earth has been given to me. Therefore go and make disciples of all nations, baptizing them in the name of the Father and of the Son and of the Holy Spirit, and teaching them to obey everything I have commanded you. And surely I am with you always, to the very end of the age (*Matthew 28:18-20*).

The purpose of the Church, while it may be communicated in various forms, is to make disciples of Jesus. All nine vibrant churches shifted from *fuzzy* to *focused*. And the focus for each church was clearly disciple-making.

Few churches will argue with the notion that they should make disciples. Agreeing that disciples should be made is not the point. The point is that these churches focus all their energy, time, and resources toward the goal of making disciples over the long haul. It's never enough to have a mission statement or a stated purpose unless it changes how you function.

Making the shift from *fuzzy* to *focused* first requires listening—listening to God to determine direction and listening to the people to determine how to bring them in that direction. Beginning with the end in mind, vibrant churches began asking questions like *What is a disciple? What qualities should a Christlike disciple exhibit?* and *What are the key components of a fully devoted Christ-follower?* As you might imagine, there is never complete agreement in the answers to these questions. But some of the common answers were *regular worship service attendance, connecting with a small group,* and *finding a place to serve others.* Each church, given their personality and context, wrestled with these questions and came to its best possible conclusions.

Then came the hard part. Each of the vibrant churches directed all their efforts toward the end of making disciples. They measured current ministries and programs to determine if they were contributing to disciple-making. Some of those ministries and programs were ended. Others were altered. Sometimes painful changes were endured. All the ministries of the church were aligned. Every sermon, every event, every small-group gathering, every training effort—every activity was aimed at making disciples.

68

MAKING DISCIPLES OF THE NEXT GENERATION

As vibrant pastors submitted to a three-year process of surveys and summits, one specific aspect of disciple-making became clear. All nine made a priority of making disciples of children and teenagers. At Crossroads Community Church of the Nazarene in Farmington, New Mexico, the disciple-making process begins in the nursery. Written lessons are communicated in story form to infants and toddlers. And age-appropriate homework is sent home so parents have basic tools to begin the process of spiritual education for their children.

With great intentionality, they believe that discipleship isn't something that begins later in a child's life.

Other avenues for making disciples of children in vibrant churches are Bible quizzing, Sunday School, small groups, camps, one-on-one mentoring, Caravan, and children's church. Many of these examples are common church programs for young people. The key is not whether they are offered. The key is the intentionality with which they are used to make disciples.

Several vibrant churches report involving children and teenagers in service to others in efforts to make those young people into disciples. At Clarksville, Tennessee, Grace Church, the children's pastor would regularly assign ministry tasks to children. They assisted with sound, lights, music, and clean-up for events. They also brought children along for visitation. At Crossroads Community Church children and teens are regularly involved in service projects for the elderly. They also participated in Hurricane Katrina relief work in Louisiana. And they often serve the homeless in an area soup kitchen.

At New Hope Church of the Nazarene in Princeton, Illinois, children frequently lead food and toy drives for others. The church also zeroes in on child-to-child evangelism. Because of these efforts, some of their children have led other children to Jesus. And several of the vibrant churches open doors for children to serve in regular worship services. For some, that includes ushering, greeting, or playing in handbell choirs. At the Latin American Church of the Nazarene in Owings Mills, Maryland, children actually lead the worship service at least once every two months. Much could be said about the value of teaching children to focus on others. Because selfless service is a core component of the life of a disciple, these churches make room for children when it comes to service opportunities.

Several of our vibrant churches used the word *intergenerational* when describing their discipleship of children and teenagers. Instead of always segmenting age groups, these churches make an effort to include people of different ages in various ministry settings. At the Waverly, Tennessee, Church of the Nazarene, the children's group partners with a different adult Sunday School class once a month. These intergenerational service groups have assembled care packages for missionaries and crisis care kits for disaster relief. They have also visited nursing homes and cleaned up the city park. When different generations of Christ-followers serve others alongside one another, not only is Kingdom work accomplished, but disciples are also made in the process.

These intergenerational efforts include resourcing parents to disciple children. Pastor Laura Root of New Hope Church says,

> Parents are the greatest spiritual role models for kids and have the greatest impact when discipling kids. So we give parents devotions and send weekly e-mails to help parents disciple their children on the very topics that we are teaching in children's church. Thus, the children are getting the same messages at home and at church. Our plan is to come alongside parents and assist them in discipling their children. We recognize that our time investment opportunity in each child is limited so the best thing we can do is invest in the parents and help them to be confident in being their children's disciplers.

Instead of segmenting age groups on Wednesday nights, the Waverly church implemented Family Fusion, a service designed specifically for family worship and teaching. At the close of each service, families are given devotionals to practice together for the next six days until the next Family Fusion. The content of the devotionals follows up on the worship service and leads toward the next week's service.

In another effort to resource parents, the children's pastor sends home a weekly letter to parents providing a summary of Sunday morning's message and three follow-up questions parents can ask their children. This resource opens conversation between parents and children. Additionally, the pastor and children's pastor periodically preach the same sermon series. While these are not the exact same messages, the texts and focus of the messages are the same. This allows children and parents to go home ready to discuss the sermon material.

Vibrant churches realize that discipleship of children and teenagers cannot adequately take place without equipping parents to disciple them. Pastor Root stated this mind-set well when she said that her church "comes alongside parents" to resource them in the disciple-making process. Vibrant churches regularly preach about the importance of discipling young people. Classes are taught toward that end. Children's pastors, teen pastors, and lay volunteers understand that they have as much responsibility to the parents as they do the children and teenagers. In multiple ways, vibrant churches are intent on "coming alongside" parents for purposes of discipling children and teenagers.

71

DISCIPLESHIP RESOURCES

Because this book aims to be a practical resource for local churches, we asked vibrant pastors to name discipleship resources that have shaped their understanding of disciple-making. Programming isn't everything. But the right strategy for a given church can help provide the necessary framework and guidance for disciple-making. Each of the following discipleship resources has been adopted by more than one vibrant church. They were not merely used as material for a group study at some point along the way. Instead, these resources are philosophies that have informed the disciple-making processes of our whole churches over extended periods. In other words, these strategies shaped the DNA of our vibrant churches over the long haul. And not only did our pastors adopt the following strategies, but they adapted them as well. Our pastors noted that they tailored these strategies to fit their local settings.

Several of the vibrant churches have been impacted by *Simple Church*,[2] by Thom Rainer and Eric Geiger. And a few of them found their way to the *Simple Church* paradigm prior to the publication of the book. In summary, Rainer and Geiger's study of over four hundred churches determined that the most effective churches in terms of spiritual and numeric growth are those that have a simple process of disciple-making. Such processes contain the following four elements: clarity, movement, alignment, and focus.

Three of the vibrant churches have been heavily influenced by *The Master's Plan*, which originated in Colombia and is sometimes referred to as G12 (groups of twelve). The Master's Plan is a disciple-making model that begins with a weekend retreat. The retreat is followed up with a year-long intensive series of courses. People join discipleship groups. Leaders are trained to mentor new leaders. And leadership groups hold leaders accountable to the task. The central role of groups in the Master's Plan is not unlike John Wesley's intricate system of groups, which served the same purpose. Craig Rench develops the methodology in *The Master's Plan: A Strategy for Making Disciples*.[3]

Stan Toler and Louie Bustle's *Each One Disciple One: A Complete Strategy for Effective Discipleship*[4] is another discipling resource used by several of the vibrant churches. The first section is about "Becoming a Disciple." Toler and Bustle provide simple, practical material that covers the basics of faith and the life of discipleship. The second section is about "Developing a Disciple." Recognizing that mature disciples make new disciples, Toler and Bustle equip those who use the curriculum to lead others to become disciples of Jesus.

Another resource that has impacted more than one vibrant church is Rick Warren's *The Purpose-Driven Church*.[5] Warren lays out the following six purposes of the church: worship, ministry, evangelism, fellowship, discipleship, and service. These six purposes serve as umbrellas under which the ministries of the church operate.

In addition to these overarching resources, vibrant churches carefully select discipleship curriculum for their groups. Because small groups are integral in disciple-making processes, such curriculum is chosen or created prayerfully. It is vital that the curriculum fit the overall disciple-making process. Some of the vibrant churches create their own curriculum, and all of them piece together components from various sources. While each of our pastors is drawn to specific resources and tools, we are aware of the pitfalls of blindly swallowing the biggest, shiniest, or newest curriculum fad. Instead, with great discernment, vibrant pastors take their context and local church vision into consideration when weighing curriculum. Many use the Nazarene Publishing House material to ensure a Wesleyan-Holiness biblical perspective without the necessity of vetting each lesson.

In addition to regular discipleship ministries such as Sunday School or small groups, several vibrant churches have created a course specifically for discipleship training. These courses focus on spiritual practices, scripture memorization, basic theology, local church vision, and leadership training. The Core Church of the Nazarene has a thirty-six-week discipleship training course combining classroom instruction with practical application. Like several other vibrant churches, people are required to complete the course before they are placed in leadership positions within the church.

In the end, there is no better resource for disciple-making than on-the-job training. While classrooms and courses are not without merit, they are no substitute for following Christ throughout everyday life. Jesus' own method of making disciples was "Follow me." The idea that we can make disciples apart from service, evangelism, and community life falls far short of biblical disciple-making. The above-mentioned plans and strategies and programs are worthwhile only when they propel people out to live as faithful disciples.

LIVING WITH FOCUS

Proverbs 29:18 offers a well-known truth: "Where there is no vision, the people perish" (KJV). These vibrant churches once operated without a clear sense of their mission or vision. After accepting the challenge of shifting from *fuzzy* to *focused* on making disciples, vibrant churches began discerning and developing God's vision for their particular context. In doing so, they have learned that with *vision* people flourish. With *vision* Kingdom work is accomplished. With *vision* people realize their potential to be disciples and disciple-makers. With *vision* we are more faithful to Christ and His Commission. With *vision* churches experience vibrant renewal.

NEXT STEPS

Chapter 5: *Fuzzy* to *Focused*

1. Chapter 5 key thoughts

74

a. *People shifts* are changes in mind-set, attitude, and action that lay leaders and entire congregations embrace in order to welcome a new day in their local settings.

b. Our five *people shifts* are (1) *fuzzy* to *focused*, (2) *inside* to *out*, (3) *single-cell* to *multi-cell*, (4) *established worship* to *energized worship*, and (5) *obstacles* to *opportunities*.

c. Busyness may be a great disguise for lack of life. Churches can suffer from blurry vision. Narrow the focus: Identify a single purpose. Make disciples of the next generation. Find solid discipleship resources. Live with focus.

2. Discussion starters

a. Read Matthew 28:18-20. Does your church have a clearly defined mission? What is it?

b. Are there activities your church is engaged in that do not contribute to your mission? Which ones?

c. Are there any potentially painful choices that need to be considered in order to better focus? What?

d. How does your church define *disciple*?

e. What is your church's process for making Christlike disciples?

f. Does your church involve children and young people in ministry? How?

75

3. Suggestions for further reading

Thom S. Rainer and Eric Geiger, *Simple Church: Returning to God's Process for Making Disciples* (Nashville: Broadman and Holman, 2006).

Craig Rench, *The Master's Plan: A Strategy for Making Disciples* (Kansas City: Beacon Hill Press of Kansas City, 2011).

Stan Toler and Louie E. Bustle, *Each One Disciple One: A Complete Strategy for Effective Discipleship* (Kansas City: Beacon Hill Press of Kansas City, 2008).

Rick Warren, *The Purpose-Driven Church: Growth Without Compromising Your Message and Mission* (Grand Rapids: Zondervan Publishing House, 1995).

six

SHIFT INSIDE TO OUT

The Owings Mills Church of the Nazarene, in the
Baltimore area, is primarily a Hispanic congregation.
Given the unique needs of the surrounding Hispanic
population, this church has an active presence in their
community. Every Saturday morning they have a prayer
meeting at their campus. But prayer is only the first half
of their Saturday work. After the last "Amen" is spoken,
Pastors Walter Argueta and Fernando Ibanez lead the
church to Home Depot. Many people spend Saturdays
at Home Depot with work in mind. But the people of the
Owings Mills Church have a different kind of work on their
agenda. The parking lot is a gathering place for unemployed
Hispanic people, an unofficial meeting spot for workers
and contractors. Many Hispanics spend their Saturdays
waiting for someone to hire them. The church's work is
to go where the people are. So they show up at the Home
Depot parking lot with coffee and doughnuts. They meet
and build relationships with those looking for work.
They invite them to worship and
church events. And they lead them to Christ.

LOOK OUT

Vibrant church pastors were asked to describe their churches' reputation in the community prior to renewal. None of them believe their church had a poor reputation. In fact, each of the nine said their church's reputation was virtually nonexistent. They used phrases like "not known" or "mostly invisible." Pastor Jeff Griffith of Waynesboro, Virginia, Community Fellowship Church points out that even though the word *community* was in their name, they were not well known in their community.

The vibrant pastors were then asked to describe their churches' current reputation in the community. All nine gave responses like *tremendous, highly visible, well-known, stellar reputation,* and *good name in the community.* Our intent is not to make *ourselves* known. It is to make *Jesus* known. All nine churches clearly shifted from being internally focused with little impact on the community to an outward focus, actively engaging unchurched people with the gospel.

Jesus said to his disciples, "Open your eyes and look at the fields! They are ripe for harvest" (John 4:35). When I read this exchange between Jesus and the disciples, I imagine Jesus literally taking one of the disciples' heads in his hands and gently turning it away from their inner circle. Jesus was helping them make a shift—from internal to external, from *us* to *others.* Vibrant churches have made this shift. Instead of being consumed by matters of personal preference and institutional preservation, they have turned their collective heads. There is a strong connection between holiness and outreach. Realizing *It's not about them,* the good people of these churches have laid aside their agendas and opinions in order to *look out* and *reach out.*

PERSONAL EVANGELISM

Once heads are turned, hearts are broken. In each of our vibrant churches is a culture of personal evangelism. Starting with the pastor and filtering throughout the congregation, people hold to the common belief that without Jesus, people are eternally lost. And we don't just believe that truth and leave it at that. We believe it's our business to do something about it.

As stated previously, it begins with a pastor who moves from the *desk* to the *field*. At the same time each vibrant pastor engages in personal evangelism, his or her preaching and teaching play a vital role in cultivating an outward focus. First, vibrant pastors preach evangelistically. They preach for response. Their messages are aimed at helping people make decisions for Christ. And second, through preaching and teaching they challenge their people to cultivate relationships with unchurched friends and invite them to accept Christ. When a pastor models, preaches, and teaches personal evangelism, the people of the church are more likely to respond by living evangelistically.

Vibrant churches offer training in personal evangelism. People are taught to develop relationships with unchurched people (the process) and to help them pray to receive Christ (the crisis). Evangelistic calls are made. Events are designed to connect with people who don't yet know Jesus. The story of salvation is told in worship services. Altars are opened, and people are invited to begin a personal relationship with Jesus. All nine of our vibrant churches are marked with a sincere burden for lost people. They truly have broken hearts for broken lives. And they offer the wholeness of the gospel to those in need.

MISSIONAL/ATTRACTIONAL

A recent dialogue has to do with whether churches should be *missional* or *attractional*. *Missional* refers to going out, engaging spiritual and physical needs of people where they are. *Attractional* is about attracting people to church services or events, inviting them to respond to the gospel. While many churches actively engage in both, whether a church is missional or attractional has to do with its starting place, which is informed by its basic philosophy of mission.

Aware of the tension between these two models, we asked vibrant pastors how they identified their churches. We also asked each one to list their ministries to determine to what extent they are one or the other. Interestingly, of nine churches, two are purely attractional. Two are mostly attractional with some missional ministry. Two are nothing but missional. Two are mostly missional with some attractional ministry. And one church falls right in the middle, with fifty percent missional and fifty percent attractional ministries.

Several conclusions are clear from this portion of the study. First, both missional and attractional models are effective. A church can be either and be vibrant. Second, these groupings had nothing to do with the age of the pastor. While some might assume that older pastors lead attractional ministries and younger pastors develop missional ministries, our survey says that is a false assumption. The vibrant church with the oldest pastor engages totally in missional ministries. And some of the younger vibrant pastors lean more toward attractional ministry. Third, whether a church is missionally oriented or attractionally oriented depends more on the given context, the pastor's personality and philosophy of ministry, and the identity of the local church.

Furthermore, we concluded that missional is attractional. In other words, people are drawn to missional work, and attractional ministry is carried out for missional purposes. The distinction between these two ends of the spectrum is not always as clear as it is made out to be. Whether a church is missional, attractional, or somewhere in the middle of the spectrum, what matters most is ministry directed toward those outside the church.

COMPASSIONATE CONNECTIONS

Vibrant churches have turned not only their eyes but also their hands toward the fields of their respective communities. Following the example of Jesus' own ministry, these churches engage their communities with both evangelism and compassionate ministry. Realizing that the two go hand in hand as seamless Kingdom work, vibrant churches refuse to opt for one or the other.

In *The Habits of Highly Effective Churches*,[1] one of George Barna's nine habits is "serving the community." When vibrant pastors rated the strengths and weaknesses of their churches according to Barna's nine habits, six of the nine rated "serving the community" as their strongest habit. Vibrant churches look for people with needs in their communities and engage those needs. They do not shy away from the brokenness and sin of their surroundings—especially when it isn't easy.

On Pastor John Stallings' first Sunday morning at the Massillon, Ohio, Church of the Nazarene, he encountered in the parking lot a man still drunk from the night before. Pastor Stallings began conversation with him and invited him into the sanctuary. At the close of the worship service, the man walked to the altar and gave his life to Christ. Eighteen months later, this man became the children's pastor of the Massillon church.

Pastor Laura Root tells a story of how New Hope Church (Princeton, Illinois) reached out to a lesbian dying of cancer. Because of the church's love, she accepted Christ and ended her lesbian relationship. She then actively witnessed to her friends, telling them about the love of Christ. Three years later she died. Her funeral was an amazing service of worship and witness. Pastor Root tells the rest of the story:

One lady who came to her funeral and was also gay and hated God ended up coming back to our church six months later when she was in a crisis. She said she woke up one Sunday and felt the need to come. She brought a friend with her. They both got saved. She has decided to be celibate as she discovers what God wants for her. She was baptized two weeks ago. She attends small group with me, and I watch her dog every night while she works. She said, "In all my life I have never been loved like this." The entire church has embraced her and loved her. She is sober for the first time since her teenage years. Her mom and sister came to her baptism out in the country in a muddy hole of a creek. Both of them were previously unchurched and came to our church this week for the first time. At the end of the service they were both at the altar.

This series of compassionate connections was not without cost. Two families left the New Hope church because they believed the church should not reach out to homosexuals. It wasn't the first time religious people got their feathers ruffled because a hand was extended toward sinners. And if Pastor Laura has her way, it won't be the last.

Pastor Dave West also tells a story of how a challenging funeral became an opportunity for redemption.

In 2002 I was approached by a local mortuary concerning an individual who had died and for whom no church wanted the funeral at their facility—because it was a young man who was involved in criminal activity (drug dealing, gang affiliation, and so on). I said, "Yes—we'll do it!" The memorial service was a great test for our people. On that day our church was packed with over three hundred gang members and their families from California, Texas, Arizona, and New Mexico—all dressed in blue. Our church not only received the families of the deceased but provided a reception dinner and covered the cost of the memorial service. As police officers lingered outside due to the nature of the individuals who attended, our church people hung out, tended to their needs, and never shrieked in fear. The family was overwhelmed by our love and compassion. And one who was in attendance that day is now a strong leader of our church.

The Waynesboro Community Fellowship Church held their annual Easter outreach to the community at the local elementary school. Along with music and games for children, they gave away food, haircuts, clothing, and door prizes. Pastor Jeff Griffith says,

I met a young lady with two kids who had been recently taken away from her because of her inability to provide for them. She was skeptical about me, the church, and our motives. Her piercings and tattoos told her story. We talked for about twenty minutes, and she ended the conversation with "I don't think your church would accept someone like me. With my tats and piercings, I haven't found too many accepting churches." I told her to come as she was and if one person said something to her or gave her an "I can't believe you're here" look, to let me know and I would be sure to address it. That was four months ago. She attends every Sunday. She has regained custody

83

of her children and has received new employment. Caring for people where you find them is the key. We can't leave them there, but we need to minister where we find them.

The Waverly, Tennessee, Church of the Nazarene ministers weekly to ladies in the county jail. It began when the Holy Spirit started speaking to a godly lady who had never seen the inside of a jail. "I have no reason to go to jail," Tish said, other than the prompting of the Holy Spirit. Each Tuesday night Tish leads a team of ladies who visit ladies in the jail. They get to know them, listen to them, share Christ with them, and pray for them. As a result, several inmates have accepted Christ. Thus far, six have been brought to the church on weekday mornings to be baptized, with shackles on their wrists and ankles, escorted by deputies. Dozens of people from the church gather to talk with them, worship with them, and celebrate their baptisms. I had the privilege of baptizing each one—chains and all.

Vibrant church pastors listed the following compassionate ministries in which their churches regularly engage:

- Pregnancy help center
- Hope House for women
- A booth at a local beer festival, where the worship band played and the pastor preached the gospel
- A "moms to work" program in which vehicles are purchased, repaired, and sold to single mothers at no cost
- Services at nursing homes and veterans' hospitals
- Food banks
- Clothing giveaways
- Street outreach with free hygiene packs and hot dogs
- A yearly flu clinic
- Birthday parties at a youth prison
- Home repairs for the elderly and poor

84

These compassionate connections are often messy and costly but are practical examples of what happens when Jesus gets hold of His people and turns their gaze outward.

OUTREACH TO FAMILIES WITH CHILDREN AND TEENAGERS

The previous chapter highlights the intentionality with which vibrant churches disciple children and teens who attend their churches. With equal intentionality, all nine of the vibrant churches gear many of their outreach efforts toward families with children and teens. Pastor Jim Asberry expresses the mind-set of vibrant churches in this regard: "We have an intentional focus on children. We believe that the children's area has been the biggest area of growth for our church. Making children's ministry a priority has allowed us to reach many new families in our community." Pastor Jeff Griffith shares that sentiment: "I believe if we reach the children, then we can impact the family and the community. Our commitment to children goes beyond the family structure at church and into the community, specifically in the schools."

Vibrant churches' attractional events include Easter egg hunts, children's friend days, baby day Sundays, block parties, fall festivals, movies, "trunk or treat" events, concerts, summer camps, and Upward sports. These churches have a genuine desire to reach young people for Jesus. But they also realize, as noted earlier, that children are often the gatekeepers to whole families who need Christ. So they plan and organize services and events for children. In doing so, they become magnets for families.

With a strong emphasis on outreach to children, four of the nine vibrant churches have adopted a total of five public schools. These churches serve the schools, students, and em-

85

ployees in a variety of ways. They offer prayer support, school supply giveaways, tutoring help, and other types of assistance. Determining the unique needs of each school, the churches serve the schools on the schools' terms.

The Owings Mills Church offers a tutoring ministry specifically for Hispanic students of public schools. Many of their parents are limited when it comes to homework help. These parents don't always know enough of the English language to sufficiently assist their children. Without this tutoring program for Hispanic students, many of them would suffer academically.

The Waverly, Tennessee, church's adoption of the local elementary school allows the church to serve in several ways. Employees are regularly offered appreciation dinners, prayer cards, and gifts. Because many teachers use their own money for classroom expenses, a select number of teachers are given $150 annually to help purchase classroom items. Larger items such as workroom microwave ovens and benches for playgrounds have been purchased. Administrators have said that these efforts have increased employee morale, which has a direct effect on students' education.

86

The Waverly church also directs ministry toward the students of the school. Church members volunteer as greeters at the front doors of the school each morning. And the church takes part in a backpack ministry. Many children who receive free or reduced lunch during the week do not have healthful eating options on weekends and over holidays. The church gathers easy-to-prepare, nutritious food items and has them placed in select backpacks on Friday afternoons. In addition to fulfilling biblical commands to feed the hungry, this ministry has impassioned more of our members than any single ministry in the last ten years. People get excited about being involved in such vital service.

All nine vibrant church pastors agree that their emphasis on outreach to children and their families has become a catalyst for vibrant renewal. A mother in the Waverly church once shared with me a statement of profound wisdom: "If you love me, that's fine—but if you love my child, you've won my heart." Vibrant churches understand the reality of those words. Vibrant churches love children. And as a result, they win families and impact communities for Christ.

GIVING THE GOSPEL

Phineas Bresee is often quoted as saying, "We are debtors to give the gospel to every creature in the same measure that we have received it."[2] A vibrant church's services, events, and programming are directed toward those outside the church. Outreach is a priority in the budgeting process. Vibrant churches attract unchurched people. And they are sending churches, deploying members into their community for evangelism and service. Vibrant churches preach, teach, equip, model, and celebrate missional living. Vibrant churches are not receptacles for the love of God—they are conduits, channels of grace for those in need. Vibrant churches have made this all-important shift. In efforts to *give the gospel*, they have been turned *inside-out*.

87

NEXT STEPS

Chapter 6: *Inside* to *Out*

1. Chapter 6 key thoughts
   a. *People shifts* are changes in mind-set, attitude, and action that lay leaders and entire congregations embrace in order to welcome a new day in their local settings.
   b. Our five *people shifts* are (1) *fuzzy* to *focused*, (2) *inside* to *out*, (3) *single-cell* to *multi-cell*, (4) *established worship* to *energized worship*, and (5) *obstacles* to *opportunities*.

    c. Look outward. Practice personal evangelism, both missional and attractional. Create compassionate connections. Reach out to families with children and teenagers. Give the gospel.

2. Discussion starters

    a. Read Acts 1:8. Does your church place an emphasis on evangelism? How?

    b. Does your church provide training in personal evangelism? What methods? How many are trained?

    c. Do you know how many people live within your church's sphere of influence? How many?

    d. Do you know how many people in that sphere of influence attend church regularly? How many are unchurched?

    e. Do you know how many different people groups live within that sphere of influence? How many?

    f. Does your church presently have compassion ministry connections? What are they?

    g. Does your church's budget reflect an emphasis on unchurched people through compassion and evangelism? How?

    h. Does your church have intentional outreach ministries to children and teens? What are they?

3. Suggestions for further reading

    Hugh Halter and Matt Smay, *AND: The Gathered and Scattered Church* (Grand Rapids: Zondervan, 2010).

    Reggie McNeal, *The Present Future: Six Tough Questions for the Church* (San Francisco: Jossey-Bass, 2003). (The DVD curriculum is also a worthwhile resource for leadership groups.)

Thomas G. Nees, *Compassion Evangelism: Meeting Human Needs* (Kansas City: Beacon Hill Press of Kansas City, 1996).

seven

SHIFT SINGLE-CELL TO MULTI-CELL

There has been a great paradigm shift in our church. When we began our ministry at London First fifteen years ago, there were no true small groups—only four traditional Sunday School classes. Our first attempt to implement this ministry met with great resistance. People had no desire to meet in small groups. We persisted and began using small groups as a means of training and sharing life together. Today we have healthy "holistic small groups" that meet on a three-month rotation system. This past year we developed "TGIF" (Together Growing in Faith), which meets at our church every other Friday evening. Everyone comes together and shares a meal. It is intergenerational and open to unchurched individuals. Everyone is encouraged to bring a friend, and after the meal we break out into small groups. Some groups are age-based. Others are topical groups like those focusing on "grief-share," parenting, recovery, Bible study, The Kingdom Experiment,[1] *and doctrinal study. This has been a tremendous success and has also become a form of evangelism with many visitors who have continued attending. Praise the Lord!*

—Pastor Junior Sorzano

Much has been written and discussed in recent years about the value of small groups for discipleship, church health, and growth. Our vibrant pastors affirm that their small groups played a vital role in each of their churches' vibrant renewal. Their renewal would not have taken place without serious attention to their small-group structures.

Prior to renewal, each church *was* a small group. They experienced intimacy within the church as a whole. For the most part, everyone in the church knew everyone else. They related to one another as a close-knit "family." In other words, each church was a single-cell organism. Recalling Biology 101, these churches underwent *mitosis,* or the process of cell division. With great effort, each of our vibrant churches went through a deliberate strategy to stretch the structure of their churches. They shifted from being single-cell to being multi-cell organisms.

The pastor and leadership of each of the vibrant churches viewed this shift in terms of infrastructure. They realized that it was necessary to expand the base or structure of the church as a whole. By adding groups in an effort to become multi-cell, these churches removed a major obstruction to God-given growth, laid the groundwork for future growth, and opened up potential for vibrant renewal. In other words, small groups were not added *because of* growth. Instead, they were added to make way for anticipated growth.

While the addition of small groups is necessary to make the transition to a multi-cell organism, this shift is about more than adding groups. It's about decentralization, releasing groups of people to be centers of community life, creating space where cells or clusters of people can experience spiritual growth together.

Like all the shifts, this one did not take place without challenges. The greatest challenge related to this shift was a crisis of community. People often perceive this transition as a loss of intimacy. They might verbalize frustrations such as "We don't know each other anymore" or "I miss the way we used to be like a close-knit family." But intimacy is *not* lost. It is experienced within groups instead of the church as a whole. While making this change, vibrant church leaders had to address the issue of intimacy, educating people about the importance of relationships within small groups.

We identified three specific changes vibrant churches made to their small-group structure in order to shift from *single-cell* to *multi-cell*.

MORE GROUPS

Pastor John Stallings says, "Our vision is to continue to start new groups." That vision includes small-group leaders who mentor assistants who eventually begin their own groups. Like the Massillon church, each of the vibrant churches simply added groups. They continually sought opportunities to divide existing groups or to start new ones. Prior to vibrant renewal, these churches averaged fewer than five Sunday School classes or small groups. Currently these churches average almost nineteen groups. Pastors and leaders of these churches constantly have the next group in mind.

The types of group structures vary. Three of the vibrant churches have Sunday School programs. Two churches are organized around small groups or life groups. And four of them have both small groups and Sunday School. Some of these groups meet on the church campus, while others meet in homes. Some even gather in restaurants. When they meet, where they meet, and what name they call it matters little. Whatever form it takes, structural expansion is taking place. Most often these groups are age-based. But groups are also based on geography, affinity, topical studies, felt needs, and so on. Following the *sticky church*[2] format, all the Princeton, Illinois, New Hope Church's groups are sermon-based. Their curriculum is drawn directly from each week's sermon. From groups that offer financial guidance to groups that attract fishing enthusiasts or motorcycle buffs, these churches look for reasons to get people to meet together.

These churches did not wait until more people came before they started more groups. They started more groups in order to prepare themselves for more people.

GROUP LEADER TRAINING

At the same time that vibrant churches multiply groups, they are diligent about training. Groups are not left to themselves to set their course. Instead, pastors and staff members maintain constant contact with small-group leaders. When specifically asked, "What do you train small-group leaders to do?" vibrant pastors shared the following responses: "Catch the overall church vision," "Understand our philosophy of small groups," "Teach the Bible," "Make disciples," and "Communicate expectations when it comes to tasks and character."

Training small-group leaders begins with orientation. Several of our vibrant pastors mentioned the necessity of providing orientation to leaders before they are entrusted with a group. Tony Miller required every new Sunday School teacher to first meet with him for an hour-and-a-half orientation. Waverly church also requires potential group leaders to meet with the pastor and staff to equip them for the work ahead. The purpose of these orientations is to clearly communicate

93

expectations. Doing so helps groups and group leaders begin on the right note.

Small-group leaders also experience ongoing regular training. Leaders of groups gather quarterly or even monthly. The content of the training itself is important. But just as important is the fact that leaders and pastoral staff consistently touch base with one other. They maintain contact for purposes of accountability and agenda harmony. The Owings Mills Church has developed a thorough training program for leaders. Weekly contact is made with them. Monthly trainings are offered. The pastor invites an outside expert for training once every three months. And the leaders gather for a retreat once a year. The purpose of the retreat is to share and celebrate blessings and accomplishments.

The best leader training often comes from within the groups themselves. When groups are consistently multiplied, existing group leaders learn to develop emerging leaders. They are taught to locate and mentor those who have the potential to become leaders of future groups. This culture of leadership development within groups often becomes the most effective tool for training future leaders.

Small groups are the front lines when it comes to disciple-making. Realizing the vital role that small groups and their leaders play, leader training is taken seriously. Effort is made to align each leader and group with the overall direction of the church.

HOLISTIC GROUPS

In one survey, vibrant pastors evaluated their churches in certain areas prior to renewal. They used the same criteria to give current evaluations of their churches. The area that received the largest bump was holistic small groups. Prior to renewal, these churches averaged 1.4 out of 10 in this area. Currently, the average grade for holistic small groups is 7.4 out of 10. Because this area received the largest improvement, we turn our attention to the holistic nature of small groups. "Holistic" groups are those that simply share life together. In Acts 2:42-47, the Early Church's practices offer insight into this understanding of holistic groups.

They devoted themselves to the apostles' teaching and to fellowship, to the breaking of bread and to prayer. Everyone was filled with awe at the many wonders and signs performed by the apostles. All the believers were together and had everything in common. They sold property and possessions to give to anyone who had need. Every day they continued to meet together in the temple courts. They broke bread in their homes and ate together with glad and sincere hearts, praising God and enjoying the favor of all the people. And the Lord added to their number daily those who were being saved.

These verses provide a window through which we see the holistic nature of the Early Church. From this description we see at least six practices:

95

- Teaching
- Fellowship, breaking of bread
- Prayer
- Common (shared) possessions
- Giving to/serving those in need
- Praise

One of the most important words in these verses is *together*. It appears three times in six verses, and the concept of *together* lies at the heart of the meaning of the whole passage. This scripture could be summed up by saying that the Early Church *shared life together*.

Many churches' Sunday School classes and small groups are anything but holistic. While teaching and prayer often take place within these group settings, attempts are not always made to be holistic. Groups are often information-driven and lecture-based. People in these groups may interact with each other during that one designated hour each week—and that interaction may be limited. Prior to renewal, our vibrant churches' Sunday School classes and small groups resembled this format.

A significant part of the shift from *single-cell* to *multi-cell* is making sure that each group is holistic. Groups are encouraged to *share life together*, inside and outside the weekly designated gatherings. Holistic small groups engage in service projects together. They eat meals and have fellowship regularly. Practicing brotherly and sisterly love, they share possessions and tune in to each other's needs. They even provide pastoral care for one another. Each small group becomes its own sphere of shared life.

Pastor Tony Miller says, "We equipped teachers to be the pastors of their groups." And Laura Root explains, "We encourage them to treat the group like a small family. We ask them to care for each other and look after one another as if they were family. We also ask them to choose a 'Be a Blessing' project every year in the community." A large part of the previously mentioned leader training serves this purpose. Group leaders are consistently resourced to help their groups become more holistic.

At the Waverly church, each group is asked to organize themselves by designating leaders within their group. Each group has a prayer leader, a contact leader, an event leader, and a food leader. Some groups additionally have compassionate ministry leaders or other positions that they deem necessary. The small-group teacher/leader is the point person when it comes to identifying other leaders within his or her group. The designated leaders within each group are entrusted with their ministry area. For example, the prayer leader may spend fifteen minutes of group time directing the group in prayer. They may organize a group prayer chain. They may e-mail the group with a list of weekly prayer items. Whatever form it takes, the prayer leader makes sure the group is actively praying. The contact leader is responsible for the group's contact ministry for those who are potential group members, those who are sick, or those with other needs. The contact leader does not necessarily *do* the contacting. He or she leads the group to make contacts. Again, the manner in which this takes place is not prescribed. Whether the contact is by phone, card, or social media, people are regularly making contacts. The event leader makes sure parties, dinners, and other events are on the calendar. This person is responsible for organizing and gathering the group for times of fellowship. And the food leader is the person who gathers the group's cooks to prepare meals for those who are sick, grieving, or in need. This leader makes sure the group's love is extended in the form of filled bellies.

97

This group structure aims to accomplish at least three purposes: (1) The teacher/leader of the group is free to teach without the burden of having to lead all the ministries of the group. (2) Leadership is shared. People who have passions and gifts in certain areas are able to experience the joy of fulfilling their respective callings. (3) This structure creates a framework for intentional, holistic small groups. The goal of this organizational structure is to provide leadership and accountability for *holistic* to happen. When it does, these groups are more likely to be cells or clusters of a multi-cell movement. By creating a structure for intimacy and shared life within each group, the transition from *single-cell* to *multi-cell* becomes more possible.

One last note about holistic groups: Two of our pastors discussed how they organize their church board and staff as holistic groups. When leadership teams *share life* together, they set the tone for their churches' small groups. These teams of leaders model what it means to be holistic in an effort to teach other groups the same.

DISCIPLE-MAKING GROUPS

Pastor Junior Sorzano shares a clear vision of his church's small-group ministry: "Our vision is that our small-group ministry will guide our people to deeper discipleship and build intentional relationships—to promote and articulate our mission and values and equip each group to embrace what it means to be a disciple-making church." As shared in chapter 5, the church has one purpose, one mission: to make disciples. All ministries of the church need to be aligned with that mission. None are more central to the task of disciple-making than small-group ministries. After all, the first disciples were made in a group. That is why vibrant churches constantly begin new groups, continually train group leaders, and make efforts to create holistic structure within those groups, thus creating the climate for a shift from *single-cell* to *multi-cell* ministries. In a multi-cell setting, one of the most restrictive barriers to growth is removed, possibilities for fresh ministry opportunities are opened up, and most important, the work of disciple-making is expanded and elevated. The shift from *single-cell* to *multi-cell* then becomes one of the most significant shifts in the vibrant renewal of the whole church.

NEXT STEPS

Chapter 7: *Single-Cell* to *Multi-Cell*

1. Chapter 7 key thoughts

   a. *People shifts* are changes in mind-set, attitude, and action that lay leaders and entire congregations embrace in order to welcome a new day in their local settings.

   b. Our five *people shifts* are (1) *fuzzy* to *focused,* (2) *inside* to *out,* (3) *single-cell* to *multi-cell,* (4) *established worship* to *energized worship,* and (5) *obstacles* to *opportunities.*

   c. Small groups were added not *because of* growth but *to facilitate* growth—more groups, group leader training, holistic training, and disciple-making groups.

2. Discussion-starters

   a. Read Acts 2:42-47. Discuss the six practices of this holistic model as the disciples shared life together.

   b. What types of small groups are within your church's present structure? List them. To what extent does each of these reflect the holistic model of the New Testament?

   c. Does your church train small-group leaders? How?

   d. Are there ways that your existing small groups might become more holistic by sharing life together? How?

   e. What holistic small groups might your church add?

   f. To what extent do your existing small groups see evangelistic disciple-making as their primary mission? How is this behaviorally demonstrated?

3. Suggestions for further reading

   Larry Osborne, *Sticky Church* (Grand Rapids: Zondervan Publishing House, 2008).

   Andy Stanley and Bill Willits, *Creating Community: 5 Keys to Building a Small Group Culture* (Portland, Oreg.: Multnomah, 2004).

eight

SHIFT ESTABLISHED WORSHIP TO ENERGIZED WORSHIP

*Our worship was very good to begin with. I was blessed
to have inherited a wonderful choir and worship team. All
that was needed was a little vision. The challenge to do
multiple services really made our people feel the excitement
of what we might possibly accomplish, and it added value
to their talent and abilities. I certainly agree with Vince
Lombardi when he said, "If you are not fired up with
enthusiasm, you will be fired with enthusiasm."
The leader's enthusiasm makes all the difference
in the world. Bringing enthusiasm to a service
can lift the spirits of an entire church.*
—Pastor Tony Miller

100

Vibrant pastors were asked to evaluate their churches using
Kennon Callahan's *Twelve Keys to an Effective Church.*[1] They
measured their churches' strengths in each of the twelve areas on a scale of one to ten. Five of the nine vibrant pastors
rated "corporate, dynamic worship" as their strongest of the
twelve keys. While it was not the strongest area for the other

four churches, "corporate, dynamic worship" remained very high in their evaluations.

It is hard to deny the fact that corporate worship played an integral role in the vibrant renewal of our churches. It is at the very center of a church's life. A church's worship is a reflection of its attitudes, priorities, and personality. As these nine churches moved forward, experiencing spiritual and numeric growth, each made changes regarding its weekly worship gatherings, making the shift from *established worship* to *energized worship*. *Established* refers to previous patterns that needed to be changed. Certainly we are not advocating that every established component of worship be changed. With prayerful discernment, these pastors and leaders determined the extent to which changes were made. In doing so, they led their churches toward more energized worship.

Of the five *people shifts*, this area has by far been the most difficult to pinpoint. Because each church is unique in identity, and because their unique identity is most visibly expressed in weekly worship, this particular shift revealed itself in various ways in the nine churches. While the majority embraced a more contemporary style of worship, this shift is more complex than that. Nevertheless, we can gather some overall changes that were made in these churches across the board.

101

IT'S ABOUT HIM

Vibrant churches know *why* they worship. They understand who the object of their worship is. They gather for weekly corporate worship in order to exalt Jesus. Sadly, many disagreements within churches regarding worship are more about us than Him—our preferences, our opinions, our notions. Both laypersons and pastors can be guilty of imposing their agendas instead of exalting our Lord.

Worship services are carefully and prayerfully planned. Every component of each service is designed, under the direction of the Spirit, to magnify the Lord. Songs are deliberately chosen. Multiple scripture readings that tie into the service theme are incorporated. The scriptures serve the purpose of orienting people toward the object of their worship. Sacraments, readings, testimonies, and the sermon all point worshipers toward the Christ.

In John 12:32 Jesus proclaimed, "And I, when I am lifted up from the earth, will draw all people to myself." The Greek word for *lifted up* also means *exalted*. While Jesus was clearly speaking about His impending death, His statement holds true when it comes to our weekly worship services. When the crucified and resurrected Lord is lifted up in our worship, people are drawn to Him. When Jesus is the centerpiece, worship becomes what it should be. When our worship is less about us and more about Him, our affections are rightly directed.

INCREASED ENTHUSIASM

When asked to describe their churches' worship gatherings prior to renewal, some of the vibrant pastors used the following words and phrases: *poor quality, lack of celebration, lack of enthusiasm, dying, something to endure,* and *beyond awful.* Our pastors were also asked to describe their worship gatherings presently. Descriptors include *alive, energetic, participatory, elevated, upgraded, life and freedom, inspirational, about Him—not us, better flow, spirit of celebration, high energy, relevant, passionate,* and *authentic.* Clearly, each of the vibrant churches increased enthusiasm in their corporate worship services.

Again, while each of these churches employed more contemporary models (newer songs, technology, drama, and so on) in their worship services, any notion that they jumped on a bandwagon or adopted novel tactics that translated into growth is oversimplistic. Worship styles and resources may have something to do with the level of enthusiasm. But increased enthusiasm is less about style and more about the spirit with which worship takes place. When the Samaritan woman in John 4 proposed to Jesus a worship war of sorts, He responded by saying, "Yet a time is coming and has now come when the true worshipers will worship the Father in Spirit and in truth, for they are the kind of worshipers the Father seeks" (John 4:23).

While enthusiastic worship can and should be encouraged and modeled, it cannot be manufactured. Enthusiastic worship is less about our efforts to produce something for God. Instead, our worship of the Triune God who has revealed himself as Creator, Father, Savior, Lord, and dynamic, energizing Spirit should be naturally enthusiastic. The Greek word for *enthusiasm* means *possessed by God* or *filled with God*. Enthusiastic worship is an authentic expression of people who have encountered and are infilled with the living God. We do not *make* worship enthusiastic. Instead, we allow for our worship services to be what they should be. We remove any barriers that would impede enthusiasm. Permission is granted and people are encouraged to offer genuine, enthusiastic expressions of worship to God. And when offered, enthusiastic worship is naturally contagious, inviting others into enthusiastic worship.

Unenthusiastic worship, on the other hand, is a poor offering that hinders God's activity among His people. Phineas Bresee said, "If any man loses his enthusiasm, he might as well be buried."[2] The same could easily be said for entire local churches. If it is true that we are *possessed by God* and *filled with God*, both individually and corporately, then our weekly worship gatherings should be inherently enthusiastic.

There is, of course, no formula for enthusiasm. Vibrant churches use tools such as newer songs, videos, drama, and technological upgrades to assist in creating a better climate for enthusiasm. But at the end of the day, these are only tools. There is, however, much to be said for modeling enthusiasm. When the pastor, the lead worshiper, choir and praise team members, and those who play instruments express authentic enthusiasm, they educate the congregation and lead them to do the same. Simply put, in addition to musical competence, worship leaders should worship well.

EXPANDED TEAMS

Several of the vibrant churches initially had one person who led their music ministry. Others had one song leader and one or two people playing instruments. All nine churches increased involvement in worship ministries in order to make this shift possible. All nine added additional singers on praise teams and choirs. All nine added people to play various instruments. They increased involvement in non-music worship ministries such as scripture readings, responsive readings, and prayers. And three of the nine vibrant churches expanded their preaching ministry. These three developed a regular preaching rotation that includes staff members who are called to preach. They simply got more people involved in leadership during worship.

Pastor Tony Miller believed so strongly in increasing his worship team that his very first goal and church board agenda item was to expand the worship platform in order to physically accommodate more people. Before Pastor Dave West had people playing instruments regularly, he purchased music instruments and placed them on the platform while the church sang to the accompaniment of midi-files. Those stationary instru-

104

ments sent a message. Some of them remained for six months before people answered the call to use them in worship. These two examples illustrate the fact that worship teams were not expanded because of growth. Instead, they were expanded proactively, in efforts to stimulate worship.

An expanded team of lead worshipers serves at least two purposes. First, an expanded team allows more people to exercise their ministry gifts and talents. Second, an expanded team helps create a climate for greater enthusiasm. While it may seem less important or peripheral to some people, our vibrant pastors report that increased worship team involvement became a significant component in the shift from *established worship* to *energized worship*.

VIBRANT PREACHING

Because the preaching of the word plays such a central role in the life of the church, the styles and substance of sermons were examined. In addition to surveys and summits, several visits were made to vibrant churches on Sundays to experience their corporate worship and to hear the preachers firsthand. Preaching methods vary from one vibrant pastor to another. The majority of vibrant pastors preach expositionally, beginning with the text. A few preach narratively. All of them utilize more than one style, depending on a number of factors. And most of them preach in series.

In addition to adjectives such as *passionate* and *relevant*, the word that best describes vibrant pastors' preaching on the whole is *challenging*. Vibrant pastors preach for concrete response. Their messages call for clear action. Some pastors' sermons are directed toward the heart. Other pastors' sermons engage the mind. Vibrant pastors' sermons aim for the hands. There is nothing wrong with preaching that moves the heart or sharpens the mind. But vibrant pastors are more concerned with challenging people to right doing, changed habits, and specific actions. Those actions may be things like *Come forward to pray, Leave to serve,* or *Tell others about Jesus.* The call to action is clearly communicated.

Vibrant pastors' sermons are also challenging in the sense that they call people toward deeper discipleship. These messages are accessible and relevant, but the content is not watered down. On the contrary, people are summoned away from themselves. They are challenged to greater faith. The preached word calls them outside of their comfort zone and into God's purposes. Vibrant pastors articulate the biblical call for God's people to live holy lives before Him. These pastors' sermons are challenging in the sense that they communicate the cost of being a disciple of Jesus.

ADDITIONAL SERVICES

Each of the vibrant churches had one weekly worship service prior to renewal. One of the nine still has one worship service today. Five of the nine churches have gone from one to two services. One of the churches now has three worship services. One has four. And another went to five weekly worship services.

The fact that these churches added worship services is significant. The reasons are more significant. The pastors were asked if they added services *because of* growth due to space limitations or if they added services *to anticipate* future growth. By a two to one margin, vibrant pastors added worship services to anticipate growth. They did not wait until they needed the additional services. In anticipation of God's movement, and in order to offer more options, services were often added as a catalyst for renewal.

Waverly church added one additional Sunday morning worship service a few years ago. There are several reasons the additional service has served well. First, more people are involved in ministry. Teams of ushers, greeters and other Sunday morning servants have effectively doubled. The addition of a service prompted us to recruit and equip fresh people for numerous tasks. Second, worship space was essentially doubled at no cost. While we were not at capacity when the service was added, we are beyond capacity for one service today. Third, the additional service played a key role in helping us shift from *single-cell* to *multi-cell* (see chapter 7). Adding the service made it easier to move beyond being a small, close-knit unit. Fourth, Waverly is a shift-work community. Many people work at area plants that require them to work in shifts. Having an early Sunday morning service gives third-shift workers an opportunity to come from work to worship before they go home to sleep. Without the early service, their worship attendance would be much less likely.

The fifth reason was never expected. More than a few people have shared with me their anxiety when it comes to large crowds of people. The second worship service, which usually has twice the attendance as the first service, is an intimidating environment for these people. Without an earlier, smaller worship service, many of these people simply won't come.

DEALING WITH RESISTANCE

It is no secret that the subject of worship can sometimes be a topic of heated discussion and debate. Looking at it positively, people are passionate about the manner in which they worship God. The thought of change can be met with fierce resistance. Since all nine vibrant churches made changes (such as style, service structure, introduction of new forms of media), we asked them the following question: "Because worship can often be a sacred cow, how have you addressed any resistance to changes in worship?" In their responses they spoke mostly about how they anticipated resistance ahead of time and took measures to minimize its impact. The following three responses were repeatedly given.

First, pastors were intentional about worship education. Anticipating resistance beforehand, pastors preached about worship. They addressed what worship is, who it is for, why we worship, and what matters most about our worship. At Waverly I preached a four-week series on the meaning and purpose of worship prior to implementing changes. In that series I addressed potential concerns beforehand. Pastor Junior Sorzano says, "We tried to explain and educate before, during, and after any major change. We have also encouraged tolerance and an understanding that corporate worship is toward God and not primarily about our personal and individual preferences."

Second, vibrant pastors connected the dots between the change and the mission of the church. Not taking for granted that people understood the reason for changes, these pastors verbalized changes in missional language. Pastor John Stallings responded to the *resistance* question with, "We continue to point worshipers to lost people needing Jesus." In other words, it was made known that changes were made for the sake of the greater mission.

Third, most vibrant pastors made changes at a slow pace. Pastor Walter Argueta spoke of sensitivity toward those who might be resistant to changes. Other pastors described the process by which they introduce changes in worship as "gradual" and "slow." With healthy respect for local history and previous traditions, changes were introduced deliberately and slowly.

Not all resistance can be averted by proactive measures. But much of it can. When pastors and church leaders understand their given context and take time to listen to people's voices, it becomes much easier to bring them through changes, worship or otherwise. It is at this point where a *holy core* and *energized worship* intersect. Because worship changes can often be a subject of great tension within local churches, it makes a great difference when such matters are handled with the spiritual maturity of a sanctified leadership core.

ENERGIZED LIVES OF WORSHIP

Vibrant churches paid significant attention to the quality of their weekly worship services. Raising the level of enthusiasm, expanding worship teams, presenting challenging preaching, adding services, and anticipating resistance were common components in the shift these churches made from *established worship* to *energized worship*. Without attention to these areas, vibrant renewal would have been much less possible.

The apostle Paul reminds us,

I urge you, brothers and sisters, in view of God's mercy, to offer your bodies as a living sacrifice, holy and pleasing to God—this is your true and proper worship. Do not conform to the pattern of this world, but be transformed by the renewing of your mind. Then you will be able to test and approve what God's will is—his good, pleasing and perfect will (*Romans 12:1-2*).

109

Corporate worship matters for many reasons. One is that worship extends beyond corporate worship into every other area of life. When churches shift from *established worship* to *energized worship*, that spirit of worship is more likely to permeate people's lives, and they're readier to offer themselves outside of weekly gatherings. When churches make this shift, that worship becomes less an activity and more of a way of living and being. Their efforts, in cooperation with the Holy Spirit, become a catalyst for vibrant renewal.

NEXT STEPS

Chapter 8: *Established Worship* **to** *Energized Worship*

1. Chapter 8 key thoughts
   a. *People shifts* are changes in mind-set, attitude, and action that lay leaders and entire congregations embrace in order to welcome a new day in their local settings.
   b. Our five *people shifts* are (1) *fuzzy* to *focused*, (2) *inside* to *out*, (3) *single-cell* to *multi-cell*, (4) *established worship* to *energized worship*, and (5) *obstacles* to *opportunities*.
   c. A church's worship is a reflection of its attitudes, priorities, and personality. It's about Him. Increased enthusiasm. Expanded worship teams. Vibrant preaching. Additional services. Anticipate some resistance.

2. Discussion starters
   a. Read Romans 12:1-2. How can energized corporate worship extend into every area of people's lives?
   b. What word best describes your church's main weekly worship service? Why?
   c. How "enthusiastic" is your worship service? How might you become more enthusiastic and increase newcomers' desire to return?
   d. How might your church increase the involvement of more people in participating in worship ministries?
   e. Discuss what is meant by "challenging" preaching; "call to action."
   f. Has your church considered adding another worship service? What might happen if you did? Would there be resistance? How might you deal with resistance?

g. Who are the people a new service might reach who do not attend regularly now?

h. How might your church increase the focus on Jesus in your worship services?

i. Are there obstacles in your worship services that might be impeding Spirit-led worship? How might you deal with them?

3. Suggestions for further reading

Charles Arn, *How to Start a New Service: Your Church Can Reach New People* (Grand Rapids: Baker Books, 1997).

Buddy Owens, *The Way of a Worshiper: Discover the Secret to Friendship with God* (Lake Forest, Calif.: Purpose Driven Publishing, 2002).

111

nine

SHIFT OBSTACLES TO OPPORTUNITIES

"We went through fire and water, but you brought us to a place of abundance" (Psalm 66:12) is a verse that tells the story of Waverly, Tennessee, Nazarenes. In 2009 and 2010 our facilities were damaged by a fire and a flood. The fire scorched a portion of one of our buildings and sent ash through the ductwork, damaging the entire building and its contents. The flood, brought on by rising creek water, came as high as four feet above ground level on both our buildings. These disasters delivered a one-two punch to our buildings and our people. Major portions of our facilities were rendered unusable for stretches of weeks. The church responded to both events with prayer, unity, and a sense of anticipation. God brought numerous positive outcomes from the fire and the flood. The insurance company replaced our pews with chairs, creating much-needed seating increase and flexibility. Our nursery was expanded and updated to provide more space and better space for our VIP's. Church offices and Sunday School classes were upgraded and rearranged to maximize ministry. More important, these events bound us together like never before.

*We experienced a renewed, collective dependence on the
Lord. People came together to fill sandbags, move furniture,
and repair buildings. Some of them had not served the Lord
prior to these disasters. For those people, the fire and flood
accomplished what I had yet been able to do—they got
people involved in ministry. With the Lord's help,
we went through fire and water. And He brought us
to a place of abundance.*
—Pastor Daron Brown

OBSTACLES WILL COME

The nine vibrant churches are not immune from obstacles. Like every other church, they face their share of hardship. When asked to list recent obstacles, vibrant pastors listed physical hindrances such as space limitations for worship and Sunday School, lack of adequate parking, older buildings that are ill equipped for current ministries, and insufficient finances. They listed the following spiritual and mental obstacles: *depression, low self-esteem, lack of faith, no vision, inward focus, wrong spiritual mind-sets, small church mentality, human control, locked in to old familiar ways, internal conflict,* and *apathy.*

113

Two of the nine pastors were appointments to churches in crisis. Another entered his pastorate immediately after the church split. Several of these churches experienced varying degrees of unhealth and decline prior to vibrant renewal. And five of the nine vibrant churches experienced renewal under leaders in their very first pastorate—which is a seemingly insurmountable obstacle in and of itself. These churches were definitely not picture perfect from the start. And they continue to come up against hurdles today.

WELCOME OBSTACLES

One major difference between vibrant churches and many others is how these obstacles are viewed and approached. Instead of seeing them as mere obstacles, they are welcomed as opportunities. Instead of throwing hands in the air, crying, "Woe are we!" or living with a grumbling spirit, these churches view problems as possibilities. While their attitudes are optimistic, they are more than glass-is-half full, look-on-the-bright-side, human-generated optimism. Instead, their optimism is grounded in their relationship with the God of Scripture who acts in history on behalf of His people.

This is the God who time and time again brings blessings out of barriers. Beginning with *the beginning*, God brought life out of chaos. When His people were cornered on all sides, He made a way through the sea. From a cleared, barren stump He birthed a shoot. In a valley of sun-bleached bones He raised up a living army. When faced with the finality of crucifixion, He brought about resurrection. As the Early Church endured persecution, the good news swelled and spread through the known world. Throughout Scripture and history, God's plans face human obstruction. And in each case His purposes prevail. Vibrant churches know that they follow the very same God. Theirs is the God who constantly takes obstacles and brings opportunities.

114

A year and a half after Pastor Junior Sorzano arrived at London, Ontario, First Church of the Nazarene, he conducted a church board retreat in which he presented a renewed vision. Their facilities were not handicapped-accessible. With a large group of senior adults, their lack of accessibility became a spiritual barrier for many. In addition, the church needed a van and other equipment for purposes of outreach. Pastor Sorzano's vision included the raising of $50,000 for these needs.

He challenged the historically fiscally conservative congregation by quoting William Carey: "Attempt great things for God and expect great things from God." To Carey's quote he added, "and believe all things are possible with God." Within two weeks one board member was stirred to give the $50,000 for the needed projects. The rest of the board, after first responding with disbelief, began believing that all things are truly possible with God.

Pastor Sorzano describes another instance in which a spatial dilemma had spiritual ramifications.

We are in the downtown core and did not have a parking lot. Many times families were not able to find a parking spot on Sunday morning and eventually went elsewhere to church or just returned home. I presented an investment and expansion vision that included selling the parsonage, investing the funds, and eventually purchasing three surrounding properties around the church. There were many obstacles. We had to approach the city for re-zoning and the approval to demolish buildings. Our plans were in direct conflict with city by-laws. God provided one miracle after another. We obtained properties for half of their value, which enabled us to achieve our vision with limited finances. Many of our members thought it was impossible. But God reminded us that "all things are possible to him who believes" [Mark 9:23, NASB].

This episode presented a string of obstacles. But the church continued moving forward, trusting that God would provide at every turn. "If you don't have an obstacle," Pastor Sorzano concludes, "you're not a candidate for a miracle."

115

LOOKING AHEAD

Other vibrant pastors led their churches to address physical and spatial limitations by adding worship services and stepping out on faith by building newer and larger facilities. At one point the Latin American Church of the Nazarene met in the small basement of another church's building in the Baltimore area. After they filled the meeting room, they placed chairs in the hallways. People would stretch their necks to see. They would strain to hear. Without an air conditioner or heater, these faithful believers endured extreme weather and cramped conditions on a regular basis. Pastor Argueta remarks,

> Instead of despairing and giving up, we asked God to take us not only out of that place but also to give us a better place. If we had not desperately needed a bigger space, we might have never decided to try for the beautiful and large space that God provided. Our obstacle not only pushed us to find a building but also motivated us to come up with a plan with a goal of having financing ready in two years.

Pastor Argueta identified another obstacle that is unique to the Hispanic population in his area. He explains: "Many immigrants think that they will be here for only a certain number of years. Then, after the years have passed and some of our members have the opportunity to visit their native country again, they realize that they don't quite belong there any longer." This common scenario brings about a great sense of loss. Instead of having two homelands, many immigrants feel as if they have no real place to call home. They live in a state of exile, which often affects them emotionally and spiritually. Pastor Argueta approaches this serious obstacle as a powerful opportunity for spiritual growth. He reminds them that they belong to neither nation. Instead, he points them to the apostle Paul, who said, "You are no longer strangers and aliens, but you are fellow citizens with the saints, and are of God's household" (Ephesians 2:19, NASB). This obstacle appears to rob people of their identity. But Pastor Argueta sees it as an opportunity to educate people about their true identity in Christ.

DEALING WITH FEAR

The greatest obstacle, which often lies at the root of other obstacles, is fear—fear of change, fear of loss, fear of failure. Whether we admit it or not, we are driven by fear. We often make financial decisions based on fear. We isolate ourselves because of fear. More often than not, our fears render us immobile. We fail to move or act based upon fear. Whole churches and individual Christians stay put because they are fear-stricken.

Pastors, leaders, and entire local churches must be reminded that "there is no fear in love. But perfect love drives out fear" (1 John 4:18). What is there to fear when our lives are bound up in Christ? Not even death itself has leverage over our lives. When churches pull back the curtain on this root cause of other obstacles, they experience fresh freedom, which releases them to move forward in faith. The obstacles then become catalysts for newfound life and growth.

117

The opposite of fear is Spirit-directed, forward-moving, risk-taking faith. Vibrant churches share countless examples of instances in which they, armed with faith, run headfirst into their fears. They take financial leaps of faith. They embrace risks regarding needed changes. They do not shrink in fear when faced with obstacles. Instead, they charge forward, trusting God.

PRAYING THROUGH OBSTACLES

Drawing a direct connection between chapters 1 and 9, vibrant pastors speak of the importance of prayer as it relates to the shift from *obstacles* to *opportunities*. When faced with obstacles, these churches may not have solutions at their disposal. But they have direct access to the One who does. Obstacles drive vibrant churches to their knees in prayer—but not necessarily in a spirit of desperation. Instead, they are driven to their knees in a spirit of anticipation. *What will God do now? Let's see how God parts these waters! How will God show up and show off this time?* They confidently seek God's wisdom and direction, because they "know that in all things God works for the good of those who love him, who have been called according to his purpose" (Romans 8:28).

The Farmington, New Mexico, Crossroads Church of the Nazarene was facing serious spiritual battles. Pastor David West responded by entering the sanctuary on Sunday nights for special prayer and anointing. He invited key leaders to join him. Together they sought the Lord, claiming the church for Christ. Their prayers directly impacted Sunday morning services and paved the way for renewed spiritual health. These vibrant churches constantly find themselves in front of mountains. But they aren't intimidated. They are tuned in to the *Mountain-mover*.

In addition to increased faith and serious prayer, several of the vibrant pastors mention the importance of celebrating past victories over obstacles. When new obstacles are presented, the pastor and people remind one another of what God has done in the past. Stories are told about steps of faith. People remember how God has acted. They remind themselves first of all of God's faithfulness to them. Second, they remind one another of the fruit of their past faithfulness to God. These sto-

118

ries provide a framework. They locate their current obstacle within the context of the larger history of God's activity. *Remember how God has seen us through?* they ask. *This is one more opportunity for God to do what He always does for us!* Placing the current obstacle in the right context emboldens God's people. In other words, when obstacles are approached as opportunities, momentum is created to address future obstacles.

FORWARD IN FAITH

Numbers 11 identifies one of the many instances of conflict in the ongoing wilderness drama. With the familiarity of Egyptian cuisine on their minds, the Israelites complained about God's wilderness menu. Like a restaurant server caught between disgruntled customers and the kitchen crew, Moses brought their complaint before the Lord. God responded to Moses with a question: "Is the LORD's arm too short?" (Numbers 11:23). Of course, God knew the answer. He knew there are no limits to His own power. What mattered is how Moses and the Israelites would answer such a question. How they answer that question would determine how they live. If they believe the Lord's arm is too short, then they shrink in fear and live on edge. If on the other hand they come to the conclusion that the Lord's arm is long enough, then they will live differently. If they believe the Lord's infinite reach will provide for them and protect them, they will learn to trust Him despite the circumstances. The same applies to churches today. Do we believe that the Lord's arm is too short for us? Do we trust Him enough to move forward? Do we believe that He will use our obstacles as opportunities to reveal himself?

Vibrant pastors and churches do more than endure obstacles. They embrace obstacles. After all, they know whose church it is. If this is *my* church, then obstacles are clearly obstacles—no doubt about it. But if this church is *God's* church, then obstacles truly become opportunities—for spiritual growth, for flexed faith, for increased faithfulness, for newer and better possibilities. When churches make this shift, approaching obstacles as opportunities for God's activity, then His people once again become a mighty movement, vibrant and renewed.

NEXT STEPS

Chapter 9: *Obstacles* to *Opportunities*

1. Chapter 9 key thoughts
   a. *People shifts* are changes in mind-set, attitude, and action that lay leaders and entire congregations embrace in order to welcome a new day in their local settings.
   b. Our five *people shifts* are (1) *fuzzy* to *focused,* (2) *inside* to *out,* (3) *single-cell* to *multi-cell,* (4) *established worship* to *energized worship,* and (5) *obstacles* to *opportunities.*
   c. Obstacles will come. Welcome them. Look forward, not back. Deal honestly with fear. Pray through obstacles. Move forward in faith.

2. Discussion starters

   a. Read and reflect upon Romans 8:28 and Mark 9:23.
   b. What obstacle(s) is your church facing that makes you a candidate for a miracle from God?
   c. Are there fears that your church faces that might hinder movement forward? Are they real or imaginary? Present now or only possibilities? How might you deal with those fears?
   d. What miracle are you anticipating from God to change an obstacle into an opportunity?
   e. How might you help create an atmosphere of trust and faith that would help your church deal with future obstacles?

f. Reflect upon and discuss the relationship between this book's first chapter, "Powered by Prayer," and this last chapter, "Obstacles to Opportunities."

3. Suggestions for further reading

Dwight M. Gunter II, *Deliverance from Daily Giants: The Power to Conquer Worry, Fear, Failure, and Other Goliaths* (Kansas City: Beacon Hill Press of Kansas City, 2006).

Erwin Raphael McManus, *Chasing Daylight: Seize the Power of Every Moment* (Nashville: Thomas Nelson Publishers, 2002).

CONCLUSION
ONGOING RENEWAL

The concept of renewal is a significant theme throughout Scripture. In Colossians 3:10 Paul says we have "put on the new self, which is *being renewed* in knowledge in the image of its Creator" (emphasis added). In 2 Corinthians 4:16 he says, "Therefore we do not lose heart. Though outwardly we are wasting away, yet inwardly we *are being renewed day by day*" (emphasis added).

These scriptures tell us two particular things about renewal. First, renewal is God's work and not ours. God is the subject. We are the objects of renewal. Second, renewal is not something that occurs only once. God is continually in the renewing business. Renewal is His ongoing, ever-present work. That is true in our personal lives. It is also true in our churches.

When I describe churches that have experienced vibrant renewal, I do not mean to suggest that they have arrived at some sort of finish line. Instead, renewal is the work that God is constantly up to in these churches. Renewal is an ongoing, dynamic process in the life of a church. Renewal is marked by a constant state of flux. Willingness to be changed is the order of every day. Just like individual believers, when churches believe they have arrived at a point where they no longer need renewal, their need for renewal is most apparent.

In our most recent discussion, vibrant pastors discussed how to *sustain* renewal. The question was met with resistance on two levels. First, as you might imagine, the word *sustain* doesn't sit well with vibrant pastors. *Shifting*, and not *sustaining*, is in their DNA. They are not interested in preserving something that has been. Second, we came to the conclusion that renewal is not ours to sustain—we did not manufacture it. And neither do we preserve it. Instead, we constantly put ourselves into position *to be renewed*. Most important, that happens by regularly tending to the *first things* mentioned at the beginning of the book. Local churches must ceaselessly come to their power-full God in prayer. Vibrant churches become vibrant on their knees, and they remain vibrant on their knees. They keep praying first. They keep praying much. And they keep praying forward. Their continual state of prayer keeps them in tune with the One who powers them forward.

Just as important as prayer is the growing holiness of the church's core group. Local churches will not experience vibrant renewal without the core group's willingness to die to themselves and follow Christ in a spirit of unity. And local churches will not continue in that spirit of renewal unless the core leadership team persists with a sanctified spirit. When key leaders live their lives in corporate, complete submission to Jesus, they put themselves in position for ongoing renewal. In other words, *first things* become *ongoing things* in the life of a vibrant church.

Our God is the God who specializes in *small*. Throughout history, He does much with little. Our nine shifts describe how the Holy Spirit led these nine churches from fewer than one hundred in attendance to vibrant renewal. Undoubtedly,

124

as these churches keep moving forward, there will be more shifts on their horizons. The responsibility of these churches and their pastors is to walk in step with the Holy Spirit, the Creative One who is always doing new things. The future is open. Uncertainty is certain. Every church is summoned to vibrant renewal. And every church's vibrant renewal depends on its willingness to shift.

NOTES

Chapter 2

1. Robert Murray M'Cheyne. This often-used quote is attributed to M'Cheyne without a known source.

2. The website for the Church of the Nazarene's Continuing Lay Training Program is http://thediscipleshipplace.org.

Chapter 5

1. Thom S. Rainer and Eric Geiger, *Simple Church: Returning to God's Process for Making Disciples* (Nashville: Broadman and Holman Publishing, 2006), 20.

2. Ibid.

3. Craig Rench, *The Master's Plan: A Strategy for Making Disciples* (Kansas City: Beacon Hill Press of Kansas City, 2011).

4. Stan Toler and Louie E. Bustle, *Each One Disciple One: A Complete Strategy for Effective Discipleship* (Kansas City: Beacon Hill Press of Kansas City, 2008).

5. Rick Warren, *The Purpose-Driven Church: Growth Without Compromising Your Message and Mission* (Grand Rapids: Zondervan Publishing House, 1995).

Chapter 6

1. George Barna, *The Habits of Highly Effective Churches* (Ventura, Calif.: Regal Books, 1999).

2. Phineas Bresee. This often-used quote is attributed to Bresee without a known source.

Chapter 7

1. Bruce Nuffer, Liz Perry, and Rachel McPherson, *The Kingdom Experiment: A Community Practice on Intentional Living* (Kansas City: The House Studio, 2009).

2. Larry Osborne, *Sticky Church* (Grand Rapids: Zondervan Publishing House, 2008).

Chapter 8

1. Kennon L. Callahan, *Twelve Keys to an Effective Church* (Hoboken, N.J.: Jossey-Bass, 1983).

2. Phineas Bresee. This often-used quote is attributed to Bresee without a known source.